A LOVE The WORLD Should KNOW

"ONE COUNTRY GIRLS STORY OF ENDURANCE."

YVETTE L. GAINES

TABLE OF CONTENTS

Chapter 1

HOW IT ALL BEGAN

Yvetta Lacey Fryer was born in Eufaula, Alabama, on January 15, 1976. And yes, for the history buffs out there, like one of my many spiritual fathers, Apostle Eugene Florence, January 15th is Martin Luther King Jr.'s birthday. You see, my journey started in the likes of greatness. But oh, how the tides changed during the course.

I'm the third daughter born to my mother and father, who started their family at a very young age. By the time Mom had her 4th child, she figured motherhood and marriage had taken up enough of her youth and set out to explore some of the things she missed being bogged down with children. This search for lost time included a lot of late nights and constant partying. Mom has a wild spirit, while Daddy, on the other hand, is very meek and quiet. You know the old saying, opposites attract? Such was the case with my parents. Dad's job as a long-distance trucker brought in good money but kept him away from home a lot, which meant Mom was stuck running the house solo. He was never the party type and didn't socialize as often as mom, but he wasn't perfect by far; he had his own giants to battle. While their issues in the marriage were not the same, their differences ultimately led to divorce. Daddy moved back in with his mother, and we remained with Mom. He continued to support us all financially so we didn't feel the sting of the separation or have to leave our beautiful home, and Mom made sure we were well-kept.

Around the age of 7, I remember Mom saying she looked too good to be alone and something triggered in me; beauty was to be used as an advantage, and I made a mental note to put it to work when the time came. Eventually, all the girls would grasp a hold of the beauty meal ticket. Mom's a very pretty woman, and not to toot my own horn, but the fruit didn't fall far from the tree.

Shortly after her revelation of not wanting to be alone, Mom started dating my stepdad. He was a wonderful guy and had one of the calmest spirits I have ever encountered. Now keep in mind my mother has recently set out to reclaim the freedom of her youth. Dating opens one door before closing the other, and just like her first marriage, family and commitment got in the way of her doing her own thing. Instead of leaving Mom though, my stepdad often fought with her to make her see things his way. He was a trucker of sorts himself, he drove big rigs for a moving company which periodically meant he was away.

During the course of their union and in between trips, five additional children were born: four more girls and a boy. With a grand total of eight children and a home to care for, one would think we were close like the Waltons. Instead, life was very chaotic! The only thing that made me feel normal in childhood were the two vacations we took a year as a family. However, as time went on, my nights as a child that should have been spent at home watching TV and eating popcorn became nights in the bars partying, and I realized my family was anything but normal.

Life with Mom was loud, adventurous, and very unpredictable at times. But thankfully, I have a quiet place at my grandmother Lucille's. She's my haven on holidays, weekends, and any other time Mom would get lost. She despised the way our Mom raised us and often told me, "Don't be like your mother when you grow up", and I always prayed I wouldn't. My grandmother's heart was soft, and it didn't matter that we were not all my father's children; she cared and tended to the eight of us whenever Mom would drop us off. With Dad being on the road constantly, the majority of the burden fell on granny. Still, she wouldn't turn us away; at least she knew we were safe with her. She never pretended to be happy about it, though. She let Mom know just how she felt every time she would leave us. I know it was a lot on her to look after so many children, as she worked from sun up until the sun went down again herself. Somehow, she managed though and ALWAYS kept us in church. It was those trips to church every Sunday that was responsible for instilling that much-needed word in me that would be necessary to sustain me later on in life.

My mother stopped working years ago. She said it was too much with all the kids being born so close together. The idea was to stay home and make a nice life for the husband and children. But that's all it was, an idea. Mom wasn't impressed with being a housewife; she found the night life more exciting. Mom figured she had missed her golden years, so instead of settling down with age, she got wilder. This made us more of a problem than a blessing at the time.

The back and forth continued for years, my mom dropping us off to party and my grandmother's pleading for her to settle down and be a better mom falling on deaf ears. Not to mention the constant arguing between my mom and dad as to who was the worst parent: my dad who was never home because of road trips or my mom who never stayed home because of partying. I often wondered if, and where, we fit in. The only positive thing that came out of this lifestyle was the children learning how to adapt, depend, and rely on each other. I taught myself to follow a schedule that rotated around certain activities and routines depending on which house I was at in an effort to keep some consistency in an ever-changing environment.

As we grow older, the children start to parent each other. We comb hair, do laundry, wash dishes, iron clothes, and cook (okay, anyone who knows me knows that I never quite grasped the cooking. But hey, I tried). We did all that and anything else required to keep a household operating, forcing us to become survivors at an early age.

The pattern continues as we become young adults, and things get even more hectic when my stepdad is injured on the job and has to stop driving long distances. He only works locally now, which means the checks are not as fabulous as we're used to, so we move out of our beautiful home in a prestigious neighborhood into a trailer next to my grandmother because it's more affordable. Spending more time at home causes my once laid-back stepdad to develop the same passion for the night life as my mom. I guess if he couldn't keep Mom home, he would at least be with her in the streets.

A few months after settling into our new town, someone retiring from a local bar asked my mom and stepdad to manage it once he left. This only added to our interesting childhood, to say the least. The older children are now privileged to skip nights at grandma's in exchange for nights in the club, introducing us to an environment that caused us to grow up faster than any kid should. Needless to say, I was exposed to things a lady shouldn't even be thinking about at such a young age, and I could dance and cuss with the best of them. Some nights, once the smaller kids fell asleep and my chores were complete, I would sneak into the "juke joint" (as my Grandma referred to it) because I was so fascinated with that life. On more than a few occasions, my mom was in the back cooking or on the card table, none the wiser that I was there.

It was nights I watched her play cards, dance, drink, and work the crowd, oblivious to the fact that her daughter was becoming a pro at it.

On the weekends and holidays that my father wasn't on the road, he insisted that we stay at his mother's with him. We were MADE to attend Bible study, Sunday school, and then Sunday morning services. Those visits used to stir up things inside me that I didn't understand. I would cry and complain the whole weekend about so many trips to church and how boring it was. I was starting to hate the very place that my grandmother had assured me was my safe haven. I had no clue way back then that the enemy was trying to keep the seeds being planted inside of me from taking root and growing—seeds that I would go back, pull up, and uproot years later when the devil got hot on my trail. This was my existence for as long as I could remember; going to church with grandma, then to the clubs with Mom, watching grandma pray, and observing Mom fight. And when I say she was a fighter, I don't mean catfights; she fought hard with my dad, my stepdad, and anybody else who got in her way. I, too, had a war raging as to where I wanted to be: in the world that felt so good or the church where I knew I was safe. My spirit was battling with the flesh. Fighting has become a common part of my life, and it was a fight that ultimately drove us out of Alabama to Buffalo, NY.

It's a typical night at the bar, and I'm hanging out doing the usual, watching Mom go back and forth from the kitchen to the card table. She's flipping chicken like it's nobody's business. In between kicking butt on the table and stuffing money down her bra, waistline, and anywhere else she could keep it, she was something serious when she played. Meanwhile, my auntie is in the corner being over-friendly with someone else's beau. Just like my mom, all my aunties were easy on the eyes, so male company was plentiful. However, this particular gentleman was with someone else. The lady he had come with casually strolls up to my aunt, and some heated words are exchanged. After my auntie goes up one side of her and then down the other, the lady walks away in a fury. She returns a little while later with a gun, and my heart drops at the sight of it. (My auntie is young and full of life; we have a good time every time we're with her, and the stories she would tell us would make us laugh until our stomachs hurt).

Seeing that gun to her head brings a fear over me that I have never felt before. The times when my mom and stepdad would have their drag outs didn't even compare. It seems as though things are going in slow motion! Once I find my voice, I scream for my mother and run toward the kitchen. By the time mom comes out of the back, it's too late… the lady pulls the trigger.

All you hear are gasps as the gun clicks, and then jams. Oh, to my relief, the gun isn't working. But bad news for the lady, out comes my mother's gun, and the whole place is in an uproar. The guy manages to knock the gun from my mom's hand, so she picks the lady up and throws her through the window. The gentleman then rushes out the door. Mom picks up her gun and is in hot pursuit behind him. I guess with all the commotion taking place, someone had called the police. When I make it outside, I see the lone policeman screaming for Mom to drop the gun (remember, we live in a town smaller than most big-city blocks).

No one had ever really given Mr. Leroy a problem. Mom does; she starts shooting in the direction of this poor, kind sheriff, and I remember thinking she's going to JAIL. Thankfully, he decided not to go round for round with her. He drove away, saying he would be back with the State Patrol. I guess he'd had enough of the female Wild Bill; it was time to call in the big boys. That was my mom's chance to make a dash for it. We wrestle her in the car, and my auntie convinces her that she needs to get out of town, and quickly. Even as a kid, I knew shooting at the police couldn't be good. We make it home, wake up the other children and my stepdad (who had picked the wrong night to stay home), pack all we can in our van and head out of town.

This was the last time my mom saw home for years. Thank God the van is equipped with a fridge and bed, making a longer-than-usual ride a little more comfortable. As children, we are all excited about the road trip; with Mom being a big gambler, it's nothing to pack up and go out of town on a whim. To us, this is another middle-of-the-night excursion. Little did we know this trip would be life-changing.

Chapter 2

BIG CITY/BIGGER PROBLEMS

We arrived in Buffalo, New York, with no plan, eleven children, and only the money my parents had on them. And if you are wondering if you missed something with the eleven kids, you didn't. Mom had 8, but my stepdad had three from his previous marriage that were always with us. No one can tell us we're not blood brothers and sisters. The love we have for each other outweighs DNA.

We are so excited about this new adventure and clueless to the hell that we will soon encounter. I've heard New York streets referred to as the street's dreams are made of. Well, let me tell you, I see more dreams killed than produced in the neighborhood we reside in.

Our unexpected vacation, on limited finances, lands us at an aunt's house. She's terminally ill, and Mom often talked about visiting and helping her with her three children, as if she didn't have enough kids already! But that was my mom; no matter how wild she was, she would always bend over backwards to help someone out. You could have her last dollar or the shirt off her back if you could keep in her one place long enough.

My aunt's children range from early teens to young adults. All this time, I thought I had seen too much for a girl my age until I met them. In comparison, I was an angel. The youngest was a girl and had experienced more than I had even imagined, the middle son had more women than you could count, and the oldest son was mixed up with drugs and a few more illegal activities. But for now, this was the best we could do. Being from the country, I found them to be exciting at first, but within a few months, I discovered exciting was definitely not the right description.

I adjust to city life quickly: enrolling in school, learning the bus routes, and making friends fast. I was so busy learning about new things like corner stores, rap music, and different nationalities, I didn't notice the immediate hold the city life has placed on all of us. We're handling it, though, fighting regularly along the way because we are the new kids in the town. My stepdad was busy working and providing for all of us, which meant 15-18 hour days at times, and Mom spent most of her time caring for my auntie, which left our cousins to show us around town. And it wasn't always good things we were seeing. In a few months, we were back to looking out for ourselves. Unlike the country, though, being on your own in the city is a different type of beast. No little harmless hit-and-tell catfights; you had to go for what you knew when these ruthless kids came at you. All those survival tactics we had learned growing up kicked in and had to be upgraded. They don't call it Ruff Buff for nothing.

Just as the dust is starting to settle from our relocation and we seem to catch a rhythm, my auntie passes. We maintain for a little while, but with my stepdad being the only source of real income, the bank made good on all their promises to take the house now that my auntie was gone. My mom and stepdad find a six-bedroom, within their budget, in another neighborhood on the Eastside. Keep in mind we are now 15 children strong with my aunt's three children and my cousin Edrick who recently moved up from Alabama (I know this just keeps getting better).

We settle into the tight living quarters as comfortably as we can. The smaller children all slept in one room with two sets of bunk beds and the boys shared rooms as well, but all the girls got their own space, I was thankful for that. But, I was even more excited that we didn't have to change schools. I had just made friends; mostly everyone loved the Bamas (I personally think they were entertained by the way we talked). With Auntie gone, the kids at school and my stepdad at work, Mom has a lot of free time to tend to the smaller children, keep the house clean and prepare meals. Life is as close to peaceful as I can remember in a long time.

It seemed as if I blinked, and then I was in High School! I look forward to these being the best days of my life. With so many of us at the same school in close age proximity, it should be fun! Mom is so skeptical about us roaming in this big city. We have to be our own entertainment, seeing that school is about the only place we are allowed to go. She does ensure we have a social life, though, by allowing our friends to come over and party with us on the weekends. We have unimaginable fun, my mom and stepdad cook food for days, and there's always a DJ! Everyone thinks we are IT! I mean, what kid doesn't appreciate parents like this?

As usual, though, too much of a good thing can go bad, as is the case with these parties. Eventually, people who were not in school, mainly low-life friends of my oldest cousin, started to hang around. These once-popular parties are slowly turning into something else. Mom has started having after-parties of her own, which usually end at the bar on the corner of our street. She would leave before half of us fell asleep to have a few "adult drinks". Soon, we found out that these adult drinks had turned into other extracurricular activities, and those innocent Friday night parties for us were cut off completely. Mom and her new group of friends have parties of their own now in the basement, where they smoke funny cigarettes and drink for hours, then she "steps out until later". She's grown at the end of the day, and I had more than enough siblings to keep me company. I didn't see the harm at first.

The bigger the city, the bigger the demons; that's what we soon discover about Buffalo, New York, which ends up being our final destination and the last trip we take as a complete family. The

New York night life is much faster than the Alabama nightlife, and it's pulling my mother back into familiar territory. Coming in late at night or the early hours of the morning is now every other night instead of just on Fridays. We transcend back to being parents! My stepsister and older cousin now pitch in and share chores with us; one would cook, the other comb hair, another would choose clothes for the smaller ones, and the fourth would do the dishes and vacuuming. All the while, my stepdad was working and trying to maintain because with Mom being up to her old tricks again and a few new ones, money was disappearing at a rapid pace.

This once-fun city is not so fun anymore. My stepdad is working tirelessly and Mom is officially out of control. Everyone is feeling it. I complained once to my stepdad about him working so many hours, as Mom was still receiving good money for us from my father. That, in addition to the money he was bringing home, should be enough for him to work normal hours. He sat me down and explained that he didn't know where the money was going that my father contributed, but bills had to be paid, so we had to continue helping out. I didn't question him anymore after that. My cousin lost interest in helping out after a few months of us moving and started hanging out more and more. It was strange that at such a young age, she went on so many dates with all these different men. I guess she figured anything beats being stuck at home raising a bunch of kids. My sisters and I are used to it, so we continue to maintain amidst the chaos.

Today has been particularly hectic, and I can't wait to go to bed. As I'm turning back my covers, I hear this awful loud scream and rush toward the front of the house to see where it's coming from. The smaller kids are looking on and crying. What is Mom up to now? She's been gone for at least two days at this point and has the nerve to come back with some drama! I'm fully annoyed until I hear my stepdad yell, "DIAL 911!" then I go numb with fear.

To my surprise, Mom isn't the source of this commotion, but my cousin has gone into labor. With all the hustle of our daily lives, her popping in and out on "dates", she had managed to get pregnant and carry a baby full term without anyone noticing. Teenage pregnancy, while disappointing, is bound to happen when there's a lack of adult supervision. Don't misunderstand, we run the house like we're adults; In actuality though, we are just children ourselves finding our own way. Life is hard enough, and putting children in adult situations leads to adult behavior more often than not. My dad has yet another thing to deal with while my mom's only concern right now is what makes her happy.

We hear stories at school and in the neighborhood about how wild she is and the things she's doing. She's a known partier, but it has never gone this far. Kids have started to tease us, and that means constant fights in and out of school. I don't care WHAT she's doing; she's still my mom, so when someone came out their mouth wrong, my fist would go in it. At one time, we were the coolest family on the block, and she had to feed them all, so I'm gonna need them to act like they remember that; damn what you heard.

To occupy my mind with something other than the craziness of my home life, I join every after school activity I qualify for. I like most sports, but basketball is my favorite. I play all the rest just to stay away from the madness in the hood as long as I can.

I'm goofing off at practice when I see my coach walking fast toward me. "Fryer, you have an emergency phone call." It's my sister telling me my stepdad has been hurt and rushed to the hospital. It's nothing life-threatening, but serious; she sounds upset. I tell my coach I have to go and cut to the locker room to change. I don't realize how cold it is until I'm waiting at the bus stop. My mind was so preoccupied I hadn't thought to check the schedule to see what time the next bus would come. The practice has ended, and other students are coming out, but there is still no bus in sight. I'm at another level of cold at this point.

A car drives up. "Do you want a ride?" My heart stops; it's the cute boy from practice, and his mom is driving. I want to answer, but my lips won't move. It has to be cold because my big mouth never stops running. "Someone told me you left because your dad was rushed to the hospital. My mom wanted me to ask if you'd like a ride." Sure, I finally answer.

He slides over in the backseat. His brother, who is taller than his 6 feet 4, is in the front, smiling from ear to ear… He's a clown. His mom says hi in a country slang that sounds much like my own.

I can't resist asking where she's from. Alabama, she replies. A huge smile crosses my face. "Why is that so funny?" I'm from Alabama as well (what's the chance?), and I like him even more now! I had heard kids at school refer to him as big country, but I figured it was just a nickname because he and his brother are tall as trees. B's a cutie pie; I used to daydream about him all the time. His brother is a year older, but he's so goofy he had failed and ended up in the same grade with us. I was so shocked from being so close to this handsome boy with the brownest eyes I had ever seen that I almost forgot where we were going until we pulled up at the hospital.

I get out of the car and greet my other siblings who had gotten a ride to the hospital with Art, my sister's boyfriend. The doctors are still running tests; my stepdad had a nasty fall. I am so nervous; he is the primary caregiver with Mom being MIA most of the time. I don't know what we'll do without him.

B says his mother has somewhere to be, but he offers to stay with me, and I accept. Dad's still in surgery, so we decide to feed the kids. We scrap our change together to buy them something from the hospital cafeteria, and as the kids eat, we talk and discuss our Alabama roots. My sister comes to the table and says Dad is headed to recovery. We gather the kids and head to the waiting area outside his room. The doctor informs us that Dad's injury is pretty serious and he will not be able to move around for a while. For some reason, anything he said after that was blurry. What are we going to do without Dad? I feel like if it wasn't for bad luck, I wouldn't have any.

About an hour after he is stabilized, my mom shows up. I can see she is really sad. She loves her family, but this hold the street has on her apparently wins. When the kids see her, they all start to cry. It breaks my heart. I try to hide my face, ashamed because B's here, but you can't make your heart stop what it feels. As the tears start to flow, I feel his hand on my shoulder. We stay with Dad until the nurse tells us visiting hours are over, and then we all load into Art's van to head home. Despite the fact that it's so many people packed in here, there is an unusual silence. No one has seen our mother in a while, and we have a million questions, but with B in the car, they will have to wait.

I help get the kids to bed, then walk B to the bus stop at the corner. We talk about friends and things we have in common for a little while, and then it's silent. Finally, he clears his throat and asks the dreaded question: why did everyone cry when my mother walked in? It's a long story. "I've heard about your mom through the gossip committee in school; I mean, who doesn't know the clan from Alabama…" small chuckles.

"So, if you know, why did you ask?"

"Once I saw her, I couldn't believe she was as wild as they said; she's too beautiful."

"Thank you, but I don't want to talk about that right now. Let's change the subject."

"What do you want to talk about?"

"Nothing really. I'm just tired."

"Are you too tired to answer one more question…Would you go out with me?"

I'm speechless again for the second time in one day. I see lights approaching (saved by the bell or would it be the bus?). "Can I answer you tomorrow?"

After a week and a half, Dad is released to come home. I have been avoiding B like a plague since that night at the bus stop! I have enough going on; Mom is finally home and actually being a mother again. I guess this thing with Dad scared her straight. I had missed several practices since Dad got hurt because my family needed me around the house. I have never been selfish; my siblings are always my first priority all we have is us. I'm in the kitchen washing dishes with my headscarf on, dancing to music only I can hear, when my idiot brothers walk in from school. They are so loud. I ignore them and go back to my chores, then suddenly, someone asks, "What are you listening to?" It's him… what the what, how did you get in my house?

"I know you're avoiding me, so I came over. I told your brothers to ask your parents if it was okay, and your mom said yes."

All she had done, and I never wished her any harm, but today I'm going to kill her! I look a mess! At least she could have warned me. He wastes no time getting to the point. "So that question I asked the last time we talked requires a simple yes or no."

"Listen, I think you're really nice, but I have a lot going on, and my life is very complicated, so it's best you find another girlfriend. I mean, most of the girls in the school want to date you anyway."

"This may be true, but there's just one problem with that: I don't want anybody but you."

My heart flips, and I feel a strange feeling in my stomach. I smile, and he comes closer to give me a hug. My 5-foot-5 frame feels good against his tall body. Okay, I forgive my mother. B helps me finish my chores, then says he has to go home. I take the stairs two at a time to my mother's room once he's gone. She could have at least given a sister a heads-up. Mom is helping my dad out of bed. He doesn't need as much assistance as he did when he first came home, but he's not a hundred percent just yet. I ask my dad if we can have a minute; his smile tells me they are in business together. Once the door closed, I set into her. "Did you tell that boy to come over here?"

"Yes. He asked, and that lets me know for sure that he's a gentleman. You should always get a man that will take care of you, and no one does that better than a country boy. Just look at your dad and your stepdad."

Can't argue with her there; those are two of the best men on Earth! And just like that, she's off the hook. "Now, are we done?"

"Yes," I mumble, hating when she's right.

"Good, because his whole family is coming over on Saturday!" She's too much.

This is the best weekend we've had in a long time. My stepdad is feeling well enough to grill despite the cold and having to sit occasionally to stay comfortable. We had a blast playing cards, dancing, and just laughing until we cried telling down south tales. My mom and B's mother find they have a lot in common. He and I become an instant item, and just like that, our families become one! It's funny how the most unfortunate things tend to bring people together.

Shortly before spring, Dad returns to work, and things are still going smoothly in our home. Our families continue to get together often, and every week, I look forward to Saturdays. Dad didn't want to miss work, so we started without him today, but he wastes no time calling next on the spades game when he walks in. We're laughing and having a good time when there's a knock on the door. It's my cousin; she moved out soon after having the baby, but finds her way back occasionally when there's food and people around! And every time she does, things seem to go haywire. My other cousins, her two brothers, had moved out over a year ago. They were like revolving doors in the world, the oldest boy in and out of prison and the other one with a different woman every six months, but they never came back to our house to live. The sister, however, would usually disappear for months and then resurface. I could never really stay mad at her, though, because just like Mom, no matter how bad her habits were, she had the sweetest heart and would do anything for you.

My mom invites her in. I guess she feels the resistance because she hesitates as if she's never lived here before. She finally walks in, slowly carrying a tote bag, looking drained. I guess moving from place to place and constantly getting beat down by life can wear on you. By the time she showers and Mom feeds her, all of our guests are gone and we're just hanging out in the kitchen. I hear Mom tell my cousin she made an appointment with the doctor next week, and she should be up early, ready to go on Monday morning.

For it to be the first day back to school after the weekend, I'm in the best mood. B had walked me to every class at school. Nothing could ruin this day. Within an hour, not only was my day ruined, but my life was about to change. I walk in smiling from ear to ear, only to find everyone in the house in a slumber and Mom crying her eyes out. What now!

Someone says she has AIDS.

Chapter 3

HOW MUCH MORE
CAN I TAKE

When I regain my composure, I ask Mom how she got AIDS. I have been studying about this. It's been all over the news, literature is everywhere. Why weren't you more careful? She says between sobs that it's not her, it's my cousin.

I'm relieved! I mean, I'm not happy for my cousin, just elated it's not my mother. I haven't had the best childhood, but she is still my mother, and I love her with all my heart. What's next, I ask. How is she going to care for herself? Where will she live? I have a million questions because this is way too much. My stepdad is sitting there with a blank stare because he knows it's about to be a volcanic eruption when my mother says... she has to move back here. WHAT THE WHAT! I'm horrified. I've seen all the documentaries on this awful disease, and I don't want any parts of it.

The blowout begins; everyone is yelling, kids are crying, and it is getting ugly. My mom finally yells, "IT'S MY HOUSE!" and the argument comes to an end. No one really needs this extra stress; this is a critical time in our lives. In the end, my mother wins as usual, and my cousin moves in—upstairs, of course—in the bedroom next to my mom because we refuse to have her downstairs with us. If she must be in the house, not in the next room.

I thought this would give my cousin a reality check… NOT. She continues hanging out and doing the same things. We are fed up. There is always someone looking for her, and from past experiences, we don't care much for strangers. She's constantly running in and out at all times of the night as if she doesn't have a care in the world or a deadly virus. You can believe no matter how much she runs around, though, she always makes it to dinner, and tonight is no exception. As soon as my mom yells that the food is ready, she comes strolling down wearing a tank top and shorts. It looks like she gained weight overnight. My mother turns and asks, "What have you been eating?"

She casually replies, "I'm pregnant."

Okay, where's the camera crew? Because this HAS to be a joke. Only her facial expression says it's not. She needs another baby about as much as an asthmatic needs a pack of Newports.

My mother goes through the roof. I think she kind of walked herself into this one, letting her be so carefree all the time. My mom's wild behavior had slowed down, but this sent her back in the wrong direction. She has started coming home late at night again and avoiding her responsibilities. Her disappearing acts become more frequent until finally she's full force back at it. I don't have time for this; we are preparing for Junior/Senior prom, graduation, and all the fun stuff that a teenager looks forward to this time of the year. But what does that matter to Mom when she gets on these kicks? It's all about her. I'm not discouraged by her behavior; it's nothing new. I just kick in and carry on.

I finally got my dues and affairs together for prom today. My friend Tee and I are on the phone making plans when I hear someone cry out in pain. I recognize the sound from before; my cousin is in labor! I hang up and race up the stairs to find her doubled over on the bed. I mentally thank God I can't have kids; this looks painful. We call 911, get her downstairs, and wait for the ambulance. Tonya rides in the back with her while I stay back on babysitting duties. By the time my sister makes it home from the hospital, it's rather late. I open the door to tease her and see another shadow looming. "Look what the wind blew in," Tonya says, trying to make light of the situation.

I always wonder if my mother secretly watches over us because every time we have a crisis, she just appears. Once my cousin is released, Mom helps her prepare her room for the baby. Mom has her faults, but when she is on her game, it's amazing the things she can do. She quickly produces a crib, car seat, clothing, and anything else needed to care for the baby, as the first one had been adopted by another family and all the baby things went with her. Auntie duties keep Mom calm and content for the whole month, and I'm glad. We have been too busy with preparation for prom and graduation to deal with anything else. The only thing left to do was pick out our dresses, and Mom promised she wouldn't mess that up. This would be a priority over her partying. With the money that comes into the house, I know she can make good on her promise.

I'm not worried until two days go by, then I realize she's not coming back; my heart is broken. Like so many times before, she didn't keep her word! The mail came, and Mom said she was going to the bank and would return shortly to take us to the mall. Sadly, I had to call my father who had already sent money for my dues, hair, and other necessities. That was the arrangement they had made, and he held up his part of the deal. It's only a week left before prom, and Mom won't have money again until next month; I don't have a choice. After explaining the situation to him, he said a few words I don't care to repeat and told me to head to Western Union to pick up the money. He had saved me from yet another letdown. He wasn't around daily, being that we lived in another state, but I can never remember my father telling me no. I decided not to let Mom's poor decision spoil my fun. I ask Ms. Mackinnon to take me straight to the mall after leaving Western Union. She helps me find the most beautiful gown, shoes, and some accessories to complete the look. Regardless of the drama that came with my mom, she had taken the time to teach me fashion and style.

One of the most exciting days in a teenager's life has come. We are dressed to the nine, hair fried-dyed-laid to the side, dates on our arms, and a few dollars in our pockets, thanks to my stepdad. This is going to be a great night. We're posing for pictures, about to load up in our chariot (okay, it's Tee's 1990 Sentra), but who cares? We are headed to the prom!

I hear a car pull up, and my mom jumps out. She looks sad. I'm sure she feels guilty that she broke her promise. I'm not even angry when I see her; I know her heart is good, she just makes bad decisions. She gives B a hug, then walks over to me. "Where did you get that dress?"

"From a boutique in the mall."

"Who paid for it?"

"My Daddy!"

Mom flips! "Who told you to call that judgmental bastard?" She launches toward me. She always said I was Daddy's favorite and he would do just about anything I asked. What she doesn't know is that Daddy would do the same for all of us. They just never needed him so much. I depend on my daddy for everything, and no matter how big or small, he always comes through.

With tears in my eyes, I ask, "What should I have done? Wait on you to show up or go naked?" Smack, right across my face. Now she trippin. I take off my shoes and earrings, but before I can do anything else, my stepdad grabs my mom and takes her inside the house. My little sisters pick up my shoes and help me put them back on and tell me to have a good time; they always got my back. Meanwhile, all the neighbors are watching in amazement because it really is some real live TV show drama that takes place at our house, only it's not scripted. I'm upset that I even let her get me out of character; the flesh responded to the slap. I know Mom is doing what she does best: deflect. She feels bad for not coming through when I needed her, and she's trying to redirect her pain.

We get in the car and act as if it never happened. We let the guys have the front so I can touch up my hair and makeup. Our dates are silent; I think they are in shock. No matter what length of time you've been around my family, nothing can prepare you for the mayhem. We have a blast despite the near riot hours before. The thing about dysfunction is you either learn to adapt to it and keep it moving or it will consume you. Unfortunately, more often than not, it consumes the best of us.

My sister Tonya moves out the week after graduation, and I cry uncontrollably once she's gone. This is a big piece of the little puzzle of normal I have. I'm thankful to still have B to help me out around the house and with the kids. He's such a lifesaver. He even stays overnight with the little ones on the days Dad needs my help at the store. You would think he has always been a part of our family, and he will be in about a year. I've decided I'm going to marry him! I had been with him all this time, and we were even voted the best couple at school; it seemed natural. My mom and stepdad love him like their own son. He eats when we eat, cleans the house, does chores, and even cooks when neither of my parents are around to make dinner as cooking is still a skill I have yet to master.

I'm relieved this is my LAST year of high school! The drama at home is at an all-time high, but I made all my sports teams again, so at least I have something else to focus on besides that. My mom is scarce most of the time, so I've been making a lot of decisions on my own or consulting my teacher Ms. Mackinnon, who's been my rock since I started South Park High School.

Ms. Mackinnon is simply an Angel on Earth! I can always count on her when the going gets tough, and she works overtime to keep me on track. She pressed me daily to make sure I excelled in all the classes I needed to get the proper credits to attend college, something I had not willingly considered because of my circumstances. However, I'm looking forward to it now. Thoughts of college have me consumed when my homeroom teacher walks over and slides me a note that says I have one more day to pay senior dues in order to go on the field trip, get my senior photos, attend prom, and all that other good stuff.

I have exactly $5 to my name. I see B during the class exchange, and I tell him about the deadline for dues. He shrugs his shoulders and says not to worry about it. What do you mean don't worry? Everyone waits four years just for this very thing; I have to get this money. He kind of blows me off and goes into his next class (what's that about?). I try to forget it; nothing I can do in the middle of the day.

When school is dismissed, I decide to skip practice and rush home to see if I could find my mom. No such luck! I call my brother-in-law Tank and ask if he could get me a ride to see my stepdad at work.

"You know it, sis. Just give me a minute."

He had his grandfather outside to take me before I could get my jacket on. He and his mother, Kitty, love my siblings and I as if we were their own. My stepdad tells me he just paid the bills. He looks so disappointed; he understands it's important to me. I hug him, letting him know it's okay. My last resort is my dad, but when I call, his wife tells me he's out on the road. He had married Dott a few years after we moved to New York. She's very kind and meek, like my father. I think they are a good match She's also my middleman when dad's out of reach, as we chat often when I call.

As always, we speak for a few minutes and she promises to have him call me back. With all my hope gone, I go to bed early. How can I not be a part of senior skip day or prom? This is the worse. At times like this, I really dislike my mom. I arrive at school the next day and tell the teacher over the senior committee to take my name off the list because I wasn't able to come up with the money. She looks at me and smiles. She's about to get punched in the face... and we'll see how funny that is!

"Your Angel took care of it this morning," she says, her smile growing even wider. Ms. Mackinnon has saved the day again! Whew, I'm glad I didn't hit this lady! But how did she know that I called her my Angel? And how did Ms. Mackinnon know I needed the money? I hadn't told her because I depended on her for so much already. I walk to her class, thank her, give her the biggest hug, and tell her how much I love her. Tears gather in her eyes instantly before she can respond, so she rushes me out with a kiss on the cheek. I'm flying down the hall to find B and give him the good news when the boys' basketball coach yells, "Ms. Fryer, slow it down." I break it down to a light jog. He turns around and winks at me. He's another favorite of mine. I love how he treats the kids as if they are his own flesh and blood.

I find B in the gym with a girl from the junior class. She looks captivated by what he's saying. Her blue eyes are locked on his lips, and she's twirling her blonde hair dreamingly. I clear my throat to alert them of my presence. B almost jumps out of his skin, and little Ms. Prissy frowns when she sees me. "What's up?" he asks a little aggressively, as if I'm bothering him. I tell him that my dues were paid and I will be able to hang out with him on senior day.

His excitement doesn't match mine. "After you said you weren't able to get the money, I got up with a few of my friends and made other arrangements to go with them."

I lie, saying that's cool, and walk away hotter than a pan of fish grease on a Friday night. I wasn't just pretty, I was quite smart, and it didn't take rocket science to figure out he just fed me the biggest line of BS. I'm not going to make a scene though; we spend most of our time together. If he wants to be with the fellas, oh well, I'll just hang with my girl, Tee. We have more fun anyways; we make any environment we're in HYPE. As I exit the gym, Ms. Mackinnon is coming down the hall toward me so fast I think she's going to run me over. Her face is wet with tears. I start to panic. She grabs me by the hand and tells me we have to go. I'm pleading with her to tell me what's wrong, but all she says is, "We need to get to the hospital." I really start to freak out then! We stop in the main office so I can check out, then run to her car. She instructs me to put on my seatbelt and try to stay calm.

My brother has been shot.

I try to wrap my mind around this. My brother is a sweetheart. How did he get shot in school? A thousand questions run through my mind, but the most important one is, is he okay? He is my competition, my basketball partner, and my runner when I need a snack from the store. The tears will not stop coming.

We make it to the hospital where my stepdad and a few other family members are waiting in the ER lobby. I ask what happened, but everyone is too upset to talk. All I find out is that he's stable but still unconscious. I ask the nurse if I could go back. I wanted to see him for myself. As we enter the double doors, my mom is standing there, her face swollen from crying. As I reach out to hug her, she notices Ms. Mackinnon behind me and starts to hurl insults. "What the fuck are you doing with this White bitch around my son? You know she looks down on us; she makes you think you are more than what you are. You ain't shit," she says as she's walking away. Ms. Mackinnon never says a word. She, too, understands my mom is mad at herself more than anyone else.

"You're out of line, Mom! Ms. Mackinnon has been the closest thing to a mother I've had in a while." Smack! Okay, what you not about to do is keep putting your hands in my face because I speak the truth. Lord, forgive me, but somebody has to take this pent-up frustration. It may as well be her since she causes most of it. I launch at her with all the thoughts of the past in my head: B and that dumb girl, her disappearing acts ("Where the heck were you last night when I needed you?"), and definitely the fool who shot my brother. Yep, she is about to catch a variety of beat downs. I grab her and try my best to make her feel all the pain I'm feeling. We knock over a table tussling, and everyone rushes in. My stepdad grabs me up like I weigh 25 pounds instead of 125 and sits me in a chair. Ms. Mackinnon never moves. I think she's stunned.

The nurse comes out and says my brother is awake with a face that reads, break up the ghetto shit. I learned from the police in the room he was hit in the back; the bullet barely missed his vital organs. I cry out, "Thank You, God!" Grateful it wasn't worse, even fatal.

My mom snarls, "You're so dramatic!"

I look at her dead in her eyes, about to give her a few choice words, but something holds my tongue. Instead, I turn around to tell Ms. Mackinnon I'm ready to go. I have embarrassed my family enough. I kiss my stepdad, apologize for my behavior, and tell him that I'm not coming home tonight. I'm too spent for any more drama with my mama.

I called B several times to let him know about my brother and that I will be staying at Tee's tonight. His mom answers every time, saying she hasn't seen him since school was out. My eyes are almost swollen shut when I show up at Tee's door. Her baby brother James has filled them in on what happened; he and my brother are as close as his sister and I. Tee gives me the tightest hug when I walk in, and I need it! Although she only lives a few blocks over from me, it seems a world apart from my reality when I'm at their house. Her father, my godfather Rev. James A. Lewis III, is also our Pastor and another Angel God was gracious enough to appoint me. He and his wife Zandra, my godmother, pray with me. I feel as if a thousand pounds have been lifted off my shoulders, yet I can't stop crying.

"Your brother is going to be fine, sweetheart. You said it yourself. Why are you so upset?"

"Dad, I did something so bad; I fought with my own mother." My tears are steadily pouring from shame.

He looks at me with the most serious face and asks, "Well, did you win?"

This dude is nuts! I start to laugh and can't stop. He can always lighten my mood no matter how miserable I feel. Tee takes me upstairs where she has some things laid out for me in the bathroom. I shower and lay down without eating dinner. By the time sleep finds me, the sun is coming up. I ask my godparents if I could just stay here for the day. I'm too exhausted to answer questions or hear any of the million stories floating around school by now. You know, black people, we have 50 versions of the same story within an hour's time.

I slept the ENTIRE day! I'm still in a comatose-like state when Tee flies in the house, shaking me, asking if I heard from B. Come to think of it, I haven't talked to or seen him since yesterday. That was odd. I know if everyone else had heard about my brother, so had he. I left word with my family to tell him I was here if he came by. Now I'm WIDE awake! I call his house and his brother answers. He offers a heartfelt sorry for my brother and, after a long pause, tells me his brother isn't home... I hang up.

Tee jumps right in my face. "He's an ass, and he's cheating on you!"

"What are you talking about, girl? Everybody knows that boy is so in love with me he can't see straight."

"Oh, you think so? I saw him today, all hugged up with the blue-eyed blonde that started Park a little while ago." It sounds like the chick from the gym. Oh, part two of the beat down about to start on him.

We get her dad's car and drive to his house. Sure enough, he's coming out of the house all smiles until he sees me. "And where are you going?" I ask, blocking the stairs with my hands on my hips and ponytail swinging, ready for W-H-A-T-E-V-E-R. He starts to stumble over his words, and before a lie could form, Ms. Blondie comes out of the house. AWW, HELL NO! As I start seeing RED, his brother steps out and grabs Blondie by the arm. "She's with me."

Oh, ok, somebody better tell me something. I could feel my blood pressure lower a bit. It was about to go all the way down. B suddenly finds all his words and starts explaining how he was on his way to see me and cheer me up. How could I be so stupid? I know what we have is real. Tee's not so convinced. I have to believe it, and I'm too tired to deal with what it seemed like it could be.

We go to my house to check on the kids. Andre is there watching them while my parents are at the hospital. He was my sister's high school sweetheart, and another son my mom had welcomed in love! He and my sister had gone their separate ways about a year ago, but he is still our big brother and comes by often. I'm glad my mom is not home; I can relax without reliving the foolishness from yesterday. I call my sister Tonya to keep me company. She brings a pizza, and we sit on the porch and unwind.

She was never one to judge, and her spirit was much like her dad, just cool and calm. No matter what was going on, their presence alone can bring you peace, and that's what I need right now.

As night begins to fall, she gathers her things to leave. She asks if I will be ok once she's gone. I assure her that I'm much better now. B tells me the chores are all finished and he'll be leaving soon as well. I give him the side eye.

"I have a busy day tomorrow, Chief. My friends are picking me up early from home."

No big deal. I want to be alone tonight with my thoughts anyways. Once we get the kids settled, B gathers his things and heads out the door just as my parents are driving up. Mom gets out, only saying hi to B as if I'm not there. As she passes me on the stairs, she elbows me into the rail, my shirt catches and then rips. "What's your problem, Mom?"

"YOU!" she yells. "I can't stand you, always got somebody in my damn business. I didn't need you calling your sister for food."

"Actually, you DO since you don't ever buy any for the kids to eat! But I didn't call her to bring the food; I called her for comfort, something I can get from everyone except YOU!" Tears start to fall. I fly into the house and start packing my things; I give up! I call Tee to pick me up, and she makes it here before I can zip up my luggage. "I need to go to the greyhound station, girl." I had called my dad to send for me.

"We only have a little while before graduation, Vett. It would be crazy to go back down south at this point," she says fast talking. "You also hate Alabama. Remember, you complain about the heat every summer after you return."

I consider my own words for a minute. I did say the only way I would live in Alabama again would be dead. The thought vanishes quickly; I'm not listening, and I yell for her to take me! Wait, where the heck did B go? Who cares? I'm leaving anyway. She tries with all her might to talk me out of it. I'm not having it; once I make my mind up, that's it. I ask her to open the trunk for my bag, and she pulls off, leaving me standing in the yard. Oh no, she didn't. Fine! I'll walk until the bus comes. I got my $5 on me.

I'm barely to the next block when I see her zooming up again. Only she's not alone; her dad is with her. Great, just what I need: a lecture! He doesn't lecture me this time, though. He quietly gets out, grabs my bag, and puts me in the car. "Thank you, I just want to go to my daddy." He smiles and says, "you're with your daddy baby, let's go home."

We stopped by my house and he talked with my stepdad, asking if he could have the rest of my things. My stepdad reluctantly agrees. I'm his only real help with the kids since my other two sisters moved out. More so, he understands that this is the only way I will survive. He gives my godfather a hand putting the rest of my belongings in the car, and kisses me goodbye. I never lived in my parents' house again. I spent the rest of my senior year with the Lewis's. I vacationed when they did, shopped when they shopped, everyone had dinner at the same time and split chores equally. I go to bed every night, wondering if this is what normal feels like. I still go to my parents every day after school to see the kids and make sure they are ok. They are my world; after all, my sisters and I had practically raised them. And apparently, they were paying attention. The older ones have picked up where we left off. They wash dishes, comb hair, and assist with school work for the children under them; the cycle continues.

I'm kind of relieved I didn't leave for Alabama. A scout from Wisconsin is at South Park for B's signing day, and I would have missed this exciting moment for him. He received a football scholarship for the Badgers, and I've been accepted into the State University of New York at Buffalo. I'm really happy for both of us, but we are going to be so far from each other. We are not as tight as we used to be. My godfather, being a Pastor, isn't with all the male company, so we haven't spent a lot of time together lately. I can tell we're drifting apart, but I love him just the same.

The school conference room is full of media, administrators, and his family. Once it calms down a bit, I ask if he wants to go out that evening and grab a bite to eat. He says his mom has something planned.

"That's cool. I'll just come over there."

"Nah, it'll just be family."

My feelings are hurt a little. I had chosen this special night to discuss getting married before our lives spiraled away from us. Oh well, we have a week left of school and the whole summer.

The next week came and went so fast; We never got a chance to talk, but I feel today is perfect; it's GRADUATION! I notice him watching me from the opposite side of the stage and blow him a kiss. He winks and smiles. He's so handsome. I feel a twinge of sadness thinking of the beautiful babies we would never have. I had a terrible accident one summer when I was 13. It caused some serious damage in my reproductive area, and the doctor said that having children would be impossible. I was raising babies already, so I wasn't too concerned then, at this very moment, I feel it. Oh well, it's a happy occasion. I can't think about that right now. Speaking of babies, his mom is holding the most adorable little girl with the curliest hair and the bluest eyes. I step down the back stairs, scanning the room for my mom, who's not here. I do spot my siblings and my stepdad…That'll work. I go over and hug them, and he starts to make an excuse as to why mom isn't present. I save him the embarrassment by assuring him it's okay. I excuse myself to go and speak to B's mom, his little sister, and his brother.

"You look beautiful,"his mom says, appearing uncomfortable.

I try and change the atmosphere. "Big W finally messed around and got a baby, huh?" Lord knows his brother had a different woman every day of the week. Black, white, hispanic— he didn't discriminate.

"That's not Big W's baby. She's B's!" his little sister blurts out.

Everything got really quiet for the next few minutes. It was as if time stopped. Once I gather my senses, I run backstage like a bat out of hell. He never saw it coming; I came up behind him and punched the daylights out of him. Before he could recover from the first punch, I threw a storm of haymakers, catching him from every angle I could. Out of either shock or anger, he slaps me so hard he busts my lip, but it doesn't stop me. I'm used to getting smacked in the face, it only makes me madder, and I continue to fight.

We are wrestling for a few minutes before Coach and a few other people separate us. Coach drags me into another room and asks what set me off. I told him that baby in his mom's lap. I guess the pain in my face and voice prompted his next question, "You didn't know he had a baby?"

I shake my head no as tears start to fall, even though I'm trying my best not to cry. Well, sweetie, everyone knew but you," he says with compassion in his voice. "That's why she transferred to another school." That would explain all his strange behavior and absence lately.

I'm not going to let these people see me cry! I quickly dry my tears, hold my head up, fix my hair, and go back to find my place in line. Needless to say, we walked across the stage a little disheveled as if we had been in the limo in the movie "What's Love Got to Do With It", but hey, we graduated. Good thing I didn't embarrass myself with the conversation of marriage; he is history. Hope it works out for them. It's certainly over between him and I.

Summer is definitely what the doctor ordered for a broken heart. Even though I'm not visiting Alabama due to some prerequisites I have to complete so I can start school in the fall. At least I have something to keep my mind occupied. I keep busy with school and entertaining my siblings during the day, but nothing helps at night; when everything gets quiet, I cry myself to sleep at the thought of losing another piece of my normal. No matter how badly B had hurt me, the feelings would not just disappear like I prayed they would. Spending years with the same person and then having to let them go is painful, and I don't know how much more pain I can take.

Chapter 4

COLLEGE BOUND

Fall 1994 came around fast, and a new chapter has begun: I'm college-bound. As I stand in line to receive my room assignment at SUNY Buffalo, for the first time since I was a little girl, I feel I have a chance to become someone who will make a difference in this world. Tee and I are staying on Campus instead of home even though we're not leaving the city. We have big plans to experience every aspect of college, including the parties and all the other wild things that come with it. We would be studying too, of course, but we were both good students, members of the National Honor Society even—we had the education part down to a science. It was the social skills I needed to expand.

Orientation day is hot, busy, and confusing. Boy, this is a big place! It's strange what a difference 15 minutes and a zip code can make; it's a whole new life in the same city. Tamara's family is all here to help her set up, and I, of course, have the help of my faithful Ms. MacKinnon. She was here bright and early in tow with all the things a girl needs to start her freshman year. We haul all the bedding, dressers, food, etc. to my new residence. My dad had sent me the money to purchase everything I had asked for. And the few things I had forgotten, Ms. Mackinnon or my stepfamily had gotten. They all joined forces to see that I succeeded. No matter what it looked like, God always gave me just the right people at the right time, even when I wanted to find an excuse to give up. Moving in took up most of the day, and it was well after dinner time when everyone left. Tee and I make plans to freshen up and meet in the Common area.

We never made that date. I woke up to sunlight, fully dressed, and starving. I had showered and sat down on my bed to rest until Tee called and fell asleep. I guess I was more exhausted than I thought. I got myself together for breakfast and called Tee to meet me. I don't know what looks better, the food or the boys, H-E-L-L-O.

Breakfast is light, and I stare more than I actually eat, Where in the world did all these people reside? I know for sure Buffalo could not claim them. Through some upperclassmen, I discovered my assumptions are correct: SUNY has students from all walks of life, and it is fascinating. We meet people from at least 10 different states and a few other countries in just a short while we're at breakfast. I can't wait for dinner!

We take the shuttle to the North Campus, walk around, see a few sites until we work up an appetite, and then take the shuttle back to the dining hall. No different from breakfast, dinner is packed full of hotties. I'm so happy I didn't listen to that little voice in my head telling me college was a waste of time. Hold the phone! My thoughts are interrupted by a rather noisy group walking in. The whistles around the older gentlemen's neck suggest it's some sort of sports organization, and whichever sport it is, I support it. A Resident Assistant sitting at our table says it's the UB football team. I don't know what their record is, but in the looks department, they are winners; fine as wine, muscles for days, and smiles blinding every girl in the room. I can tell more than Tee and myself are enjoying the pre-game show from all the whispers and lip gloss popping out. We, however, have passed the needing approval stage. We think we are the best thing since sliced bread. I'm drooling mentally, but I am way too cool to let it show. We talk amongst ourselves and leave the desperate chicks to their business. I was taught by the best when it pertains to male company: make them come for you.

I'm so nervous about my first day of class! All my new things, decorations, and cute outfits do nothing to console me. It's time to dance to the music of the real world. No more good morning love taps from Mrs. Lewis or faces from little James behind her back that would make me laugh so hard I would snap right out of my sleepy fog, ready to start my day. It was all me, my alarm clock, and a new adventure.

My first class isn't until 10 a.m. I took advantage of the late classes when I made my schedule; the last 4 years of being up early and at the bus stop were over. I walk to the commons to grab something quick before jumping on the shuttle. I was never a coffee drinker. I had only stopped to get a bagel. However, the tall stallion at the coffee machine made me purchase a cup; I had to get a closer look.

I attempt to make coffee for the first time in my life; It can't be that hard. I pour the coffee, sugar, then cream into the water. It looks like it should, I guess. I stir it and take a big gulp… OH MY! My mouth is on fire, it's burning! He's staring. The heck with it; I spit it out everywhere. The Cutie runs over to help; my mouth is really burning! I need a fire extinguisher! I try to clean up quickly. Oh gosh, my outfit is ruined; I am thoroughly embarrassed. He grabs some napkins and hands them to me. I can't look up. He starts to assist with cleaning up the mess I made. "Are you okay?

I can't talk, it's a mixture of pain and embarrassment. When he touches my hand, the pain subsides and I tell him I'm okay in hopes that he will just leave. He doesn't, so I leave the mess and start to walk away.

"Where are you going?"

"To the North Campus," I respond and start speed walking, hoping to put some distance between us. "Oh, I'm headed there myself."

I don't want to talk to him now; I look CRAZY!

"If you're headed to class, you might want to change."

NO, HE DIDN'T! He doesn't know me like that. He is about to get the old one-two. I turn around to give him the business, but all I feel is pain when I open my mouth. As he grabs my face, he looks concerned. Seriously, Are you ok?

I want to lie, but I refrain. I try to save my lies for an as-needed basis. "No", I whisper in absolute SHAME! He suggests I go to the on-site triage. What is that? It's a clinic for students. I'm not familiar; I had slept through most of the orientation. He offers to escort me. I don't want company, but pride is out for now. I'm desperate. We walk silently across campus until we reach the building with big, bold letters. I'm relieved. I think the staff is more humored than concerned when I explain why I'm here (there is nothing much you can use to treat stupidity). They rinse my mouth with a solution and tell me, luckily, the mouth heals quickly. I'm instructed to eat soft foods only for a few days, and if anything is smoking, blow it first.

He was waiting patiently for me when I walked out from the triage, despite me telling him numerous times that I was ok. I now know you're Yvette LaShun Fryer. It's nice to meet you. (At birth, I was named Yvetta Lacey Fryer. Once Mom and Dad divorced, she dropped the a for an e and changed my middle name to LaShun. She had to have the last word on everything, so that was her chance to one up him. She said she never liked that name, so when he left, the name went with him.

He extends his hand, bringing me back to the moment. Thanks I say, realizing I have been with him almost two hours and didn't know his name. "And what might your name be, sir?"

"A.B.," he replies with a gorgeous smile, shaking my hand firmly. "You have a strong grip for a girl."

I chuckle, and he smiles again. Okay, that was worth the pain. He is more beautiful now than two hours ago, or is it the way he had turned his hat to the back (I love a hood nigga)? He clears his throat and brings me out of my daze. Oh God, how many times am I going to embarrass myself in one day? I thank him and walk away quickly toward my dorm, opposite the direction he's going. He turns and follows me. "Are you not going to class?"

"Yes." "Well, you're headed away from the shuttle."

"I have to change, remember?"

"Do you mind if I walk with you?" You want to carry me, I ask in my mind, but my mouth simply says, sure." He waits in the hallway while I change. I daydream about being on campus with a hunk like this, and I make a mental note to invite him over this weekend for cards. Not only do I love to play, but that's also my way of seeing if a guy can REALLY tolerate me. This mouth can be brutal…On the card table; it gets even worse.

When I come out, he's sitting on the couch listening to headphones. Goodness, he's good-looking, or have I already mentioned that? We talk like we are old friends during the shuttle ride until he proudly says he's in his junior year. The conversation stops there for me. He mentioned earlier at the triage clinic he was in the same freshman class I was headed to. I might not need the card game to test his strengths, after all. He redeems himself, saying he needs this class to graduate but has been avoiding it until necessary. Typical male. I resume my investigation. So, what are you doing this weekend?

"Not much. Going to a party with some buddies."

Okay, I'm with partying; cards can wait. "Is it an all-male party/sports type of deal?"

"Oh, definitely not; anyone's welcome."

YEESSS! Wait until I tell Tee we are officially about to experience our first party as free women with no curfew.

"My girlfriend and some of her friends will be there. You should come."

Now, why did he have to kill my vibe? He has a girlfriend? Why has he been in my grill all morning? I hope he doesn't think I'm easy or desperate because I'm a freshman. I'll give him B's number if he wants to know how I feel about cheaters. I become reserved, not sure if I should be angry or not. Why did he spend all this time with me if he knew he had a girlfriend? But he's telling me now, so it's not like he lied. I will just let him talk the rest of the way, and when we get to class, I'm so sitting on the other side of the room.

We arrive at the North Campus, and I exit the shuttle without saying goodbye. Even though I had started to act as if he was getting on my nerves, I was secretly hoping he wouldn't leave me before we reached our class. And he didn't. I knew from the professor's name on the door we had arrived, so I made my move and zoomed to the left of the class once he walked to the right. I sit quickly, hoping to get lost in the large crowd wondering in; apparently, no one wanted the first class. As I start to remove my things from my bag, I hear A.B. yell my name. I try ignoring him, but his voice is as loud as his muscles are big, so after the second time, I look over at him, irritated. He gives a hand gesture for me to come to his side of the room where he's surrounded by at least six or seven other guys who are just as big as he is. I recognized a few of them from the student commons the other night. They are members of the football team. Great, more testosterone and arrogance. Not wanting to make a scene, I politely shake my head no and pray he doesn't call me again. He didn't. Goodbye Mr. A.B. Go on with your jockey life. I don't want any part of that Minutes later, I hear a commotion and turn around to see all of them walking my way. Good grief.

They all sit in the row immediately behind me except A.B. who makes himself comfortable in the seat right next to mine. Okay, now it's time to let him know I'm not the one. Before I could blast him, he says, "Yvette, these are my homies. I was just telling them that you're new to campus and how cool you are."

I smile, flattered that he thinks I'm cool. Wait, is this a trap? One of them suddenly yells, "Is it true you from Alabama?" in a drawl any true Southerner recognizes. I smile again and lighten up a little. They might be alright. He extends his hand and introduces himself. "Eric. E. O. to my friends. I saw you moving in. Your mother's white, isn't she?"

"No!" I'm confused, then realize he's talking about Ms. Mackinnon (she was my acting mother that day, as she had been often). "That was my teacher. We're just really close."

"Humph, I thought you looked pretty black to be half-white."

What does that even mean, I ask, as everyone laughs as hard as I do. A string of introductions takes place, and then the professor announces he's ready to begin. They may as well have stayed in bed; they clowned the ENTIRE class. College is going to be interesting.

Back on the South Campus, I go looking for my girl, and I find her in the hallway of her dorm. "What up, Tee? You look cute!"

"Girl, why didn't you wear the outfit we picked out for you last night?"

I'm forced to tell the coffee story. She dies laughing. She laughs so hard she almost falls off her chair. Okay, she's about to get uninvited to the party this weekend. When she gets herself together, I break the news that we are officially invited to our first college party. She is as excited as I was! It's only Monday, but we start planning outfits anyways. It briefly crosses my mind that I only have one person to look out for now: me. A flash of guilt hits me for not having to be responsible for my siblings anymore. I dismiss the thought as quickly as it comes; I'm young myself, I don't have any children, and I have to live my life. I can't continue to be a help to them if I don't better myself.

It's the weekend, BABY! A.B. is at the entrance of my dorm as he is every morning with juice. He had told me he'd better not see me near coffee ever again. "You still coming to the party tonight?"

"Yep!"

"Cool, I brought you directions. I'll catch you later."

We are friends now. I made a point to establish boundaries to keep down any confusion. I had asked how his girl would feel about us hanging out, and he told me she had her own life and he didn't really care for her highly fluent friends. I left it at that. His friends became mine, my one friend is his, and that's all it is.

The party is located in a nice area, so we decided to walk with some other girls from our dorm. And I must say we turned a few heads on the way. You can tell from all the people on the porch and the music blaring that the party is jumping. Tee and I venture off to find a bathroom as soon as we walk in the door. We have to make sure the walk didn't disturb one hair on our head. My feet are also telling me, next time, choose another pair of shoes. I sit on the toilet to rest them for a minute. Tee laughs. "Those dogs barking, huh?" I flip her the finger; she had warned me about these shoes. I told her it was some hotties that we had yet to meet and I was going to be wearing these shoes when I met them. You only get one chance to make a first impression. Now, if they ever see them again, that's a whole different ball game.

I say a prayer for my toes, and we leave the bathroom to get the night started. We run smack into E. O. on our way out, the funniest of the whole crew. I introduce him to Tee; they become fast buddies. Tee is just as silly as I am, so Eric's accent is entertaining to her. I had almost forced mine away. My drawl creeps out every now and again, but he has it bad. He offers to get us drinks, so we follow him to the kitchen. I'm on my third drink before Tee finishes her first. Freedom doesn't taste as good to her, I guess. I drink until I'm ready to dance. I have been a dancer since I was a little girl. I don't need any assistance. I don't even need a partner, just a floor. But as always, Tee is closely behind. We dance in a circle to keep strangers and unattractive men out of our faces.

The dance space is crowded, but the music is on point. I dance until I sweat. That's not cute. It's time to take a break. We are trying to make our way through the crowd when someone grabs my arm. I snatch around to give whoever it is a piece of my mind and notice it's A.B. I check my attitude quickly; he is F-I-N-E! I remind my hormones that he is my friend and he has a girlfriend. He and Tee hug; I can't do it. Touching him would be a bad move full on alcohol.

"You're so rude," he says, playfully punching me in the arm. "I invited you, and you haven't spoken all night."

I apologize; I don't like disrespecting. "I'm not sure where your other half is."

"You're being silly. We are just friends."

Cool. Now that I know, it won't happen again. I punch him back playfully in the chest and continue outside to cool off. The fresh air feels great. We are enjoying it and trying to revive our hair when we hear screeching and yelling inside. There are 10-12 females stomping and yelling chants in the middle of the room. E.O. tells me it's a female sorority. They command attention, and they are cute. This looks like it's worth checking into.

People scream and clap loudly in approval once they are done. One of the prettier girls walks over to A.B. and takes a drink out of his cup; I guess that would be the other half. Well, at least they look good together. Sometimes you see couples and wonder how the hell did that happen.

Tee, Eric, and I head back to the kitchen to get another drink. A few of the other guys I had met in class were in the kitchen as well, so I introduced Tee to the ones she hadn't met. We chill in the kitchen until they start playing some jams I can't ignore. We all break to the dance floor, and since I'm familiar with them, we let them in our circle. I dance until I'm literally about to pass out from exhaustion. I haven't danced like this since those house parties my mom used to throw on Spiess Street. I'm HOT! I have to sit down.

They start to play Boyz11 Men, "I'll Make Love to You". That's my JAM. I'm going to have to pass, though. My feet are killing me. Tee and I are trying to make our way to the wall or a seat, whichever comes first, when Ant and Cle, two of the hotties from A.B.'s dorm, cut us off and take our hands. All the pain in my feet ceased. They are so cute they can make you cross-eyed. Ant is that grown mankind of sexy, and Cle is a magazine model fine. I thank this school for free therapy; all these fine men seem to have gotten me over B in a New York minute.

Ant smells so good; I'm becoming dizzy but in a good way. This song needs to end soon. All my cool is out the window, and I'm glued to his chest like I'm a part of his shirt. As the song is almost over, he asks what I'm doing after the party. I hadn't thought that far ahead, but it is getting late. I look behind me to find Tee. She looks like she's as mesmerized as I am I laugh to myself. It can wait. Why ruin her dance?

My feet are happy when a new song starts to play, but I'm mad I have to let him go. The crowd has thinned out, so we decide to take it in for the night. I see Ant as we are walking out. "Y'all want to grab something to eat?" I can never say no to food. We continued the party at Denny's. In total, it has to be 30 of us. I kept wondering when they were going to ask us to leave because these people are so obnoxious, but we stayed for over an hour without incident. I guess the staff is used to this. We caught a ride here with some girls we knew, but they left a while ago. Ant had one too many and is leaving with a couple of his friends. We may be freshmen, but we know enough not to get in a car full of guys that's been drinking, no matter how cute they are.

Tee and I are attempting to hail a cab when A.B. walks out with his girlfriend closely behind him. "Would you like a ride?"

Before I could answer, his girlfriend stepped in front of him, asking if he had heard what she had said. He looks frustrated, and she looks mad. I tell him we're good (It's too late for drama). I start to walk away when A.B. says we can catch a ride with them if we want. Ok, it's all good with me! I turn to walk to his car when his girlfriend says rudely, "HOW DID THEY GET HERE?" Ok, she's about to get punched smooth in the face.

I'm good, I assure him, and we hail a cab back to the dorms. Tee decides to crash with me; my roommate practically lives with her boyfriend. I don't think she's slept here more than twice since we moved in. We get comfortable and recap the highlights of our evening. We are sharing a good laugh when there's a knock at the door. It must be Alice; she would pick tonight to come here. But why in the world is she roaming around at this time of the morning?

I swing the door open with my t-shirt and panties on. It's A.B. Oh crap, I slam the door. Tee burst out laughing as I trip, trying to get on my sweatpants and fix my hair. When I open the door again, he's grinning from ear to ear. "What you want?" I'm visibly pouting. "You made me hurt my toe, boy. Every time I see you, I get injured."

His voice gets serious. "I just want to apologize for the way my girl acted."

"Boy, please, it's like 4:30 in the morning; that could have waited. Maybe you should have introduced us at the party, and she would have been okay."

He retorts, "I would have if you weren't all in Ant's face!"

He got some nerve. Did he have an attitude? "Whatever the case may be, homeboy, I'm sleepy…It's all good. I will see you later." "Are you coming to the football game tonight?"

"Yes, Sir!" I speak as if he's my father because that's the vibe I'm getting.

"Don't be a smartass," he fires back. When I attempt to close the door, he stops me, then leans in and kisses me on the cheek. "I'm really sorry again," he says and walks away.

I'm like Whoopi in "The Color Purple"; I can't move. Tee is in the background tripping. "I thought y'all were just friends." WE ARE! She jumps up, shuts the door, and flicks on the light because I really can't move. She starts with the interrogation. "Why did he come here this late? Why did he kiss you, and why are you looking like that?"

I couldn't answer. For one, she was asking the questions way too fast, and honestly, I didn't understand what had just happened myself. I flip the light off, lie down, and try to figure out what had just taken place and why it made me feel so jittery inside. Tee says to the dark, "I'm going to have to watch you," before she drifts off. I'm no longer sleepy; I'm dazed and confused.

We won the game with ease that evening; the opposing team was whack, but let them tell it they are just good like that. The after-party was being hosted in Ant and Cle's dorm. They also had another roommate, Derek, who was equally as fine but not as wild. I think he's so cool. I'm introduced to a few of the female crew members I hadn't met as of yet. They are mostly upperclassmen and are nice enough to school me on what is what: which parties not to attend, walk to, etc. Some people have different agendas. I'm all for fun, but not at the cost of my life or health. I know first-hand that the other life leads to destruction. I mean, I drink my share, but not to the point of being unsafe and destructive.

My mom dropped street knowledge on us females often. One of the more important lessons was to never leave your drink unattended or get so intoxicated that you can't protect yourself or make wise choices; that sticks with me closely whenever I'm in a crowd. I can also spot game when I see it, like this random guy walking up asking me if I want to drink with him. I politely decline. He's apparently offended and gets in my face. Ant steps over and tells him to take a walk, saving him from a good beat down because I don't play like that. Loud talking is just as bad as putting your hands on me, it sets me right off!

Ant finds it amusing that I go from one to ten so fast. This temper is also an inheritance from my mom. Ant asks if I want to dance the stem off and starts imitating a stripper when I don't answer, and it cracks me up. I reach for his drink; I need to calm my nerves. He grabs my hand and pulls me close to him. "I like you," he whispers in my ear.

"I like you back," I whisper just as A.B. is walking in, and we lock eyes. A.B. smirks at me and waltzes to the other side of the room, never taking his eyes off me. I don't know why, but I feel uncomfortable. I put some space between Ant and myself, then scan the room for Tee. "Girl, can you step outside with me? I got issues." We have to walk down the hall a bit to find a private spot; people are everywhere.

"What's up, Vette?" She is rocking and grinning, indicating she was approaching her limit.

"I think A.B. likes me."

"Duh! He kissed you."

"On the cheek!" I shout back. "Do you kiss your friends on the cheek?"

"Good point! Ok, so what's the problem?"

"He has a girl, remember, genius?"

"Do you think it's serious? You never see them together."

"This is true, but the fact still remains! Ant just said he's digging me, and the feeling is mutual."

"Well, let's go with what we know, chick. A bird in the hand is better than two in the bush." Ant is the safer choice. Oh Lord, she's been around my family way too much; she's using the sayings. I think she's right, though. The dilemma is over. Let's get back to it.

A.B. immediately grabs me when I walk in and escorts me back outside. "Can I get my party on?" "What's up with you and Ant?"

"First of all, don't press me like that! What's your problem?"

He simmers down and apologizes. "Look, I've been chilling with you and looking out since we met. But it seems like every time we cross paths, you're all up on Ant."

"You are tripping, nigga! You got a girl, so check yourself!"

"We're not talking about her!" he yells.

"The hell you say!" I yell right back. "You are not talking about her, but I AM! I don't play second fiddle, not even for you, Mr. A.B. So sorry to burst your bubble, but this ain't happening. This conversation is over!" I count to 3 to calm myself down because he is about to get beat up. "Listen, dude. If you want to remain friends, I would love that. If not, speed on." I leave him standing there and go back to find Tee. I spot her dancing up a storm with some other people we hang out with. Ant and some chick are also going strong on the dance floor.

I'm out. I make sure Tee has an escort from the party, tell her to call me when she makes it in tonight, and walk back to my dorm. She knows from experience when I get like this, it's best to let me be. I hear a knock on the door as soon as I slip on my nighties. Tee had followed me anyways; she's not going to let me pout alone. I always ruin my girl's fun with my drama. I open the door, and A.B. is standing on the other side. I have to start using my peephole.

"What?" I ask with an attitude.

"May I come in?"

"No!"

"Why not?"

"Alice is asleep," I use one of my lies. He has gotten on my last nerve tonight.

"You liar. I saw her with her boyfriend a little while ago."

Dang… I should have saved that one. "Well, how about the truth? I don't feel like talking to you!"

"I deserve that, but I need to talk to you." His voice is low and controlled.

I give in and walk away, leaving the door open. I'm afraid of what I just felt and hope he makes it quick and to the point. When I hear the door close, I turn around to A.B. standing right behind me.

"I was rude!"

"I agree. What's wrong with you?"

"I'm jealous and don't know why; I think you're so pretty and smart. Most girls like you are not fun." This is working; the madness is fading. He continues, "My full intentions were for us to be friends and hang out, but all my friends talk about is how sexy you are, and it's been bothering me lately."

"Why does it bother you?"

He grabs my face. "Because I want you."

I almost collapse when his lips touch mine. My mind is telling me this is wrong, but my flesh gives in. I'm intoxicated by his embrace, and the alcohol does not help my rationale. As the sun is coming up, I drift off with a strange feeling of guilt and pleasure. He treated my body with so much respect, but I know what it feels like to be cheated on. This will not happen again! He wakes me up, telling me he has to get to practice.

"Listen, A.B. We made a horrible mistake."

"I thought it was beautiful."

"Not the act itself, boy. The circumstances." He looks puzzled. "Are you ready to leave your girl?" I ask point-blank.

"She's not as nice as she used to be. You're exciting."

"NO... I'm new to you! I'm sure that's all this is, but I need an answer."

"I'll be honest. I've thought about leaving, but I'm not sure."

"I respect your honesty, but this is not a game I play. Friends, we will remain; that's it! I don't want to be in this predicament again."

"I can respect that; I didn't even come with the intent of going this far."

I believe him. You should never make decisions when you're emotional; it can get you into some bad situations." I didn't find that out for many years. Needless to say, I make a few more detrimental decisions before I read Juanita Bynum's "No More Sheets" and some AFTER! "What now, will this stay between us?"

"Yes, I think that's best." I know us includes Tee, but hey, she'll never tell.

The rest of the semester goes smoothly. A.B and I still see each other in class and around campus, and despite the first few times being weird, we are good. We don't hang like we used to, but we run in the same circle, so we can't avoid being in the same place occasionally.

Ant and I are in an unspoken relationship, I guess that's what you would call it. We haven't said we are officially a couple, but we do almost everything together. I also see A.B. around campus with his girl from time to time. Guess he still hasn't decided. Good thing we had agreed to leave that alone. I am delighted this term is over, and if I must say so myself, I did well for being on my own for the first time! Even with mad partying, late nights, and crazy family drama, I managed to handle it all and end strong.

Chapter 5

COUNTRY CLEANSE

As much as I love being in college and out on my own, I can't wait to get to Alabama and spend the summer with my family. I need a break from New York. I never want to live that deep in the South again, but it's always a good getaway from the fast-paced city. Tee is vacationing out of state with her family as well; we will have a lot of catching up to do when fall rolls around. We are going to be sophomores, no more new kids on the block—not that we felt that way last year. We had made our mark at SUNY UB.

The heat index is hell when I pull up to my grandmother's house. We usually spend all day inside because it's unbearable until the evening, and sometimes it's still too hot to come out then. The nightclubs are still the hole in the walls I remember with new names. However, we party as if it's a three-story convention center. Fun is what you make it! Southern people are funny to begin with. Mix that with some alcohol, and you're talking about a laughing good time. It doesn't matter how much I party, though; my grandmother still makes me go to church on Sundays. She never lets me forget to give God His time. She was sure to tell me, "You can stay at the Juke Joint all night if you want, but you gon' be in church on Sunday morning."

I never understood that. I felt like God would be offended by my actions the night before. I would party until the sun came up, then exchange my mini-skirt for a dress that passed my knees; that was a must. Grandma was strict; she didn't play that. I attempted to wear a dress that was above my knees the last summer I was here, and she talked about me so bad I felt naked. I've never tried her again. Grandma will still pull her switch out, never mind the fact that I'm in college. My dad also inherited that trait with a different weapon of choice; he pulls his belt off with the quick if you didn't move fast enough when asked. Kids have it made these days.

This Sunday morning starts like any other: hymns, collection, me struggling to keep my eyes open, and my grandmother waiting for me to nod so she can pop me. What she was really chastising me for was staying out all night, but I played along with her. My siblings and I took turns nodding so one could tell the other whenever Grandma was on alert.

It was my turn to take watch, and since I couldn't find two toothpicks to hold my eyes open, I decided to at least focus on the Pastor. His message is on "Forgiveness". I'm not going to survive this; my eyes are blinking rapidly, and sleep is quickly winning this battle. Suddenly, he says, "When you have Christ in your heart, you can love people even if they've done you wrong; you have to forgive them to cleanse your own heart." This chases all my fatigue away; he has my full attention. I've asked God for years why my heart is so cold, and I think I just received my answer. I am very mean, and it doesn't take much for me to flip! I know I have plenty of unforgiveness in my heart. His statement makes perfect sense to me. I had not forgiven my mom for the way she ran the streets, nor B for the betrayal after all those years of loyalty to him, not even my dad for never rescuing me from my mom.

I started to cry like a baby. Somewhere deep down, something was released. For years I searched inside of me for what made me so hot-headed and quick to dismiss people. Jumping so quickly from one relationship to the next, hoping it would make up for the last failed one, be it friendly or romantic. As the Pastor lays his hand on me and tells me to confess my sins and give my life to Christ, I release the hurt in my heart and tell myself I'm going to stop using it as a crutch. It took me coming back to the country after all these years to get this cleansing of my soul and make me realize I have to forgive the people whose betrayal cut me the deepest because it's not hurting them; it's damaging me.

No one discusses what happened in service during the drive home. I think my grandma understood my tears. The party in Clayton tonight crosses my mind. It's always the event of the summer, but I will not be attending! I had told my country crush who I've been sweet on since elementary school that we would go. We always hook up when I come home and I really look forward to spending time with him. I've never really been into dark skin men. However, he DOES it for me every time. But for some reason, I'm not excited anymore. My mind is still on what took place at church. This Sunday was different. I didn't feel like just another body in the pew today; something happened.

I can't stop my mind from racing, so I take a long nap! I wake up and find my grandmother sitting in the living room watching "In The Heat of the Night". I sit quietly next to her and lay my head on her lap. This is her show, I wouldn't dare interrupt. However, when her hand touches my head, I feel it's ok, so I ask if she is proud of me. For some reason, at that moment, the little girl in me needed to know that. Like my father, she was never really affectionate; they have a tough time showing emotions. It's strange. As wild as my mother is, and even with all her stunts, she is the most lovable, affectionate human being to know. When she wasn't leaving me for days at a time or smacking me around, she would hug and kiss me like I was her only child in the world. She gave us all much love that way. I get all my affection from my mom. I learned how to maintain from my dad.

Granny gets up and walk away. I don't think she wants me to see her cry. However, I hear her tears when she speaks. "I'm proud of all of you for making it through the hell you were raised in."

"You know you're a big part of the reason I never gave up, Grandma." Even though I know she wouldn't hug me back, I hug her tight anyways. She hits me across my bottom with the fly swatter.

"Come on. I'll teach you how to make my biscuits."

That's as close to "I love you" as you're going to get from her, and that's fine with me.

She tried for three days straight to teach me that recipe, but I kept putting her off. I hate being in the kitchen; it's too hot, and cooking doesn't hold my attention. While learning to make biscuits from scratch didn't interest me, I was very attentive in church every Sunday for the remainder of the summer. Whatever it was that I felt, I wanted more of it. Those seeds that were planted when I was young seemed to need that water.

It seems like summer comes to an end just as I got excited about church again—like I used to be when I was small. It's gloomy as I load up the car to head back to New York. I'm going to miss my family. I'm trying to hold back the tears as Granny gets in her car to leave for work and Dad loads up his big rig to go back on the road. Life goes on for us all until next time, or so I thought! Granny died a few years later of cancer. I didn't make it back for a few summers because I started working. I wish I had taken the time to learn to make those biscuits. Guess I'll have to survive off the memories.

Chapter 6

BACK IN THE
SWING OF THINGS

I return to Buffalo optimistic about the future, looking forward to calling B and my mom to clear the air. He and I were together a long time, and now that I'm working on healing properly, I know there's a conversation to be had. Making amends with my mom will be harder, so I need time to work on my approach. I call Tee to see if she was back on campus, but she won't be returning for a few more days. I could use her moral support, but declined to tell her about my need to make amends; no use in burdening her with my problems while she's still having fun.

I decide to call B and at least get that part out of the way while I have the nerve. I dig through my things and find my phone book. I will have to call his mom. I have not spoken with him since the week after graduation. He had called before he left for college, but I hung up soon as I heard his voice. My stepdad had told me he also made a point to call and say goodbye to the family. As if that was supposed to ease the pain! I feel the anger rising again. I hurry and dial before I change my mind. His sister answers, and we have a surprisingly pleasant conversation before I ask to speak to her mom. I'm not sure how his mom will react. I'm a little anxious as I wait. However, she is very polite and easygoing, just as I remembered when she came on the line. After we catch up a bit, she gives me her son's number in Wisconsin, and asked that we talk more often in the future.

I dial B as soon as we disconnect, and low and behold, a female answers the phone. My immediate attitude is an indication that my tears may have helped me realize I need to forgive, but they definitely hadn't healed the wound. She calls for him in a voice that's a little too perky, and it annoys the hell out of me. I'm debating my decision to make amends when I hear his deep voice come on the line. "Hello."

I hang up; I no longer remember what I wanted to say. Oh well, another lifetime! Since that didn't work out, I will use what's left of my nerve to call my mom. My stepdad answers.

"Hey Dad. Where's Mom?"

"You just missed her, sweetheart. But I will tell her you called. You okay?"

"I'm fine," I lie and hang up before the tears fall. I'm not okay; I'm dying inside, as if all of my hurt started with that call and not years ago. I cry for what seems like forever until sleep is all I have the strength to do. I wake up to darkness and an empty stomach. I stir around to find myself something to eat. After some weird encounters with Alice and her boyfriend, who was a little into the Gothic scene, I decided on a single room this term. She had taken her refrigerator, though; I do miss that. I make a note to ask Dad to get me one.

This snack thing is for the birds; I need some substance. I'm on the prowl for something to quiet the rumble in my stomach when my phone rings: It's Ant.

"Hey, what's up?"

"Nothing much. What you up to?"

"Shit, I just wanted to see if you made it back."

"Yeah, I came back yesterday."

"Why didn't you call me?"

"I was just trying to get myself together…" My voice cracks.

"What's wrong, Yvette?"

I can't find my words; the tears make it first.

"I'm on my way." He hangs up before I can object. I dash to the other side of the dorm to wash my face and fix my hair. He's just walking up just as I make it back to my door. He is such a sight for sore eyes; his already curly hair is thicker than I remember. He wraps his arms around me, and I feel better already. Maybe today, I'll finally talk to someone about my troubles instead of doing what I've been doing for years. It's a problem I have that no one knows, not even Tee; I use sex to mask my pain. When he asks me to sit down and talk, I kiss him instead. I remove my shirt and turn out the light. In my bed, I'm in control; nothing has the power to hurt me here. Never mind confronting my issues. It's easier to put on a band-aid.

Daylight is creeping through the window when I wake up to him kissing my forehead. "You wanna talk now?"

I do, but I'm not ready to give my demon a voice; that makes it real. As long as I don't discuss it, no one knows. I lie and say I'm just sad about leaving my family.

"I'm sorry." He hugs me tightly. "I can't relate, though. I'm from Ruff Buff; all my peeps are right here."

"I still want to hear about your summer," I insist, trying again to change the subject.

"WHY, it was boring as hell." He makes this stupid face, and we share a good laugh. His pager goes off, and he ignores it, pointing to my stomach, which has been growling loudly for the last half hour. "When was the last time you ate?"

"I was trying to eat when I was distracted." I sarcastically pointed at the bed.

"Wasn't that better than food?"

I burst out laughing. "You're so childish."

He stands and pulls me into his chest. "I just love to see you smile."

"And I love the fact that you turn my tears into a smile." We stay embraced in silence until my stomach reminds me again that I'm on the brink of starvation.

"We better handle that, girl. You up to some Denny's?"

Just when Ant's visit had gotten me back in the swing of things, Tee returned to campus and broke some devastating news to me: this will be her last year at UB. She and her family decided she's going to mortuary school in Upstate New York, and I'm crushed. I can't believe she's leaving me. I could never go that far away from my siblings, and I'm terrified of dead people. I may be tough for a female, but corpse is where I draw the line.

We make a pact; if this is going to be our last year together, we are going to make it good. "Have you seen A.B. since you have been back?"

No, luckily, we haven't bumped into each other. I live in a different dorm this year, not as close to the commons. It's better this way. It's hard to see him when I'm with Ant. The fact that A.B. and I had crossed that line always made me feel uneasy. When you give your body to someone, it's not a casual thing; it stays with you, and it CHANGES you. I wish I could stop, but that's the only medicine that works for my pain. These people take a part of your soul and stain your temple. That's why sex is supposed to be reserved for marriage; once you give your body away, you can't get it back. But when you're young and unlearned, you can cause so much physical and emotional damage without even realizing it.

"Girl, you know who I can't get rid of is your boy Ant!" We laugh our hearty laugh that no one else would understand. Man, I missed my girl.

I don't know about him though, Tee. He spends mad time with me, but I'm still having my doubts. He rarely answers his pages when we're together, even if he is near a phone. He always says it's not important. I mean, I'm trying not to bug out, but my intuition never fails me. I have to be careful not to get too caught up in that, though, and I need to focus on my studies. My partying has slowed down drastically this semester, but still I try to attend enough events to keep my work life and play time balanced.

This weekend calls for some play; life is winning by a big margin right now. I had spent most of the money my dad had given me and maxed out one of my credit cards, getting my siblings toys and clothes for Christmas; they will be happy when it comes around. Mom is still partying and doing her own thing, and I pray every day that she will think about the kids more. Someone had once told me she would never change as long as we kept picking up the slack. We had tried drawing the line and forcing her to be more responsible, but the only ones who suffered were my stepdad and the kids. I decided from then on no matter what anyone else did, I would do what I had to do until they could care for themselves.

I had tried that reconciliation call to my mom a few months ago, only to be called everything but a child of God. She had told me to save my forgiveness for someone who gave a fuck. I cried for two days and now only speak to her when it's absolutely necessary. I need to get all of this off my mind. This Friday, I'm unwinding; I need to clear some mental space!

I look extra sexy tonight. I took my time with it. No matter what I had going on, I thought if I looked good, no one would ever figure out how much I was hurting inside. There are several parties tonight; we decide on one at a Frat house off campus. We take Tee's car. I'm not even attempting to walk in these heels. Experience is a good teacher.

We have to park down the block. There's so many people here. Off with the shoes. I'm almost to the driveway when Ant appears out of nowhere. I rush to put my shoes back on; it's straight Country to be walking bare feet, looking like a million dollars. My hair is flawless, yet he's looking at me like I have on a cheap wig and some cut-off jeans. "Why are you looking crazy, boy?"

"I called to see if you were coming, but you didn't return my call." He spoke with aggravation in his voice. Okay, is it that serious? I started looking around for my dad because, apparently, he got me bent. Since he likes the way I go from one to ten so fast, I'm about to give him a quick demonstration. As soon as I roll my neck, Tee grabs my hand and escorts me away; she knows after the second neck roll, it is on. She whisked me off, half laughing because I had just finished telling her not to waste any more energy on that dog Stevie J she had been dating. My girl had been so down with this dude, but he decided fame was more important than love. Now here I am, less than an hour later, about to put the smack down on Ant! These niggas!

I shake it right off. I'm wasting time; we are here to party! I head for the alcohol immediately. My trusted friend and bartender, E. O., never fails me. He is all smiles when we enter the kitchen where the alcohol is well supplied. I start with a gin and juice, strong. Tee decides to take baby steps and grabs a wine cooler. Eric sees my face screwed up and asks if I want to dance; I accept with pleasure. He is dating Eva, and she is cool people, so we all head to the dance floor. You could always count on Eric to lighten the mood, and it was working until I spot Ant trying to pull some girl toward the door, and she doesn't look too happy about it. This looks like it requires my attention, being that he just spent the night with me less than 48 hours ago.

I excuse myself from the dance circle, using the bathroom as my escape. I discreetly make my way to the other side of the room, close enough to hear Ant and this rather attractive female having a heated discussion. Apparently, he was ready to leave, and she wasn't. I need to know why he cared if she stayed or not. You know, I'm quickly about to find out. I step around the people separating me from the two of them and right into Ant's path. He looks at me like I have a third eye.

"What's up?" I ask calmly. No need to let this chick see me sweat. I'm looking to fly to let the crazy come out and ruin my good time.

"Yvette, can we step outside for a minute?" We attempt to walk out, but the young lady isn't having it. She starts with some neck rolling of her own and gets really loud. Tee has made her way over to the scene by now.

"Who's the chic?"

"I haven't had the pleasure," I respond loud enough for the chic to hear me, testing her temperature. I deal with females accordingly.

"I'm Shan, and you are?"

Okay, she has some manners, so I can converse with her. "I'm Yvette. What's the deal here?" I point from her to Ant.

"I'm going out with him, and he's been trying to make me leave ever since I saw him outside talking to you. Maybe you can tell me what's going on."

I hit him with the death stare. "Ant, will you be kind enough to share why you would like her to leave?" Now he has two necks rolling; he clearly won't be enjoying himself tonight.

"Let me explain." Here we go! That was the wrong response girlfriend got all up in his grill.

"EXPLAIN WHAT!"

Ant, being as smooth as he is good-looking, says I need another drink and walks away, leaving the both of us standing there fuming. This is too much for me. I'm not with it. Tee and I leave, but not before I catch a glimpse of A.B. with a look of gratification on his face. He can kiss my grits too.

My phone rings before I can get inside my room. It better NOT be Ant. "HELLO," I answer, still fuming.

"What's up?"

It's A.B. I was hoping it was Ant. I had a few unfiltered words to lay on him. "How can I help you?" I say with an attitude. He quickly checks me, and I pipe down; he's not the source of my anger. A little more politely, I ask, "What do you need?"

"I'm just seeing if you're okay."

"I'm good," I say as calmly as I can. "I'll call you later." I hang up, shower, and grab a book to read. I'm too wired to sleep, or so I thought until a knock on my door jolts me out of a slump at my desk. A.B. won't fool me tonight. I pull on my robe, secure it tightly and check my hair. Mad or not, I still have a reputation to uphold. I swing open the door to find Ant and the female from the party standing on the other side. Oh, he's about to catch these hands for real. This Negro must have been smoking some good drugs bringing this chic over here. He apparently notices the stem coming out of my ears and puts his hand up to call a truce. He speaks slow and carefully. "I just want you to tell her that you and I are just friends."

I go numb. What!!! This punk has been sleeping in my bed, eating my food, taking me to parties, escorting me to balls, boat rides, you NAME IT, for a year AT THAT, and we are FRIENDS! As a matter of fact, we just went to the opening of "Waiting to Exhale". No guy goes to see a girly movie with you unless he's digging you or wants to sleep with you, and since we crossed that line a long time ago, I was sure he was digging me.

All this is running through my mind, and I'm trying to see which curse words I'm about to put on him and in what order when she speaks. The pain in her voice catches me off guard, "I'm his girlfriend; we've been dating for three years, and I love him. But the way he acted with you tonight, I know he is cheating. He only brought me here because I begged him to. If you tell me that you two are together, I'm done with him."

I've been her, and I know the pain she is feeling right now. I wouldn't wish it on my worst enemy. Sparing her heartache is worth a lie. I'll pray about it later. "Girl, please. Ant and I are just friends! He was supposed to give me and my girl a ride to the party, and he left us. That's why I was pissed at him!" In mid-sentence, I spot A.B. strolling down my hall.

What the hell? I'm already lying; may as well make it worthwhile. I decide to give Ant a dose of his own medicine by throwing in, "Besides, I go out with A.B. anyways." Ant chokes, on what I don't know, but he recovers just in time to see A.B. walking up. Ant looks MAD as hell. A.B. smiles and extends his hand for some dap, unaware I just used him as a pawn. Shan seems relieved when I excuse myself, telling her I have some business to handle. A.B. looks confused as I step aside, telling him to come in, but he comes in anyway because he's a man.

As I'm closing the door, Shan thanks me for clearing things up and apologizes for stopping in so late. I assure her it's cool and hug her tight. This is my secret; I'm sorry for sleeping with your man, who I didn't know was your man. She turns to walk away and when Ant attempts to speak, I slam the door in his face so hard the dorm rattles. I know this conversation with A.B. is about to be dramatic, so I brace myself for the sarcasm. The tears in my eyes must soften his approach. Instead of the "I told you so" I'm sure he came to deliver, he strokes my hair and gives me a hug. "Why are you crying?"

These tears are just as much for her as they are for me; she is so beautiful. Men ain't shit! That explains all the ignored pages and canceled dates that had become more and more frequent. "I can't understand why men always play with women's emotions."

"You really want to know the truth?"

"Lay it on me."

"It's because woman allow it."

Now he has pissed me off. "She couldn't possibly know he was cheating; she didn't attend this school."

A.B. insists, "As much as he's with you, she had to know something."

"Whatever," I shout back. "How about we just trust what men tell us? Did you know he had a girl?"

"Yes!"

"Well, why didn't you tell me?"

"I'm not a sucker."

"What kind of answer is THAT?"

"If I had told you, I would have seemed like a hater."

"So, you allowed me to get played to protect the guy code."

"I knew you would eventually find out; I just didn't know it would take this long."

I want to slap him, but instead, I ask him to leave. He tries wiping my face, and I push him away. I just want to be alone. He sits down on the bed, pulls me in his lap, and listens to me sob. After my tears subside, he pulls back my cover and tucks me in.

"I should get going."

"Can't you stay?"

"No, I need to leave now before we do something we'll regret. I only stopped by to see if you were okay. I heard how upset you were when I called and wanted to make sure you were good before I went in. I felt a little guilty for enjoying that scene at the party."

Well, thank you. "Now go home to YOUR girlfriend," I say, smiling, wondering who's going to comfort me tonight. He looks torn as he leaves, but we both know it's the right thing to do.

I had a killer headache the next day; the gin and crying were a bad combination. I pull myself together and write Ant a long letter telling him to die a slow death... Okay, actually I just tell him I don't ever want to see him again. I ignore the phone every time it rings. I need to do this while I have the nerve and before my flesh gives in to those lips that I will miss so much... focus, Yvette.

I'm tired of being hurt, and I haven't lived that long to have endured so much heartache. I should write a book. I put on my SUNDAY BEST to take the letter to his room; I won't dare get caught looking like I feel. If I haven't perfected anything else, I've become a master at hiding pain. I tap on his door. Not hard, though. It's crazy. Even after last night, I will miss him. I have spent a good amount of time with him and given him a part of my soul. I'm sure now that it was just sex to him, but it was special to me. Men always get away easy.

I knock again, much harder. He doesn't deserve another minute of my time. His roommate Derek opens the door. "Hey, if you're looking for your girl, she went to eat with Cle."

"Actually, I'm looking for Ant. Umm, he's… not here."

The hesitation lets me know he's heard about the episode last night and is probably wondering if I was really THAT desperate to be coming back. "I just want to leave this letter for him."

He steps aside for me to come in. I notice luggage by the door and a matching tote on his shoulder. "Going somewhere?"

"Yeah, my son is really sick, and I need to get home. I dropped my courses last week and have to be back in Cali by Monday."

"I'm sorry to hear that!" Derek is a cool dude, calm and sexy as all get out. He is very easy on the eyes as well, but he and Ant were close, so I never considered him as anything but a friend. He excuses himself to answer the phone when it rings; he is always such a gentleman. "Hello... Oh no, I really need to be there. Do you know anyone else?"

I'm only hearing one side of the conversation, but I can tell he's irritated. He lets out a sigh of frustration when he hangs up. "Are you okay?"

"That was my ride to the airport canceling on me. I guess I will have to get a cab. I don't know if I'll make my flight now."

"I can drive you. I have a key to Tee's car. It's still out front. I just need to call her and see if it's ok."

"I'll get in touch with Cle. I had told him I'd call before I left for the airport anyways."

Cle answers the page in a couple of minutes. After they finish, Derek hands me the phone. "Tee, are you cool with me using your car for a minute?" "You know it's fine. But are you ok, Vette?"

"I'm straight, girl."

"You sure? I called you last night and all morning. I was worried."

"I know. It's a long, long story, Tee. Let me call you later."

Derek gathers his things and leaves the room. I place the letter under Ant's pillow, along with the feelings I have for him, leaving them both behind as I close the door.

There's an awkward silence before Derek finally asks about last night! I feel super stupid; I know he's seen that girl as much as he has seen me with Ant. I let him talk for a while before I ask, "Did you know about her?" He gives me the "are you serious" look. I give him the "answer me, boy" look right back. He smiles. "You know I did."

"Why didn't you tell me?"

"Because that's my boy!"

R-E-A-L-L-Y. I'm dismayed. I wish men were as loyal to their women as they are to each other! I better hurry and get Derek to the airport before this good boy image I have of him is ruined.

"You honestly didn't know he was seeing someone else?"

"NO!" I yell with my voice cracking.

"Dang, that's messed up. You are pretty and all, but you're from the hood; you are supposed to be up on the game."

"Now I have a serious attitude! I don't play games, that's why I'm not good at them. And what the heck does one have to do with the other?" I ask with a neck roll. He looks shocked and starts to laugh. His laughter is contagious. My issue is not with him. I take a deep breath, and we talk calmly for the rest of the drive.

I step out to assist him with his luggage when we arrive at the airport. Once we reach the ticket counter, I hand him the bag I'm carrying and extend my arms for a hug. He lets the bag drop and pulls me in close to him. I hold him longer than I should. I feel the realness of his goodbye, and it magnifies the emptiness in my life. He kisses me softly as we end our embrace.

"I always hoped you'd find out about her so we could have had a chance, but now we will never know."

I'm dazed as he walks away and disappears into the crowd, leaving me in a trance. The ride back is quiet and lonely; I have a million thoughts going through my head. I turn on the radio to drown my thoughts, and Babyface is on. I turn it back off. I don't need to amplify the sadness I feel. I'll mess around and be in a state of manic depression by the time I get home, fooling with him. Why do I always end up more emotionally confused than when I started after each episode with men? It seems the method I've been using—getting under another man to get over the last one—only assists temporarily. I think Mom missed the mark on this one. Her advice is usually pretty solid, but she either got this theory wrong, or her heart is stronger than mine because each time, it's getting harder and harder to recover from the pain. Time and prayer are the permanent fixes I need. But of course, I will foolishly bruise my heart and body a few more times before I apply this remedy.

I returned to campus, not planning on coming out or seeing anyone for the rest of the weekend. It will take at least that long to figure out how you can feel so many emotions at once. Tee refuses to let me sulk alone; she comes over, and we order pizza and cry together. She is my friend. This is the one thing I can be sure of in the middle of all this madness.

This semester seems to creep by. I know it's partially because the campus is not as fun as it was last year. I avoid Ant like a bill collector. I haven't talked to him in over a month. He did call once he had gotten the letter, saying he was sorry and never meant to hurt me. He thought we were just "hanging out" and didn't expect things to happen the way they did. I told him I wasn't mad anymore, and it was not his job to protect my heart; that was solely my responsibility. We agreed to be friends. It is what it is.

I still talk with A.B. occasionally on the phone. I don't risk being around him; my emotions always seem to get the best of me. I practically had to sit on my hands the last time I was alone with him. I keep my distance from the two of them; our only encounters are in passing on campus. Both of those chapters are closed. I have a few more rendezvous trying to get over my heartache, but none of them end up leading to anything permanent. My heart's too guarded now. I spend most of my time off campus these days because it's always some drama in the hood to keep my mind off things.

Chapter 7

SOMETHING NEW

Tee dropped me off to take my stepdad the last of the gifts I had brought for Christmas. She had plans with her family, though, and couldn't stay, so I'm stuck taking the bus back to campus. I'm waiting at Bailey and Genesee for the Metro. It's a beautiful Sunday afternoon, but quite chilly despite the bright sunshine.

I see a black Maxima coming down the street. What a nice car! It stops at the light. The guy in it is just as nice-looking, I pretend not to notice. He looks over at me and says hello. I play it cool. I don't know him from a can of paint, and he looks like he's a lady's man. "Hi," I say dryly, turning my back.

He giggles and yells out, "That's cold!" realizing I was purposely throwing shade. "You have a name?"

"Doesn't everyone!"

He pulls into the McDonald's parking lot and gets out. Let me take my razor out of my purse and stick it in my pocket. Dang, these jeans are tight. He almost catches me. He walks to my left and takes off his sunglasses. He has the lightest eyes. Oh, Lord, I'm mesmerized. He's too fine, and his walk demands attention. Denzel Washington is the only other man to get that praise from me. No other man's walk ever rattled me, but this one is smooth! I've had my share of fine, though, and that comes with heartache. I'll pass.

My silent assessment is interrupted by the oncoming bus. I look at him one last time and pick up my things.

"What are you doing?

"Getting on the bus."

"I don't know your name."

"Shun," I call out, walking to the street.

"You just gon' leave me standing here?"

"You look like you can handle yourself!"

He smiles again. Why, Jesus, is he so beautiful? If he asks me to stay, I will.

"Can you at least wait for the next bus?"

BINGO! Without hesitation, I step back, indicating to the driver that he can keep going. "Look, I don't have time for games. I told you my name, now what else could you possibly want?"

"You can calm down and stop rolling your neck, for one thing."

I smile slightly. I don't even know him, and he's already getting the business.

"All I want to do is get to know you."

"For what? Oh, let me guess… I'm pretty!"

"You alright," he says with a straight face.

WHAT the WHAT! He's stuck on himself. "Well, since I'm just alright, get in your car, press the gas, and go straight to hell. I didn't ask for any company."

I can tell by his expression that he's entertained. He takes a seat on the bench and crosses his leg, one over the other. I turn my back to him. After a few minutes, he asks, "Did you lose the attitude yet or you need some more time?"

What the heck? I already missed my bus. I turn back around, and he's smiling again. I wish he would stop; it's making me dizzy. He extends his hand. "I'm Jimmy."

"Shun," I say again.

"I heard you the first time. I just wanted you to say it nicer." I smile wider this time. "You are very pretty, by the way." I manage a thank you, not sure how, because his touch has taken my breath away.

"Have you eaten?"

"What kind of crazy question is that? Do I look hungry?" I stare at him, puzzled.

"Well, McDonald's is right there, and the bus is gone. We can talk at this stop like we're homeless or go inside.

I giggle. "I don't care for McDonald's. I'm headed back to campus."

"What campus is that?"

"UB."

"The college?"

"Yes."

He raises his eyebrows. "How old are you?"

"21," I blurt out. He looks at least 23 or 24, and I don't want him to think being 19 makes me a kid. I've been grown for a long time.

"You mind if I wait with you?"

"I'm good," I assure him.

"I could give you a ride if you trust me."

I think for a minute. He looks harmless. I throw my bag over my shoulder and follow him through the parking lot. I remove my razor from my pocket as he starts the car to let him see it, just for good measure.

"You violent or just crazy?"

"Neither. Just don't start, none won't be none. I don't care how good you look." He shakes his head and smiles again. Thank God I'm sitting down; my knees are weak. "Where are you from, Jimmy? I haven't seen you around before."

"I'm from Buffalo, but I lived in Charlotte for a while as well. And you?"

"I'm from Alabama."

"Deep down South, huh? I can hear it."

I continued with some general questions while I built up the nerve to ask what I really wanted to know. "How old are you?"

"27!"

Dang, I wouldn't have given him a day over 23. I think briefly about telling him my real age, but for what? I'll be 20 in a few weeks and will probably never see him again. I give a little history of myself, leaving out the drama about my family life. We arrive at campus a little too quickly. I was enjoying his company, and he smelled delicious. I attempt to open the car door, and he grabs my hand. "Slow down. I want to finish talking."

"About what?"

"Anything." We sit and talk for over an hour about any and everything. The going down of the sun signals the fun must come to an end. I tell him I have to get ready for finals tomorrow, and this time, he doesn't object; he even gets out and opens the door. "Education is important; it's good to see you doing something positive."

"Thanks for the ride," I call over my shoulder.

"You're welcome. Let me get your number!"

I think for a minute and decide it's not a good idea. I'm only 19 with drama for days, and nothing good can come of this. I ask for his instead and promise to call when I go on break.

I'm overjoyed when exams are complete, which means FREEDOM until the New Year. I'm leaving campus today to go home. I want to make sure I'm up early tomorrow with the kids when they unwrap their gifts. As soon as I open the back door, I know I've made the right decision. My stepdad has the house smelling heavenly with holiday favorites. I go in and give him a hug before I put my things away. The kids are all gathered in my room, giving me my usual hugs and kisses, when I hear my mother coming down the stairs. I didn't realize she was home.

I prepare myself, not knowing what type of mood she's in. I avoid eye contact until she comes and stands in the doorway. "I saw you getting off the bus. Are you staying all break?"

"I plan on it."

"That's good. By the way, I appreciate you dropping off the presents for the kids. Are you hungry?"

"I'm starving, actually!"

"Ok, I'll fix you a plate."

I want to cry. This is the mother I know and love. I'm just scared to enjoy it too much; you never know when she will flip on you.

Dinner is just like old times; all the family is here. After we finish eating, my brothers, Tank, and I sneak out to smoke a joint before the Spades game gets started. Bro always got the good stuff. We laugh and play cards until well after midnight, then call it quits to get the kids to bed. They had fallen asleep in random places watching us rotate on the card table. As I change into my t-shirt and slide into bed, I can't help but wish my family was always like this. Jimmy crosses my mind; maybe I will call and just wish him Happy Holidays.

I search my purse for his number, but can't find it. I'm a little annoyed, but no need to spoil a good time. He has probably forgotten about me by now anyways. I decide I'm going to enjoy my family while things are good, and to my surprise, the whole break is uneventful. Mom seemed more content than I remember, and it's a good feeling!

Christmas Day was a success for the kids, but I could see a look of pain on my mother's face occasionally as the children unwrapped their gifts, knowing they hadn't come from her, but everyone else, in fact, had made a sacrifice so they could be happy. The streets have a strong hold on her; I'm just thankful they have loosened the grip for the holidays. I have never stopped loving my mom nor given up hope. I know God is real. I always trusted in what He could do, and I know for a fact my mom loves the Lord, and we are all His children. I've seen testimonies of murderers, prostitutes, and pimps becoming Pastors, motivational speakers, etc. I'm holding out hope that one day Mom will change. For now, I'll just cherish days like this!

Tee picks me up when it's time to head back to campus. I have accumulated new things thanks to Ms. Mackinnon, and a few of my family members, and I don't feel like hauling them on the bus. We catch up on what we missed over the break, and I give her the 411 on Jimmy.

"You're crazy, Vett! You never called him?"

"I'm sure it's not going anywhere. Girl, I told him I was 21, and he's damn near 30." I'm scared to see him again now; that deal is closed.

We laugh easily. I'm disheartened that my clutch will be moving away in a few months. I can tell her anything; she's the one person in my whole life that never judged me, and that is hard to find, especially in another female.

"What kind of car did you say the guy from the bus stop has?"

"A Maxima, but why does that matter?" I follow her eyes to the entrance of the dorm. Jimmy is leaning against his car, looking like he just stepped out of GQ.

"Is that him?"

"Sure is!"

"If you don't want him, give him my number."

I burst out laughing again. He is a Beautiful Sight. Good thing I had passed on wearing sweats and decided to get cute. I act calm, trying not to drool as I get out of the car. Tee steps out, acting like she is helping, but she's getting a closer look. Nosey.

Jimmy walks over when he sees me getting out of the passenger side. I tell my heartbeat to slow down as I try and figure out what to say.

"Well… you are hard to find."

"Why do you say that?"

"I have been here three times looking for you."

"Oh," I say, still acting like I'm not fazed. I really want to scream, "YOU HAVE?!" But I'm way too cool for that.

"So, where have you been?"

Questions already. This could be good! "Home."

"Oh yeah, where is that?"

"East side."

He smiles; he knows I'm playing a game. "Okay, if you don't want to be bothered, just let me know and I'll leave you alone."

Time out! I want him to stay. I want to play cool, not uninterested. I'm stuck! Ms. Nosey sees me struggling and clears her throat to bail me out. I almost forgot she was there. Look at her posing hard as ever; she's a MESS. After I introduced them, she turned and told me I had to get my things out of her car; she was in a hurry. Smoothly, she asked if he would help get my stuff in the dorm so she could get going. Now, if he wasn't my type, I would be mad. But I'm going to let her have this one. It gives me time to think of my next move.

I block the entrance to my room with my things and leave the door ajar. I invite him to have a seat on the couch in the hallway, using the excuse that my room is cluttered, instead of having to tell him, "I don't know you like that." We talk without fumbling about the holidays and discover we both have large families and share some pretty similar traditions. He looks at his watch; I don't know why but I'm not quite ready for him to go.

"Have you eaten?"

"No, not since earlier."

"Why? You cook?"

I giggle. He REALLY doesn't know me! "No, but I was going to grab something before I go to bed, if you want to join me."

"That's cool. You want me to take you somewhere?"

"No, it's a few places within walking distance, if you don't mind that."

We decide on a small pizzeria around the corner on Main Street. I find myself staring at his eyes and lips as we wait for the pizza to come out; it's an addiction I have. Some pretty eyes, straight teeth, and full lips will get my attention every time. But it only takes one stupid action or comment to turn me right off. I can't stand conceited or childish men; I'm OUT at the first sign. He doesn't come off as either, and I'm very comfortable with him. It's still a question I need answered though, so I can see how fast I need to eat this pizza and jet.

When the conversation fades out a little, I take the opportunity to ask if he's seeing anyone. "Sort of."

"Yes, or no, buddy!"

"I'm kind of seeing this girl. She lives far. Don't know where it's going."

"Hmm, well, let me help you. If she walks in right now, what would you do?"

He moves closer to me and says, "Invite her to sit down." I relaxed, satisfied with his answer. "What about you?"

"I'm single!"

"You sure?"

"Yes!"

It is a guy I chill with regularly in my old neighborhood, but it's nothing official. He's a friend of my brother's, and he's too close to my family for me to start something serious.

"Now my feelings are hurt."

"Why is that?"

"I thought you were seeing someone because you never called, but you really just dissed me."

I laugh as he holds his heart in shock. I feel nervous like a little girl when he looks directly into my eyes and says, "You have a pretty smile."

Thank God the pizza comes. We laugh more than we eat; I'm enjoying getting to know him. The food we did consume was excellent, though. I definitely plan on coming back, hopefully with him. He walks me back to my dorm and, without even asking, strolls into my room behind me.

"Listen, Negro. That wasn't a pizza-for-sex type of deal." I look at him cross-eyed. It's a shame I got to curse him out so soon. I put my hand on my hips to drive home my point. He slides his arm through mine and around my waist. "I just want your number. If you want to give me anything else, it's all up to you."

I blush, a little embarrassed, and turn to find a pen and paper. "Thanks for dinner." I hand him my number while holding the door for him to leave. I'm a little unraveled by his cologne. He asks me with his eyes if he can kiss me good night, and I respond with my lips on his. He tastes as good as he looks.

I get him out of my room quickly.

Jimmy seemingly enjoyed that kiss as much as I did. We spend all our free time together; he had even stopped by my mom's a few times when I was there on the weekends. We've been having so much fun I didn't realize the semester was so close to the end until the school wrote to me concerning my housing. My grant had only covered my Freshman and Sophomore years. I would have to kick in big time financially or find off-campus housing next year. I'm on the phone discussing the issue with my dad when Jimmy walks in.

"Are you ready? Call to see if Tee wants to come along."

"Well, excuse me, bossy. How are you today?"

"Oh hey, but anyways, I have a friend from out of town that wants to tag along, and I don't want him to feel like a third wheel."

I apologize to my dad for the rude interruption and hang up to call Tee. She says to give her a few minutes to get dressed

On the way to the club, I told her about my housing dilemma, and she suggested an apartment next to my sister that had just come vacant. Off-campus housing is much cheaper. Jimmy chimes in, suggesting it's best to stay on campus. He feels it would probably be hard to focus off campus that close to my family. I take that into consideration, then push it all to the back of my mind to deal with at a later date.

We have a blast at the club! Jimmy is a grown man, so the atmosphere is different from the house parties for sure. Tee and I dance until the lights come on. Jimmy drops his friend off at the hotel and then drives us back to campus. I invite him to come up once we are all alone. "It's late," he says, looking at his watch.

"Well, what time is your curfew?"

He laughs and parks his car. Every step we take makes me more nervous. He's grown. I am emotionally scared, young, and unsure how to interact with someone so mature. I wonder if it's any different; I guess I will just have to see.

I talk nervously for a while, trying to build the courage to take the next step. He finally takes my hand and places it on his chest when he realizes I'm stalling. His chest is solid as a rock; I'm terrified! I've lied about my age, and he will hate me if he finds out. My heart is racing. I better not do this.

He strokes my hair and kisses me softly on the neck. Okay, just once, and then I won't see him again. I undo my blouse, then take off his shirt. He never moves; he just stares at me with those sultry eyes. I think he wants to be assured I know what I'm doing. His body is just as beautiful as his face. I start to relax once I remember what a friend had told me a few months back when we were hanging out: sex is like riding a bicycle. Once you've learned to ride one, it's all the same.

I turn the lights off and experience something I NEVER felt before. He asks if I want him to leave as I lay in silence. Maybe he thinks I didn't enjoy it because I haven't said a word. The truth is, I'm speechless. I reach for the covers, pull them over us, snuggle up next to him, and fall asleep in his arms. The theory was WRONG; sex is not at all the same. In the last hour, I learned some things I didn't know my body was capable of.

He's not getting dressed fast enough the next morning. I have to call Tee. Whatever happened between us was special. I want him forever. But of course, I wouldn't DARE tell him that after the first night. But I gotta tell somebody.

"Good morning," Tee answers all cheery, as if she knows what I've been doing.

"Giiiirrrl, that man means business in the bedroom!"

"Breathe," she says, laughing.

"It's just been a while."

"I'm certain that's not the case, but try not to sound too sprung."

One thing is for certain; I know this is a feeling I will never forget.

The next few months also prove Tee's theory of something new to be incorrect. He's not just new; he's the best thing that has happened to me. My heart and body have been taken to a level I have never known. He's so fun and exciting. I feel like a different person around him. In fact, it's going so well that I've decided to make it official. I'm having dinner at my family's house this weekend, and I asked him to come.

Tee's eyes buck when I tell her that news. "Are you sure?" She was aware we had played cards there and had a few drinks, but

I had not formally introduced him to the whole family. This is a big step for me, letting him see where I really come from. My family separates men from boys, you have to be strong to hang with us, and our longevity will depend on this gathering. Lord be with me. I like him a lot, but I know my family can chase the white off rice; we're a rough crowd.

I'm a little shaky pulling up to the house. Jimmy senses it, asking for the third time if I'm sure about this. I dismiss his suspicion, saying I'm just hungry. I am actually concerned about everyone being on their best behavior. I can't be certain how the evening will go, but I'm more than confident the food will be a hit. We have two of the best chefs in town under one roof, and the aroma in the air when we walk in proves they are at it again. Mom looked very pretty in her yellow suit when she did it... She did it, a brand new hairstyle and all. You're not getting much more than a T-shirt and jeans out of my stepdad, and that is fine by me. I love him just the way he is.

I feel my nerves settling when my dad and Jimmy start to talk easily about the desserts spread on the table. Jimmy's mom could throw down too, food tasted so good it would make you slap your mama. He used to bring me dinner when she cooked sometimes. On more than a few occasions, it was so good I made him drive back across town for more. While he and Dad chat, I sit down to watch TV with the kids, Mom is finishing the kool-aid and iced tea.

By the time dinner is served, we are carrying on like he has been in the family for years. Jimmy had even called in some reinforcement for the Spade game; we told him it was a must after dinner. Rashid knocking at the door prompted us to put the plates away and pull out the cards. Mom and I choose Jimmy and his friend as our first prey. Turns out we fall victim; they beat the breaks off us! Mom can't stand defeat. She swears it is anybody's fault but her own every time she loses. She tells me to get up and let someone else play like I was the problem for sure. I'm tickled because I'm as competitive as she is and would probably be just as mad if Jimmy wasn't here, but I don't care tonight. I want to get next to him anyways.

"You want a drink, big head?"

"No, sir. I'm getting ready for round two on this table. No distractions."

"Yeah, ok!"

He's so sure of himself, but in an attractive way, not conceited, I like that. My brother says, "I'll have a drink, Jimmy."

"Heck, no, boy. You're too young. You have to be 21 to drink with me, my man."

"Don't act like that. I'm a man!"

I want to laugh. According to life standards, his statement couldn't be truer. The responsibility he had taken on after we left definitely gave him a right to feel that way, but legally, he had a few years to go.

"Boy, get out of here. 21 or nothing."

"That's messed up. You drink with Shun."

"Your sister's grown!"

"No, she's not. She's only 19!"

I felt the conversation going south, but it was out of his mouth before I could stop him. When my eyes lock with Jimmy's, I know It's about to be a train wreck. His body freezes in place.

"How old did you say she was?"

I try to look away, but I'm held by his hard stare. My brother says 19 again, and I want to DIE. Jimmy puts his cards down and speaks directly to me this time. "Shun, how old are you?"

"20," I answer.

"So, you just turned 20? Because on your birthday we celebrated you turning 22. YOU REMEMBER THAT?" He yells the last part.

"Yes," I say, barely audible.

He stands up so fast his chair falls. "Let's step outside."

Everyone is staring in silence. I'm scared. I stand up slowly, hoping someone will save me, then Mom comes to the rescue. "What's the problem, Jimmy?"

"Tell them the problem, Shun," he says between his clenched teeth. I can't find my voice.

"Shun."

"WHAT!"

"Tell them the problem," he says a little too loudly, and my attitude kicks in.

"I don't have one," I say, rolling my neck.

"Oh, you don't." He steps closer. Oh hell, wrong move! "Let ME tell them, then. I'm a 28-year-old grown-ass MAN!"

Everyone looks puzzled because he really doesn't look his age. My mom repeats, "So what's the problem?"

"Ain't nobody trying to go to jail!"

I play with my hands, too embarrassed to do anything else. It's an awkward silence, then my mom says, "Who the hell said they were calling the police?" Mom is crazy as a bat; nothing is ever too serious for her to touch. The room erupts in laughter; even Rashid is dying. But I know it's no laughing matter to Jimmy; he never cracks a smile.

"Rah, let's go!"

"Jimmy, can we talk?" I nervously follow him to the door.

"Talk about what?" He keeps his back to me and never loses his stride.

"I'm sorry. I didn't think we would get this serious. I was going to tell you. I didn't drive… Can you drop me back off?" I was babbling. I just wanted him to talk to me.

"I don't play games," he says, walking out the door, never turning around to look at me once. My chest starts to tighten, and my eyes fill with tears. My feelings for him are even deeper than I thought; this is hurting me. I ask my dad to drive me home as soon as he pulls off. I can't enjoy myself like this.

I cry all the way there with my stepdad assuring me Jimmy will be back. "No, he won't, Dad. Did you see how mad he was?" I say between sobs.

"Yes, he will, sweetheart."

"How do you know?"

"I saw the way he looked at you. He'll be back, trust me."

Before I knew it, the semester had come to an end, and it was time to exit the dorms. I've been in such a trance I didn't realize that much time had passed. I called my brothers yesterday to help me move. It's almost time for them to get here. I have to get in gear. I have decided to take my chances off campus, and it's a bittersweet decision. Despite the heartache and problems in the last two years, this campus has changed my life in positive ways. I've become totally independent and expanded my horizons so much. I will miss this place! I'm sure living off campus will not be the same.

The knock on the door makes me jump in place. I open it to let my brothers in, but Jimmy's standing there. I'm so shocked I can't speak.

"Hey!"

"Hey, what are you doing here?"

"Your brothers said you needed help moving." They were supposed to help. I guess this is their way of fixing it. They must have called him. "If you're busy, I can find someone else."

"If I was busy, I wouldn't be here. Now, get your butt in here and sit down. We need to talk." I take a seat on the bed and touch the spot beside me for him to join me.

"I'm good," he says sternly. I guess he's still upset. It's understandable.

"What do you want to talk about?"

"Why you lied to me, Shun? That's what."

"Honestly, I didn't think this would be anything serious. But then one thing led to another, and before I knew it, I was hooked."

"Hooked on what?"

I stand up and walk closer. I figure if he was done, he wouldn't be here, so I take a chance. "I'm hooked on you," I whisper before I kiss him. At first, he just stands still, and then I feel his hands moving down my back, telling me my apology is accepted.

The sun is setting by the time he wakes me. "What time do you have to be out of here?"

"Not until tomorrow. I was just getting an early start."

"Good, I'm tired."

"From what?"

"That apology. If that's how you say I'm sorry, you can lie to me every day."

I laugh so hard that it makes him smile. "Jimmy, I'm really sorry. I shouldn't have lied."

"It's all good. We can't take it back now, Shun. Just know you don't have to lie to me. Just keep it real. That's how I operate."

I lay on his chest, and he kisses my head. At this very moment, I know I'm in love, but I will keep my feelings to myself. We have emptied out enough for now.

He lifts my chin and looks me in the eyes. "Are you still sorry?"

"Very sorry," I whisper and turn off the lights. The sunrise brings me gloom; another chapter in my life will be closing today as I leave the dorms for good. I'm so thankful to have this handsome guy beside me to make my transition a little easier.

Chapter 8

ALL GROWN UP

Moving is stressful! Lights, gas, cable, and all these other things I never had to concern myself with before are a little overwhelming. Arranging my things—some new, some used, and some donated—helped ease my mind. I love to decorate. My mom, Tee, and I have a good time shopping and making my small place cozy. I had a lot to do and only a little while to get it done.

Once I had decided to move off campus, I also found a job. Daddy had purchased me a car as well because he wanted me to have reliable transportation. Jimmy and I are going to North Carolina to pick it up this weekend. Jimmy had assured me he was fine driving me around, but I knew that couldn't be a permanent thing. He had his own life, and Tee was leaving soon. I was actually good on the bus, but Daddy wasn't hearing that. He is such a MAN; he sets the bar high and tells me never to settle for anything less. If we would only listen to the wisdom of our elders, we could save ourselves a lot of heartache in this world.

Being grown up isn't all it's cracked up to be. I don't have much of a social life anymore. It's work then home, except for an occasional trip by Mom's to play cards and talk smack on her front porch. My life is boring now.

Mom is becoming more stable in her older days, not roaming the streets like she used to. She and her friends either partied in the basement or upstairs. I don't think it matters much to anyone as long she's home and we know she is safe.

Jimmy and I are going strong. He is like a permanent fixture in my apartment, although my dad doesn't know it. We spend most nights together and have a routine that works for us both. We are supposed to be just hanging out and eating tonight, but he and Rah are playing video games (yes, video games. Men never grow up).

I'm tired of watching them fight like kids. I go into the bedroom to slip on something comfortable and prepare for bed. I'm pulling off my jeans when I hear a loud bang on my window that causes me to duck. What in the world is going on? I slip on my shorts and join Jimmy and Rah, staring out my window. I see a light-skin, short chick yelling up at my apartment, and Jimmy looks like a deer caught in headlights.

I ask, "What's her problem?"

"You sleeping with my man!" Jimmy's facial expression let me know which man she's referring to. "I've followed him over here for the last week, and I know he's been with you."

I turn around toward Jimmy with the face of Death. This is deja vu! "Yo, Jimmy, you better go down and handle that!"

"Bitch, I want you to come down!"

Oh, say less. I run toward the door like a flash of lightning, I was going to be a lady and let Jimmy deal with it, but since she wants to call names, I'm about to dust her. Rah and Jimmy run a thousand miles per hour, trying to get to her before I do. The rules we were raised by are clear: if you come to someone's house, oh you gon' get what you came for.

Jimmy has the chic wrapped up, putting her in the car by the time I get downstairs. She looks all kinds of upset, so I back off. She's trying to wiggle out of his grip, but he knows she's safer in that car, so he won't let her go. He attempts to shut the door, but she blocks him. "How long have you been seeing Jimmy?"

"Look, I don't know what's going on, but you are out of bounds, girl. Go head on now."

"You sleeping with my man and you don't think I deserve an answer?"

YOUR MAN! I had been with him nearly every day since we met. Now he has some explaining to do. Jimmy finally gets the door closed and convinces her to leave, then attempts to talk to me after she pulls off. I give him the finger and walk back to my apartment. He's pleading with me to stop and listen, but I'm not hearing it. I'm tired of games; so much for keeping it REAL.

All the commotion and wrestling must have thrown my body off balance, I go to the bathroom, and I'm bleeding like crazy. I call my mom and she tells me to go to the emergency room. They checked me in and gave me a series of tests before saying I had a miscarriage. Whatever, idiots. I just had my period, and I can't have kids. I guess that's the best they could come up with.

The nurse says to stay put, and a different doctor will be in to see me. I get dressed and leave as soon as the nurse walks out. Bet they want to keep me all night playing the guessing game and running up a bill. I'm positive it's stress. I didn't tell them about the near royal rumble a few hours ago.

I'm so miserable for the next few weeks. It actually felt like a year has gone by. All I do is work, eat, and sleep. Thank God school will be starting soon. Between classes and work, I won't have time to think about anything else.

When I walk into work on Monday, my supervisor tells me that the administrative assistant had resigned. He says if I want the position, I could start next week, full time with a pay raise. I'm so excited, I immediately think about all the new things I could buy.

My supervisor clears his throat loudly. "You want it or not? Before I put in the paper."

His fat self gets on my nerves. "Yes, sure. I will definitely accept it, sir," I say in my most professional voice. Something Jimmy said comes to me. If I moved off campus, I would become distracted, and the semester did start soon. Oh well, forget him. I'm grown, and I need money, not school. I had taken a Civil Service exam to work for the County right out of high school; college was never my first choice anyways. When I hadn't received my results before school started, I went with the next best thing. I guess my opportunity to make money and leave school behind has come. My anger toward Jimmy really fueled my decision not to go back. Making life-changing decisions based on temporary emotions will, more often than not, come back to bite you.

I'm so hyped about my new position I decide to stop by my mom's instead of going straight home to waddle in my misery like I've been doing for the past few weeks. I see Jimmy's car in front of her house as I'm about to park. What the heck is he doing over here? I speed right past. His face is the last one I want to see. I had been dodging him since that night, and I planned on keeping it that way.

I catch a glimpse of Jimmy, his friends, and my brothers standing on the porch. I pretend to be looking straight ahead. I turn on the next block, cut down a couple of side streets, and race home to shut back up with my thoughts. I drop my clothes at the door and run a hot bath; my first method of coping with a stressful day. Wine is my second. I turn on my music and step into my bath. Thoughts of my new job make me smile. This wine is going to take it all away in a minute. I must have really impressed my boss to get an opportunity like this so soon.

I'm toasting to myself when I hear a key in my door, followed by the squeaking hinges as it opens. It's only two people with a key, and Tee is out of town. Jimmy comes strolling into the bathroom looking too good to be true. I remind myself that I'm mad at him and try not to react to his presence. I have to work on the tear ducts, though; my eyes tell on me every time. I have missed him so much, even though he hurt me deeply. Emotions are so dangerous they will make you stay when you need to go and go when you should stay.

He comes over and wipes my face. "I just want to apologize for how things went down."

My heart sinks deeper. I feel like punching him, but an explanation is more important. "Why did you lie?"

"I didn't. I told you I was seeing someone."

"Then why were you ALWAYS with me?"

He's silent for a long time, probably can't think of a lie fast enough. I tell him to get out! He drops his head. "I love you, Shun," he says in a near whisper.

No one else can make my name sound so sweet. I start to cry uncontrollably at this point. I mean, we've said "I love you" a few times while making love, but I never really put any stock into that. It could simply mean I love the act of what we're doing. To hear him say it so unexpectedly catches me off guard. My heart softens immediately, and even though I want to stay mad, I can't. This man has been here through every transition, good or bad, since the day he walked into my life. Hell, I was scared to change lanes on the expressway before we met. I mean, it seems small, but that's one of the things that make me love him so much. He has patience with me; nothing was ever too small or too big for him to take the time to teach me. Not to mention the way he makes my heart feel. I've never felt that with another man. It's not just a sexual attraction I have for him; he has helped me to GROW.

He stands in silence, waiting for my sobs to slow down before asking if I am ok. "I will be." He walks over and kisses me.

"I just wanted to check on you. Call me later if you want." He turns to walk away, but I grab his hand and squeeze it in mine, then I extend my other hand for him to help me out of the tub. He does and leads me to the bedroom, where we get lost for the rest of the day. Nothing at all has been resolved, but my physical gratification was easier to achieve than my emotional satisfaction, so I placed on another band-aid.

At dinner the next evening, I took the opportunity to tell Jimmy about my new position. He's not as excited as I am. "Leaving school even to work is a stupid idea. You need your education more than the money!" he says rather loudly. I remind him that he's not my father and storm out of the restaurant to the car. We give each other the silent treatment all night, and it continues for the next few days. He's angry that I'm not going back to school, and I'm angry that he won't choose. He finally leaves and goes to his mom's. He doesn't come back that night or for the next two weeks, for that matter. So be it. I had other things to worry about.

It doesn't matter how mad I am at him; every time the phone rings, I still pray it's him. I've had five calls today, and every time, it was my mom. I almost hang up when I hear her voice this time. "WHAT, ma?"

"You better check yourself, lil girl!"

"I'm sorry, Mom. I'm waiting on an important call."

"Oh, ok. Well, anyways, I forgot to tell you earlier I'm giving your dad a party tomorrow. He's been a little under the weather lately. I just want to celebrate him feeling better." Unaware that we are on the outs, she tells me to be sure and bring Jimmy.

The news cheers me up some. I'm glad my dad's feeling better. Also, it gives me an excuse to call Jimmy without him knowing how desperately I miss him.

He's not home. I leave a message for him then page him once I hang up. I curl up with my book, satisfied, knowing that I can at least hear his voice when he calls back, even if he doesn't come. I drift off reading on the couch, and I'm awakened by the ringing of my phone. It has to be Jimmy this late. "Hello."

"Hey, Chief." It's B. That's a nickname I hadn't heard in years. "Am I calling too late?" Silence. "Hello," he says into the phone.

I clear my throat. "I'm here."

"I'm in town, and my mom told me that Mom's is giving Big Dad (also another nickname I hadn't heard in years) a party. Will you be there?"

The part of me that's still angry wants to say, "Why MF?" But the part that needs some closure simply says yes.

"Will it be okay if I come?"

"It's a free country."

He laughs. "Well, I guess I'll see you then. Hey, Shun?"

"WHAT!" I retort, slightly annoyed that he doesn't seem to remember he busted my heart into.

"Will it be too much to ask to see you before then?"

"Don't push it, Negro!"

"I understand. See you at the party." I hang up without saying goodbye. The call bothers me, and I don't know why. I need Jimmy. I push all my pride to the side and dial his number again, but he doesn't answer. I'm desperate, so I call his mom's house phone. I know he is there. I also know she hates my guts and will blast me because it's late. His mother doesn't think I fit her image the way Little Miss Prissy does. Too bad I love him, and I need him right now.

I hold my breath and pray I get anyone besides his mom. After the 3rd ring, someone says hello. I freeze where I stand; you have to be *careful* what you wish for. The voice I hear is female, but definitely not his mom or sisters. I've only talked to her a couple of times, but there's no mistaking the voice on the other end. I am confused as to why she's answering Jimmy's mom's phone at this hour. I tell her to put him on the phone and she hangs up. I immediately pull on my jeans and sweatshirt; he has played with me for the last time.

I leave with my car on two wheels. I'm going so fast. I guess Ms. Thang must have been as heated as I was because when I made it to his mom's, she was flying out of the house with him hot on her trail. I turn off my headlights to see how Mr. Smooth wiggles his way out of this. Sure enough, his charm seems to be working.

It appears they are walking back into the house. I'm about to open the car door when his mom comes out yelling. I can't make out everything she is saying, but they start going at it again, one trying to out-talk the other. His mom takes her hand to soothe her and yells at Jimmy, "I told you that girl was trouble and you should leave her alone!"

"I did!" he screams back. "I don't know why she called."

I had heard enough. Time to get out of this car.

I walk up to the porch, and I can see the shock on his face. "Surprise, nigga." How is it that you know a person is dead wrong, but you still feel sorry for them? Oh well, I must stand up for myself this time. I put that sympathy in the wind and went in on him. "When did you stop seeing me, or do you mean spending the night or sleeping with me? Which one is it? Because I'm confused."

He opens his mouth to say something, and the chic tries to charge past him. He grabs her arm, and she starts to cry.

"Why do you keep lying?" He looks at me like he wants to answer me, but doesn't. My voice is starting to crack, but I need to know the truth. "Why is she here so late? Are you still seeing her too?"

He looks from me back to her, drops his head, and says, "We're engaged, Shun."

Chapter 9

LOVE AND PAIN SOMETIMES
EXIST IN THE SAME PLACE

I turn and walk away, SPEECHLESS. I'm crushed going back to my car; there is no fight left in me. I'm a magnet for unfaithful men.

I hold my tears until I'm off the block completely. They will not see me defeated. I make it home, prepared to lock myself in with my thoughts, until I remember Dad's party! Guess I'll have to put my big girl panties on and push this pain to the back of my mind with all the rest of it. No pain is worse than the pain you hide; that excruciating, deep, dark hurt reserved just for you. The kind that is heavy on the heart, but you carry it alone because it's too shameful to share. That pain is dangerous, and it will change you if you're not careful! For my stepdad, though, I'll show up all smiles as if all's right with the world.

My head is spinning. I lay down to clear my mind, but all I can do is cry. Fatigue eventually gets the best of me, and I fall asleep. I'm awakened by pounding on my door. I grab my razor;

Jimmy's getting cut for sure. Don't think you can do what you want and come over here like you running something. I had fixed his behind and put the chain on the door. Wasn't no strolling in this time, brother. BAM BAM BAM! I snatch the door open with fire running through my veins and find Tee standing there dressed to kill! She is always fly, but she put something extra on it tonight.

"Tee, what the heck are you doing here girl?"

"I called you a hundred times to tell you I was coming. You know I'm not missing it."

Missing what…OHHHH. Dad's party, ugh. I should have set my alarm. "Give me 30 minutes to get dressed." I knew what I was wearing. I was mad at Jimmy, and seeing B for the first time in a long time… definitely something short and tight. I yell for her to get the black outfit hanging on the door in my guest room, which also substitutes for a closet.

"You're always late, Vette."

"Girl, relax. This is my mom we're talking about! If she says the party starts at 5:30, that's 7:00 pm. If you're lucky, you know Ma operates on CPT." We both giggle.

"You been sleeping all day?"

"Yeah, long week at work," I lie, opting not to tell her the Jimmy story in fear that we wouldn't make it to my parents but end up having a pity party, and I don't want to think about that anymore. I need this time with family to take my mind off the drama with Jimmy and strengthen me for this conversation with B.

I shower and get dressed quickly. All I have to do is unwrap my hair and we can get this party started. I have to hype myself up so no one detects that I'm really dying inside. I was more upset at myself than anyone; I love fast and hard. If I care enough to give someone my body, it's not temporary. I'm convinced that's part of the problem; I pretend that I can have nonchalant sex, knowing good and well if I make it to the point of sleeping with someone, I care for them. But men tend to run when they feel an emotional attachment, so I lie and play the friend game and always end up hurt.

Tee catches me zoning in the mirror. "What is up with you?"

This time I tell her a partial truth. "I have a lot on my mind with the new job and not going back to school." I know my dad will be hurt, but I have to do what's best for me. That's way too deep to be getting into right now.

"Chic, we got moves to make."

She is absolutely right. Game face activated! I proceed to get my hair and lipstick on the same page as the outfit. As I pass the floor-length mirror, I realize how beautiful I am in my leather get-up. If that Negro wanted to play games, his loss. On to someone that deserved all this. Ok, I'm only 120 pounds soaking wet (all that eating in college, and I had managed to lose 5 lbs), but my big boobs still made me appear thicker. This particular outfit even made my non-existent behind quite round. "How do I look?"

"Like a sophisticated tramp," Tee replies. Mission accomplished! I had on an official F-you outfit. I hope B gets the message, and I hope Jimmy shows his face so he can get it as well, a two-for-one deal. I'm sure someone in my family had gotten around to telling him about the party, even though I didn't. They think he's the man; if only they knew the games being played.

I follow Tee to my mom's, opting to drive my own car to ensure I can make a quick getaway if I feel the need. It's almost 6 pm when we arrive, and in her true fashion, Mom is only half prepared. Guests had already started to show, so we jumped in to help out. I would do anything to take my mind off of this heartache. I place the drinks and finger food on a table while my other sisters help Mom transfer food from the pans into the serving dishes. At least she's close to being finished, I tease, feeling a little more upbeat already. Mom comes around to the table where I'm standing and looks me up and down. I try and pretend I'm too busy to notice. She was never strict on our fashion; in fact, she was quite the opposite. She let us make our own mistakes. She believed the more you shielded a child, the more rebellious they would be. But you better believe if you took her kindness for weakness, what a price to pay.

Still, she's not one to judge. She's pretty carefree in fact, so I find it strange the way she's eyeing me. "I guess you know B's in town, huh?"

"Yeah, he called and said he would be coming."

Tee looks puzzled. "Who?"

"B, girl," my mother says in a matter-of-fact tone, and a little too excited for me.

Tee smiles. "I can't wait to see him."

"You don't have to wait long. He's downstairs in the basement with the other boys."

My hands freeze. I give my mom a look. This is information I should have received when I walked in the door. Everybody knows this is a touchy situation for me.

Tee calls my name loudly. "YES!" I answer, irritated.

"You got this? I'm going downstairs."

Whatever, traitor. I'm your friend; you should still be mad at him too. But I'm not really upset with her, and I'm sort of anxious myself. What does he look like? Has he gained weight (I hope so)? I dismiss it all quickly. I don't care. I have a man. Well, do I... Oh right. No, I don't. He's engaged to someone else.

My eyes fill with tears. I have to stop falling in love. That's the answer from now on! I don't have any connections to any of these men, no proof I ever loved them, no returned emotions—just PAIN. Love is for the birds, and at 21, I think it's time to throw the towel in.

When I hear a commotion coming from the basement stairwell, I grab a napkin to dab the tears about to pour down. I brace myself for this awkward reunion as B comes out of the basement hand and hand with Tee. No luck with the fat thing; he looks better than I remember, oh boy.

The whole room seemed to get still when our eyes met. I was willing for my tears to stay in place. I don't want anyone to think I'm crying about us. These tears belong to all the men I have given my heart and body only to have my heart shattered and kicked back to me every time.

"So y'all gone speak or stand there all night looking crazy?" My mother ain't got the sense God gave her! She makes me laugh, though, chasing my tears away… for now.

B walks over and pulls me into his chest for a hug. I feel his compassion as he kisses me on top of my head. Our embrace isn't as strange as I thought it would be. My stepdad looked on, hopeful. He loved B like his own son and had told me people made mistakes when I had asked him to go kill him when I found out about the baby. After he almost died himself from laughter, he had said I should forgive B and move on if I couldn't accept it; babies don't ever go away. Daddy, J. D. is the best example of love a girl could ask for.

Mom shouts, "This is a PARTY, not a wake!" The famous words of my cousin Steward when the mood is too gloomy in the room. Everyone who wasn't in the dining area started to migrate toward the food, and the DJ turned the music up! If we can't agree on anything else as a family, we know how to throw a party. I'm enjoying a dance with my baby brother when I see B slowly making his way toward me. I'm careful not to make eye contact; the last thing I want to do is dance with him. The memory of graduation day is strongly playing in my head. Anger is the emotion in the lead right now.

The song stops as he gets closer. I quickly try to turn in the opposite direction, but he stops me. "May I talk to you?" he asks, a little too close to my ear. I try to act annoyed, but his cologne is more my friend than my enemy. (In case you haven't picked up on it, I like my men to smell good and look good; they just ain't ever NO DAMN GOOD).

I'm not letting emotions win; I turn and fire off him. "What would you like to talk about? You lying, the baby, my bruised heart, the embarrassment? I mean, just where do we start? Damn, here comes the tears again. He shields me with his 6'4 frame, gently takes my arm, and leads me upstairs away from the crowd. He just lets me cry without speaking; nothing we can do until this part is over. I had cried a thousand times for different reasons since we broke up, but these tears, in particular, at this moment, belong to HIM. When I felt I could form some words, I used the tissue he so readily had available. I now know where he had gone when he had left the room briefly. I assumed he had changed his mind about clearing the air and went back to the party.

"Are you okay?"

"Do I look okay?"

"I'm sorry. I mean, do you still want to talk?"

"No, but I'm ready to listen."

"I'm sorry."

"That's nice, but why did you do it, B?"

"We had started to fight so much, Chief. I had women coming at me, paying attention, noticing me when you were not… I got selfish! I heard you were dealing with the other guys at school, the dude from the café on the corner, getting a little too close with one of my friends… I heard it all, and it started to get to me; she was an outlet. You didn't listen to me half the time; you were so busy with your family, we were more like brother and sister than boyfriend and girlfriend."

As I listen to him, I realize something I had not considered before: I shared some of the blame. I did treat him like a family member instead of my friend/lover. My heart softens as I watch his eyes fill with tears as well.

"I always loved you, Chief. I just made a stupid decision. I love my daughter, don't get me wrong. I'm just sorry I hurt you." He takes my face in his hands and wipes away the tears that had started to flow steady again against my best effort to hold them. "I called you to make amends about a year ago."

"I know!"

"How? I hung up without saying anything."

"My mom told me a couple of days later that you had called and gotten my number. I put two and two together since it was a

Buffalo area code. Besides, I had to argue for two days about that anonymous call!"

"Good for you!"

We share a chuckle. "Can I ask you one more thing, B?"

"Anything!"

"Was the girl who answered your phone white?"

"Yes. Why?"

"It still hurts. Was I not good enough?"

You were too good for me, baby. I think that's what scared me. I was too young to settle down. I knew from the start you were wife material, and you wanted that family life."

"It didn't have anything to do with the fact I can't have children?"

"No baby, not at all." He leans in to kiss me.

My heart is beating so fast. What is happening right now? I love Jimmy (he's engaged). Anthony's betrayal crosses my mind; everyone hurts me… The hell with it. I give in and start to kiss him deeply.

"I'm so sorry," he whispers once his lips leave mine. I feel so many emotions; this was my first long-term relationship. My rationale is gone! When he starts to raise my shirt over my head, I lift my arms to assist him.

Someone yells, "Shun, Jimmy's here!"

I jump off the bed and quickly fix my shirt and then my face. B stands as well. "Guess Jimmy has taken my place."

"Shut up!"

He pulls me in for a hug. "What was happening?" he asks.

"Something unhealthy," I assure him.

He kisses me on the cheek. "I love you, Chief."

"I love you too."

"Guess this is goodbye."

"I guess so." This chapter is now properly closed for me. I feel both strange and relieved when B walks out. I need to get myself together fast. I hear B say, "What's up?" as his heavy feet hit the stairs.

"What's up?" The other voice belongs to Jimmy. I'm sure from all my old pictures and high school yearbooks he knows very well who B is, but he walks in and asks sarcastically, "Was that your boy?"

"No, it's my man Negro since you want to be funny." The look on his face tells me this will not be settled in a joke. Oh well, if he wanted war, I was always ready, razor in my bra and pain in my heart. He walks closer and asks a dumb question. "Have you been crying? You called him over here to cry on his shoulder?" He yells in my face.

"Back up, nigga," I say with enough force to let him know to move wisely. "You really think this is about you (I REFUSE to acknowledge he's been successful in hurting me AGAIN)?"

"We had unfinished business."

"As far as I'm concerned, you and your perfect little fiancé are made for each other. Now get the hell up out of my mama's house!"

"I was invited, so let her tell me that!"

"FINE!" I fly past him to go tell my mom and my whole family, as a matter of fact, that "Mr. Wonderful" is a two-timing DOG. He grabs me by my waist and pulls me back to him. And just like that, the faucet turns back on. They say crying cleanses the soul; mine should be squeaky clean at this point!

"Don't do this here, Shun. It's your dad's party. You're mad at me, no one else. Don't make a scene."

"Who even invited you?"

"You know, your mom called me. You think she doesn't know what's going on? She told me to come over and talk to you." He kisses my neck softly, and I feel myself becoming weak.

What is this? How many men can occupy your heart at once? How can love and pain exist in the same place at the same time? I turn around and look him in the eyes. Yeah, he certainly has my heart now. I'm glad B and I had found closure because this is my grown woman love… or is it? "What's up with you and the chic? Is that over?"

"Can we talk about it later?"

"What's wrong with right now?"

"I think you've cried enough for one night, Shun. You want to go downstairs with your family?"

"No, I want to go home!"

"You want me to take you?"

"No, I drove."

"May I follow you to make sure you get home safely?"

"I'm good."

"Well, can we at least be civil when we go down?"

"Why not? We've been pretending this whole relationship, right?" He looks hurt, but oh well, so am I.

He fixes my hair and takes my hand. We walk downstairs like we are all together when in reality, my heart is in a million pieces and my mind is all confused. I put on my happy smile for my stepdad as I kiss him goodnight. My mom comes over, looking Jimmy up and down the same way she was eyeing me when I first arrived. Guess this was a bad fallout, huh?" she asks her question in general.

For the first time, I notice what Jimmy's wearing. This tan suit fits his body so perfectly, it appears he had stood there and someone sewed it on him.

Mom says, "You thought you were doing something in that little leather outfit. I guess he said F-you back." Leave it to her to make me laugh when all I want to do is go home and release the rest of these tears in peace.

We managed to leave after 20 minutes of goodbyes. I was still a little unsettled about what had almost taken place between B and I, and was relieved I hadn't seen him on my way out. I'm not sure if he left or was in another part of the house, but I am certain that was one goodbye that would be forever. I'm confused enough. Jimmy still followed me home despite my many attempts to stop him. I'm lingering in my car as if I'm looking for something, giving him time to get out if he wants to because I'm not asking him to come in; my pride won't let me. My flesh, however, is hoping that he will. That tan suit has done the trick.

My tactic is working. I see his car door open and he emerges, stopping my heart. Who am I fooling? He has me so gone. I open my car door and let one leg hang out a minute longer than it needs to before exiting the car. I can tell by the look in his eyes when he approaches my car, that I will not be spending the night alone. He doesn't know I've already given in, so I keep him in suspense a little longer as he walks me to the door. I remain radio silent instead of laughing and joking like I do when we're in a good place. My building is quiet. Guess everyone must have been in the mood to party or fast asleep. All four apartments are dark, not a single light coming from anywhere. Our footsteps echo in the stillness, and I'm relieved to get to my apartment door. I don't know how much longer I'll be able to stay silent or keep my hands to myself; he smells delightful.

My hand is shaking so badly I can't get the key in the door. Jimmy gently takes the key, steps in front of me, and opens the door with ease. I all but run in the house; I don't trust myself. "Goodnight," I whisper as I shut the door very slowly, hoping he would stop me… He doesn't. I stand on the other side and begin to cry. Why did I care if he left? Why didn't I ask him to stay? He hadn't missed me at all. The hell with this, I'm going to tell him once and for all not to ever bother me again. I open the door to go after him, and he's leaning against the wall; he had never left.

"What are you doing?"

"Waiting for you to invite me in."

"I hate you!"

"No, you don't," he whispers, moving me back inside with one hand while locking the door with the other. How can I feel this safe with someone who has caused me so much pain?

"Are we going to talk about this, Jimmy?"

"Not tonight." He covers my lips with his and removes my tight clothes with little effort. It wouldn't be the next day, either; we didn't leave the bedroom for the rest of the weekend.

I hate that Monday has come. He had not called anyone or answered one page since Saturday, which meant nothing was more important than me. At least, that's what I wanted to believe; that's what I needed to believe.

We never got around to discussing that night at his mom's house. Deep down inside, I didn't want to know. I was more afraid of losing him than knowing the truth, so I let it go. I knew that was fine with him because Jimmy hates confrontation.

We pick up like nothing ever happened; him spending the night, weekend shopping sprees, his friends stopping over like it was his place instead of mine. I didn't mind, though; we all had a sister/brother bond. His friends and my family were close as well. No matter what goes down, if you forgive your significant other, then that's it. I'm sure my family suspected Jimmy and I had problems, but they love him the same. Heck, what relationship is perfect?

I guess the incident at his mom's had given me some cushion on the dropping out of college dilemma; while Jimmy had expressed his disappointment several times since he came back, he wasn't pushing it anymore. I think he had just accepted that once my mind was made up, there was no changing it. We maintain the next couple of years successfully with the exception of the normal relationship issues.

We've been almost inseparable until, as of late, Jimmy has started spending more nights at his mom's. He says she's been alone too much. Being the baby and a mama's boy, I didn't question it. I can't wait for him to get here today, though. We're planning a weekend getaway. In the 3 1/2 years we've been dating, we have never had a real vacation. I'm ready. I had asked a few times, but Jimmy had always made excuses. Tonight, he's going to put up or shut up, or else I'll be in Jamaica all by myself, letting someone else behold all this beauty.

I'm admiring myself in the mirror when the phone rings. "Hello."

"Hey. I was just thinking about you."

"How's your mom?"

"Good, but I'm telling you now if I'm staying over there tonight… you're cooking!"

"I'm already cooking, boy."

"What are you cooking?"

"Pork chops!"

"Don't play yourself, Shun."

"What?"

"You know I don't eat no pig."

"Oh well, I eat all the pig from the rotter to the totter!"

"You're nasty. Don't be asking me to kiss you." I laugh hard. "I'm not coming for dinner, then."

"Okay bye!"

"Shun!"

"What, James?" I call him by his full name when I want him to know how much I miss him. And right now, I missed him something awful.

"Cook me a hamburger and some fries."

"How much you going to pay me?"

"Bye, girl." He hangs up on me. The phone rings right back. "HELLO."

"Yes, James!"

"Don't fry my hamburger in the same pan you cooked that pork in, girl!"

Whatever. I love all of him. I prepare his plate once he gets settled, then take my phone off the hook. While he eats, I shower. I haven't seen my honey in a few days, and I don't want any distractions. By the time I got out of the shower, he had finished eating and was talking about my food so badly I wanted to put him out. I start to pout, and he attempts to fix it.

"It was pretty good, considering. But how do you burn a hamburger, Shun?"

"Why do you have to hurt my feelings?"

"Girl, you know you can't cook." He pulls me onto his lap, laughing. I hide my head under a pillow; he moves it and lifts my face in his hands. "Don't worry, you can cook like a pro in there." He points toward my bedroom. He has just gotten his points back. I shut off the TV, stand up, and take his hand.

"Where are you going?"

"To bed, boy!"

"What's wrong with right here?"

I wake up to a beeping sound. I had heard it several times earlier and ignored it, but with the TV turned off, it's mad loud. I get up and search around and discover it's Jimmy's pager. Probably his mama. I swear she acts like he's a toddler. It's the same number several times, but not his mom. He's sleeping so peacefully I decide not to wake him. I lay back down on his chest, but before I can close my eyes, it goes off again. It's almost 2 am; what in the world?

Another look reveals the same number with 911 behind it. I shake him lightly, and he doesn't wake up; I push him a little harder.

"What is it?"

"Your pager keeps going off, and I think something is wrong."

He grabs it and looks closely before calmly saying, "Oh, it's nothing." I raise my eyebrow at him, and he smiles. "Go to sleep, big head. As a matter of fact, let's get in the bed; my neck is killing me."

I notice he sticks his pager in his pants pocket instead of on the nightstand where he usually puts it. 911 doesn't seem like nothing to me, but it's too late to press the issue, so we lay down in silence. I turn on the TV in the bedroom because sleep is far from me now. Jimmy, however, dozes back off instantly.

I wait a few minutes, then shake him several times, and he doesn't move. I go into his pocket and get his pager. I ease out of bed and go into the next room to find out who had an emergency that Jimmy didn't find important. My intuition had already told me who would answer the phone, but I needed to hear it for myself.

One ring, two rings. "Hello. May I ask whom I am speaking with?"

"Excuse me, you called my number; actually, you paged my man A LOT. I'm trying to see what your emergency is!"

"Bitch—" is all I give her time to say before I end the call. This Negro is still at it. I fly back in the room and throw the phone as hard as I can at him; he jumps up, looking crazy. He looks at his pager in my hand and understands the reason behind the Babe Ruth pitch I just put on him. Instead of fessing up, he did what men do best: flip it.

"Why are you going in my things? Did you call that girl's house?"

"Go to hell! YES, and get to stepping, in that order."

He jumps up and starts to get dressed. "You're crazy. I'm out!"

"No, you're leaving because you're BUSTED." I will not cry tonight. This means war. I'm tired of wasting my tears.

He starts to the door, but I block his exit. "Not yet, buddy! WHY, Jimmy?"

"WHY WHAT!"

"Why do you keep doing this? I have feelings! I assumed that was over as much as you have been here, but you are STILL playing games."

"I told you who I am, Shun. What do you want from me?"

"How about the same love I give you... and ONLY you!" I can't do that right now; it's complicated! I love you both, Shun; that's the truth."

"Not acceptable. It's me or her, Jimmy. That's it!"

"Give me my keys, Shun," he asks calmly. I had taken them with the pager anticipating this reaction. He always leaves when it gets too hot between us, but tonight he was going to give me some answers. "Give me my keys!" he says, a little firmer. I stand there like I'm deaf. He walks over close to me and asks again. I smack him dead across his face and regret it immediately. I didn't mean to touch him, but more importantly, the look in his eyes told me I was about to pay for it. Instead of hitting me like I thought he was about to do, he charged me and tried to wrestle his keys out of my hand. I try to push him off, and we knock a chair into the table, spilling water all over on the floor. Now I'm slipping and sliding all over the place. Jimmy almost has my hands pried open, so I bite him! He pushes me so hard that I go sliding right into the window. The sound of the breaking glass makes my heart race. It HURTS.

He stands there as stunned and as shocked as I am. He calmly says, "Don't move."

"I can't. I'm scared." He walks over to me and slowly pulls me to him. Glass falls to the floor, and the pain radiates as I lean forward. He touches my back carefully.

"You're not cut; the window frame snapped in half and struck you. It barely broke your skin."

"That must be the excruciating pain I feel. "Am I bleeding?"

"No, baby." The sentimental tone he's speaking with makes me mad as hell. "Don't pretend to care about me, and you can't even be faithful to me!" I yell as loud as I can.

"You're crazy as hell! I can't do this." He picks up his keys and races to the door.

"Give me my house key before you leave, Jimmy."

"Calm down, girl!"

"NOW, Jimmy. Before I lose it!"

"Shun, we will be fine!"

"I don't think so, not this time… I'm DONE!" I wake up hours later to the sound of rain and an aching heart. Oh well, another chapter to close. I will not let Jimmy waste another minute of my life. I am going to find my happy ending… or do they exist?

Chapter 10

GAME CHANGER

I'm actually excited about going to work today. I need a distraction from my pain; it feels like the walls are closing in on me. Tee came over with some comedy videos yesterday, but ain't nothing funny about a broken heart. At least work gives me something else to think about. I get all the routes together for the day and prepare for a run I have to cover for one of the aides who had called off. My boss had told me as soon as I arrived that today would be a full-on shit storm, and I'm good with that; the busier, the better.

I sit to organize my things, a job I normally do standing, but I'm unusually tired this morning. I slept most of the weekend, yet I can't stop yawning; I guess all that crying has drained me. Maybe I'll go to the break room for coffee or not; the thought of the dreadful day at UB crosses my mind. Instead, I think I'll rest my eyes quickly before my run leaves. They feel so heavy.

That doze apparently turned into a deep sleep. The office manager wakes me up screaming, "Your route is going to be late!

Everyone is looking for you, and you're in here asleep. What in the world!" Fortunately, I had managed to get everyone else's route ready to go before I passed out. I hand them to her, and she runs out like a bolt of lightning as I attempt to get myself together for my own run. The nap/doze served its purpose. I kick in full gear, and before I know it, it's time to break for lunch. I don't feel like eating, though; another symptom of my broken heart.

I close my office door, take off my shoes, and let my mind wander. It wonders to sleep AGAIN! I'm awakened by the sound of Jackie's voice calling my name for the second time today. "WHAT?" I look at her, annoyed, as I turn on my light. I can't even enjoy my freaking lunch.

"We take 2-hour breaks now?"

What? I look at my computer screen. "Jeez, I'm sorry. Did I miss my afternoon runs?"

"Yes, but I covered them because I thought you were late coming from lunch, and then I noticed your car was still here. Why are you locked up in this dark office anyways? What's up with you, girl? You need to stop partying all night."

"The last party I went to was my dad's, girl."

"Now you know that's sad." We share a laugh.

"I just don't seem to have any energy."

"Maybe you should get some vitamins."

"Maybe I should. I will call my doctor when I get off."

I failed to make that appointment that day and with the holidays rolling around, I'm much too busy now. Jimmy and I were slowly starting to speak again. It was nothing like before, but we could at least talk, and if I had an itch, he scratched it. He had admitted to not knowing how to choose, and I'm not sure I cared anymore; I had found a solution to ease my pain: SLEEP! Although I may have to find another solution; all that eating before sleeping is taking a toll, and my butt is getting big. That's a problem I never had. I'm going on a diet after Thanksgiving, but not a minute before. I LIVE for mom and dad's dinners, not to mention the holiday addition spade games that are even crazier than the normal ones. I'm going to enjoy every minute of my holiday. I'm not going to be worried about a man or a diet that day.

It feels good to have something to look forward to, the way my life has been going lately. Mom had asked me 50 times if Jimmy was coming, so I guess I would at least ask him to make an appearance. Since he hadn't made up his mind about who he wanted to be with, I decided I better start on my outfit now. I was in that room for almost two hours trying to decide on Sunday what I was wearing Thursday. I believed in preparing early because I would never get caught looking crazy, especially when my rep was on the line. Looking for the right outfit is further confirmation that I need to diet; nothing fits!

By Wednesday, I still have nothing. I'm upset! I'm just throwing on something stretchy to wear to work. I know from prior experience that most of the cooking is done the night before, and I like to eat BOTH days. I'll figure out tomorrow's attire when I get home this evening.

I go straight to mom's after work. I can smell the food when I open my car door. Jesus be a fence; I'm about to eat myself into a deep sleep. When I walk in, my younger siblings swarm me, and I enjoy their affection. I always feel like a secret celebrity every time I stop by; the way their little faces light up as if I don't live in the same city only minutes away is great! I think it's a combination of me moving away from home so early and working like crazy, but I LOVE my independence, and the reality of that is long hours. Today, I need these hugs and kisses more than they know. The extra tight hug from my baby brother is a painful reminder of my run-in with the storm window; it's still tender to touch.

I make my way to the kitchen where I find my main man getting busy on the stove. It's going to be a good night. Dad is drinking whiskey and lemonade all right now! I steal a kiss on my way to my mom's room, checking the score on the spades table along the way. I call next and head to get my partner in crime. She's only fun if she's your partner because she's known for cheating and getting mad when you catch her; don't be on the other side of it.

Mom is halfway down when I reach the back stairs. "What you up to, old lady?"

"Coming down here to kick ass and take names, I saw you pull up." She talks junk for breakfast, lunch, and dinner. As we laugh easily, I can't help but notice her appearance is starting to fade. Running the streets all those years has taken effect. We make it to the table in time to catch the end of the game currently taking place. I don't know who is getting the first whooping, but somebody is in trouble once we get on this table. Tank and my brother Jaime fall victim to my cousins Kev and Eddie. Tragic, but they still gotta get up. Mom and I are taking our seats when Jimmy walks in with his friends Rah and Will.

I think the madder I get at this Negro, the better he looks. I pretend to be preoccupied with the cards, offering a quick hello, but he's not having it. He comes around and pulls up at a chair right next to me. I'm literally about to faint; he smells so good. I force myself to focus. I shouldn't be so attracted to someone who's so nonchalant about my love for him. I'm angry at myself for being so weak.

He hasn't said much to me since he sat down. He's otherwise engaged in a conversation with the guys and sipping on the same drink he's had since he got here. He had offered me a drink that I politely declined, knowing full well where that would lead. He makes it his business to keep brushing against me, and every time he does, something inside of me flips. After his indirect antics fail, he leans over to my ear and asks if I have changed my mind about hooking up tonight. I want to say, "Yes, please take me home now." But I refuse to let my FLESH win again, so I don't answer. He needs to man up and decide. I had told him the last time we made love was the last time, and since he couldn't decide, I chose ME! I had even started to see this police officer here and there but he wasn't interested in hearing about Jimmy on every date, so nothing came of it. As bad as I want to be with Jimmy tonight, casually sleeping with him doesn't fix my heart so what's the use! Every time he left my house, a piece of my heart went with him, and it just isn't worth it anymore, even if it is the BEST I ever had!

I remained strong—it takes all the power inside of me—but I didn't give in all night. When he realizes his charm isn't working, he decides to leave. I can tell he has an attitude, but who cares? I'm tired of him. I had not slept with him in months because I meant what I said. I gave him the power to treat me like an option, and now I've taken that power back by putting myself first. Sex is not the solution to this dilemma. I want a permanent fix, no more band-aids. I invited him because my mom and dad wanted me to, and he is still my friend; he will forever be that. But that's where it ends.

He stands to leave, saying goodbye to everyone but me. Oh well! Dad asks if he's coming to dinner tomorrow.

"No... I have other plans."

"GO FIGURE," I blurt out. I was meaning to just think it, but being my momma's child, it came on out. Might as well go with it now.

"Thanks for seeing me on Thanksgiving Eve. Nothing can make a side chic feel more important than seeing her the night BEFORE the holiday. How sweet!"

"There you go with that bullshit, Shun. You told me you didn't want to see me anymore. Now you're making a scene!"

"NO. I said I didn't want to SHARE you anymore." Everyone stares in his direction. He throws daggers at me with his eyes and walks out. "Who's turn is it?" I try to mask my embarrassment of being the second-place holiday chic by pretending I'm still interested in the game, but I can't. I played the wrong card twice! I excuse myself and head home. I'm not even hungry anymore; I'm PISSED.

I don't even bother taking off my clothes; I just grab my throw and a bottle of wine and let the TV watch me. I drank more than I intended, and my head is pounding when I wake up. I turn off the TV and slide on my nightgown. I feel like crap, and I have chills. I hope I can make dinner tomorrow.

I dismiss that thought quickly. The devil is a lie. I'm not missing Thanksgiving dinner for nathing (with an a). Hope these few hours of sleep help me shake whatever bug it is that has me feeling this way. I suspect it's the love bug; love's side effects are worse than any drug if you ask me. I was doing just fine until that Negro showed up. I haven't even had a drink in a while, but tonight I killed a whole bottle of wine, hoping with every sip that any memory of what we had would disappear. Sleep helps me feel a little better; at least the headache is gone. I know the jerk will not be at dinner, nor do I wish to entice him any longer, so I put on a sweatshirt and wrestle on my favorite jeans, although they don't seem to favor me too much today. I'm usually very comfortable in these, but l can tell you now, they will be unbuttoned after my first round at the table.

The festivities have already begun when I arrive. I can't get anywhere on time. But you can count on it being enough food. My parents always cook for an army, and on holidays, they cook for two armies. The main table is full, so I get in where I fit in. I find a spot at the second table with the younger ones. They all ask "Where is Jimmy?" as soon as I sit down. I dislike this table already; I did not want to hear his name so soon. The thought of him makes me queasy, or is it the smell of the collard greens? I feel my insides coming up. I have to get to the bathroom, but I'm blocked in. As my sister is passing my favorite homemade mac-n-cheese, I lose the battle to get out and vomit all in the pan. Everyone jumps up. NOW they want to move. My brother is raising sand; I don't know which of us likes mom's mac-n-cheese better. We usually fight over the last serving, but that will not be necessary tonight.

My stepdad, having the weakest stomach in history, makes a quick exit, and mom comes over to assist with the cleanup. I'm trying with all my might to help her, but I feel like a bus has hit me. "Let me move," my sister Kenya says, almost running from the table. "I don't want whatever it is she has."

"You can't catch what she has, honey. This girl's pregnant." Everybody simultaneously looks at me. I use the little strength I got left to give my mom a piece of my mind! "Mom, stop saying off-the-wall crap like that!"

"What's off the wall about it?" she snaps back.

"You know I can't have babies!"

"Bullshit, lil girl! I've birthed nine babies and raised plenty; I know a pregnant woman when I see one."

I'm pissed off because she should learn to leave well enough alone. I hate when she runs her mouth about stuff she doesn't know. I clean up as quickly as I can so I can get the heck out of there. They can have dinner, cards and all. I should have just stayed home. I pull off, tires screeching. I would like just one thing to go right.

Tears pour down my face all the way home, and I don't even know why I'm crying! Am I tired, stressed, or just heartbroken? I wonder if there's a pill for that. I hope they can tell me what I need at my appointment in the morning. Maybe some vitamins will help. If not, I'm definitely going to explore counseling. My emotions are all over the place.

I decided to take the Metro downtown to my appointment; my brother-in-law had made plans to use my car because it's MY tradition not to leave my house the day after Thanksgiving. I don't want to ruin his plans, and I certainly don't feel like being bothered with anyone else, so the bus it is. I'm enjoying my quiet time at the bus stop when the lady in white that I've seen around the neighborhood approaches me. I never knew her name, just that she was always covered in white from head to toe. I'm not sure if she's homeless, but whenever I see her, she's roaming. Her smile and gentle demeanor suggest she's harmless, and I actually feel a sense of calm when she sits down next to me. I'm so full of emotions that her simple touch on my shoulder causes my eyes to swell with tears.

"Everything will work out, my dear!" Lord, is it that obvious that my life is a mess? "Will this be your first child?" What! I don't mean to sound harsh, but she caught me off guard! Will this be your first child? I thought that's what she said!

"No, ma'am," I say softly, "I can't have children."

"Oh, you're indeed going to have a baby. It's a little girl."

I don't feel the anger I felt toward my mom; I feel compassion. Obviously, she is convinced she has some physic capabilities. I just smile and tell her thank you as I see the bus approaching. "Have a blessed day," I whisper. She grabs my hand and tells me to hang in there. I don't know why, but her touch soothes me, and I somehow know it will be okay.

I hate doctor's offices; it's always freezing, yet they want you naked, and best to believe they're going to want to stick or poke you somewhere. My doctor strolls in, giggling with the blood draw kit. I cringe when I spot the needle in her hand. Here we go. Turn your head and close your eyes, chicken. We are very good around each other. She has been my doctor since I started high school. She completes my exam and instructs me to get dressed while she runs the blood work. It must have taken a while because I was asleep on the table when she returned.

"I'm sorry. I can't seem to stay awake."

"That's what happens when you're pregnant, honey. You're going to need vitamins, alright? Prenatal ones; you're going to be a mommy."

I'm speechless. All I can do is stare at the paperwork she handed me, with the word routine appointment in bold letters. This appointment isn't routine at all; this appointment has changed the game!

Chapter 11

POOR TIMING

I sit quietly, too shocked to say or do anything! Her words keep running through my mind like a recording. All I can think about is my mom and the lady from the bus stop. How the heck had they known that a baby was growing inside of me, and I was clueless? Then the realness of the moment suddenly kicks in, and I'm overcome with emotion. I start smiling from ear to ear. I hug my doctor, and she returns it with genuine joy. I was told that I would never be able to conceive; God always has the final say.

"You know, this also explains the heavy bleeding you had a while back when you thought you hurt yourself wrestling."

That's the story I had given her (who really wants to tell someone my man's girlfriend came to my house and it was about to be on?). "I ordered your full ER report, and your HCG levels confirmed their diagnosis."

"Why didn't you tell me?"

"Would it have helped? It was too late by then; you had already miscarried. Are you still with that same someone?"

I look at her and start to cry. "Is that a no?" The face she's making causes me to laugh through my tears. "Yep, you are definitely pregnant. You're on an emotional roller coaster."

"I'm not with him anymore, but I still love him very much."

"Well, you better figure it out, young lady. You two are going to be parents soon." She gives me a prescription for prenatal vitamins and schedules me for an ultrasound. She can't estimate a due date as I'm irregular and have gone months at a time without menstruation; oddly enough, I just had what I thought was my period the other day. I leave her office with more on my mind than when I came. I'm happy, sad, and scared all in one. The only thing definite here is the poor timing.

I need to apologize to my mom and figure out how to tell Jimmy he's going to be a daddy, but first, I have to process this in my own head. I go straight to my guest bedroom, and I take off everything but my socks. I stand in my long mirror, staring at my body. I can't believe I have a life growing inside of me. Where is it? My stomach is still flat. Well, I have a little pouch, but that's from being greedy, I thought. I can still suck that in and be good as new. I turn sideways, and there it is; my hips are spreading, and my butt is wide. The myth is true. The baby is in my hips (not literally, but all the weight is in that area). That's why I haven't noticed. Or have I? All the fatigue, the attitude (okay, the worse-than-usual attitude), the tightness of my clothes, and lastly, the fluttering in my stomach, I always dismissed it, knowing it couldn't be what I thought. I began to wonder if I would be a good mom, then regroup quickly; taking care of children is second nature. I practically raised my brothers and sisters. This would be very different, though. I will be all alone with this little guy forever.

Am I ready? I love my things—my peace, my quiet, my sleep, and my money. Oh, why now! I'm thinking too hard; my head is starting to hurt. I pull on my oversized t-shirt and climb into bed. I contemplate having a glass of wine but think better of it when I feel a flutter in my stomach. Okay, James, no wine, then. Let's go to sleep. I think James is an honorable name. Besides, every James I know, I happen to love. I pray it's a boy. I can't handle another attitude under my roof, and I hate combing hair. Most of all, I would love to have at least one man who loves me unconditionally and never hurts me.

As I drift off, I hear the woman in white's voice: "It will be a girl." her words echo in my ear until I fall asleep. She has been correct once today. We will have to wait and see if she's right about that. Whatever the sex of the baby, I'm going to love it more than anything under the sun. Of that I'm sure.

I wake up with a serious rumble in my stomach, and it dawns on me that I haven't eaten in a whole day. I feel like crap. I remember the poor baby and bolt out of bed into the kitchen. The little food that I had eaten the day before came up in the mac-n-cheese at my mom's house. Everything I look at makes my stomach hurt worse. Man, I could use Rick's Steak. Grrrrrr... My stomach won't wait. I have to get something to hold me over until I get dressed and go out.

I make myself a tomato sandwich, a dirty south quick fix. Tomatoes, Mayo, bread, salt, and pepper, no secret ingredients. That's it… That's all to it. I'm inhaling my sandwich when the phone rings. I answer with my mouth full. "Hello."

"Why you chewing like a pig?"

I smile involuntarily. Jimmy has that effect on me even when I'm not in the mood. Then I remember he's the enemy right now! What do you want? Damn, it's like that! Exactly like that, with your dog self, what do you want?

"I was just seeing if you wanted to get something to eat. Don't get smart."

I didn't want to face him so soon, but I do want that steak! "You can bring me something, if you don't mind." I'm as polite as I can be given the situation.

"What do you want?"

"Can you bring me a Philly Steak with extra peppers, tomatoes—"

"I know how you like it," he interrupts me. So rude!

"Ok, thanks. I'll see you in a minute." I place my hand on my stomach. Here we go, little boy. Time for show and tell with daddy.

It seemed like Jimmy was traveling by plane, or maybe I was just a nervous wreck, and it felt that way. He was at the door before I could finish getting dressed. I almost fall when he knocks on the door, trying to put on my socks. I don't know if I'm more hungry or scared; the noise coming from my stomach suggests hunger is greater. I eat my sandwich like I've been stranded on an island. Jimmy is amused, as always, by my love for food.

"Have you eaten since I left?"

"Shut up!" He smiles that smile that has held me captive since the day we met. My eyes fill with tears.

"Don't start crying, Shun. Can we at least talk first?"

"Okay." I try to gain my composure. "You go first, then. I need to give myself time to figure out how to say what must be said."

"I know this is hard on you. I think you should find someone who's willing to settle down and be the man you want. You're too young to be stressed out like this." He rationally highlights all the reasons he thinks we should end our relationship. "Are you going to say something, Shun?"

"Yeah, I am. I'm just not sure how to say it."

"Just say it. We need to get it all out."

"Ok, Jimmy. We're going to have a baby!"

He looks like I just pulled a gun on him. The look on his face is one I've never seen before. "What did you say?"

"I'm pregnant!"

"I thought you couldn't have kids!"

"Me either!"

"Bullshit, Shun!"

"Is that anger I hear? Wait a minute, don't go acting like I did it alone."

"Well, I would have been more careful if I knew THIS could happen!"

"THIS? What the hell you mean' THIS? It's a life, not a THIS."

"What are you going to do about it?"

"You about to get the hell out of here?! I get off the couch and storm toward the door. "Get out!"

"What!"

"GET OUT!" I yell again, louder this time.

"What you mad at me for?"

"Because you're a jerk!"

"What do you want me to say? That I'M HAPPY? This shit is complicated enough!"

"Don't you think I know that, Jimmy!" He attempts to hug me. "Get away from me."

"I'm sorry, Shun."

"NO, you're right! I got pregnant, and I will deal with it. Thank you for the sandwich. You can go."

"You know I'm not leaving, Shun."

"Stop it!" I'm so upset I'm having spasms.

He takes my arm. "Come here, sit down. You're going to make yourself sick." I allow him to pull me down on his lap, where

I cry myself to sleep. It's pitch black when I wake up. Jimmy's asleep on the other end of the couch. I ease up, trying not to wake him. I don't mind his company, but I don't want the conversation. I have to pee, which has been very frequent lately, and now I know why.

When I return, Jimmy is up, removing his jacket. I sit back on the opposite side of the couch without saying a word, pick up the remote, and scan for something to distract me. He reaches over and pulls me close to him, laying my head on his chest. "How far along are you?"

"I don't know yet."

"Didn't they tell you?"

"They couldn't estimate because of my irregular cycle."

"I don't want to hear all that, Shun."

"Well, you're asking questions, and I'm just trying to answer them. Jimmy, you know the craziest part about all of this is that we've been together having unprotected sex for years, and just like that, I'm pregnant."

"It's crazy indeed," he says, zoned out, and I completely understand.

"I have an ultrasound next week."

"Damn, Shun," he says in disbelief.

I know it is so messed up I start to cry again. Crying won't help; we just have to deal with it, I guess. "Come on. I'm tired. Let's lay down."

"Nah, I can't stay. I just came to check on you."

I don't want to pressure him even though I want to be held. I get up to walk with him to the door. "You okay?" he touches my face gently.

"I will be," I try and convince him, but the tears in my eyes tell a different story.

"Come on." He turns around, walking back to the bedroom.

"I thought you couldn't stay."

"I will lay with you until you fall asleep. If I leave, all you're going to do is cry yourself to death." I know this is the worst news he could have gotten, yet he is still concerned about me. That's the biggest part of him that made me fall in love: his compassion.

Jimmy is gone when I wake up, and there's a note on my dresser:

"Don't worry, we'll be fine, now I know
why you're getting so fat, call you later"
– Love Jimmy.

I have a good laugh, something I haven't had at his expense in a while.

With that out the way, I can go see Sallie. I know she will have an ear full for me today. I don't know if anybody else will be happy to see me either since I ruined Thanksgiving. I call ahead and tell her to fix me some salmon crockett and biscuits.

"I'll have your daddy do it. He's downstairs already. What time are you coming?"

"I'll be there in about an hour."

"They'll be ready!"

I promise nothing can make you feel better than a good home-cooked meal. As soon as I smell the biscuits, all is well with my soul! Of course, they are playing spades, so I stop and check the score. "This is all y'all do! But anyways, who got next?"

Dad comes out of the kitchen, smiling hard. "I thought you were hungry? You're in here trying to play cards, lil Sallie." I kiss him and sit down next to Mom on the couch.

"Why you not playing, Mom?"

"Me and your sister got next."

"I just put my name down for next, Ma. I didn't see y'all, so you know the rules."

"They don't apply to me."

"When y'all gon' learn Ma Dukes don't follow the rules!"

"What, Lady?"

"You heard me!" I burst out laughing.

"We have to eat first, anyways. Your dad gon' run everybody off the table in a minute."

"Whew, I'm happy to hear that." I didn't want to push the issue, but eating is what I came to do. My brothers have no manners; they reach for the food as soon as Dad sits it out. He swats their hands away and looks at me. "Let that girl eat first. She's pregnant."

I almost fall out of the chair. Did they have my apartment bugged, or had Jimmy snitched? "Who told you, Dad?"

"Your mama."

"Who told you then, Mom?"

"Hell, I told you. You didn't want to listen." I smile wide; nothing ever gets by her.

Everyone gets excited. "For real?"

"No joke. I'm having a baby." They clap like I just won the lottery.

"Now apologize for being a mean ass."

"Sorry, Mom!"

"You damn right, cause don't nothing gets past Sallie."

"I'm pregnant too!"

We all gaze in my sister Tonya's direction, which is where the statement had come from. "Well, damn," my stepdad says loudly, "both of y'all… Something apparently HAD gotten by Sallie." Tonya and I both burst out laughing again. The look on my parents' faces is priceless.

The following week, Jimmy accompanies me to my appointment to see how far along I am. The nurse has a questionnaire to fill out before the doctor comes in, and she asks if I'm comfortable talking around Jimmy. I better be seeing that I'm having his baby. He looks at her sideways, and I try to keep a straight face. Two minutes into the survey, the doctor enters. I'm so nervous. The sound of the machines and the gel in her hands make it all too real to me. I'm about to get a glimpse of the person who will call me Mommy for the rest of my life.

Even though no needles are involved, my eyes are squeezed shut. This gel is freezing, and I feel the doctor's instrument moving around on my stomach, so I open one eye to peek.

"If you're afraid of this, you are in for a treat on delivery day."

I look at Jimmy, and he looks equally as nervous. "Are you okay?"

"I'm good," he assures me, focusing on the little screen that will reveal the sex.

Well, from the size of this baby, you are at least 4-5 months."

"WHAT?" we say in unison.

"Is this your first as well, Jimmy?"

"No, I have a son."

"Would you two like a boy or a girl?"

"A boy," I answer quickly, but he never responds. Personally, I think he would prefer a daughter. He adores my baby sister Fattie, and when we babysit, he treats his nieces like queens, especially little Janae; he never voiced it, but I think she's his favorite.

I'm staring at the screen with no clue of what I'm looking for when I hear the most beautiful sound I've ever heard: bump, bump... bump, bump... bump, bump... And the doctor confirms it's the baby's heartbeat. My chest gets tight, and my eyes water; nothing could replace the joy of that sound.

"Are you ready?" The doctor asks with a fake drum roll. She has the pointer near the genital area of the baby, and we all look at the screen in silence. After a few moments, the doctor says, "It's a GIRL!"

I'm in pieces knowing there will be another me in this world. I am going to make sure she never has to feel my pain. The lady from the bus stop is two for three. I'm amazed! She knew I was pregnant and even the sex of the baby. Now I hope everything will end up fine like she said it would. The doctor tells us everything looks good, and continuing to take my vitamins correctly and maintaining a sound diet will help me to deliver a healthy baby.

My stomach looks like it has grown ten times its size since my appointment two weeks ago. I wonder if my mind is playing tricks, or had the doctor put a hex on me? If I had not seen the sonogram, I would have thought another baby had joined the party. All this excess sleeping and eating is causing me to lose my girlie figure. I need to break the monotony; I'm sick of this house. Jimmy's working all day, so I get dressed and go to my mom's. It doesn't matter how cold or hot it is; someone is always over there chillin. But to my surprise, they are not playing cards today. I go upstairs to my mother's room. She is sound asleep. I get in her bed, ease the remote out of her hand, and turn the channel.

"Now, why would you come in here touching my stuff?"

"Mom, you were snoring. How did you wake up that fast?"

"Don't worry about it. Give me my remote."

"I'm company, mom. You gon' act like that?"

"Girl, give me my shit!"

I give her the remote and call my sister Tasha upstairs to walk to the store for me. Mom asks Tasha to bring her some skins and a honey bun on top of the long list I give her.

"Oh no, I'm not walking with all this stuff, Shun. You come with me."

"Girl, I'm pregnant, and I don't feel like walking."

"You need some exercise, anyways. You're getting fat."

"REALLY, MOM!"

"I'm just saying."

I put my shoes on and waddle back downstairs. I'm not that big. It just feels funny carrying another person in your body. When Tasha and I make it to the corner of Genesee and Bissell, she points to a black maxima approaching. Isn't that Jimmy's car?"

It can't be. I just spoke with him right before we walked out, and he's definitely at work. Ok, but I know that car, and it certainly looks like it. Tasha's so sure, I take a closer look, and it IS his car. When it passes, it's a female driving, not little Ms. Light Bright. This is a burnt biscuit-looking female. I call my brother and tell him to grab my keys off mom's dresser and bring my car to the corner.

"Your lazy self can walk back, girl."

"I'm shooting dice." "Boy, bring me my car. I have an emergency."

Tasha is pacing back and forth. "Sis, you're pregnant. What are you going to do?"

"See who the hell is in this car. And don't you say a WORD because they will try and stop me or call Jimmy. I'm not giving him time to make up a story."

"What are you talking about? I'm going with you."

My brother pulls up and walks to the passenger side, drop me back off. "Negative, I'm in a hurry bro!"

"I hope you don't need nothing else. That's jive."

"I'll make it up to you, I promise." I pull off full speed.

Tasha still looks nervous. "Sis, you don't have to go. I got this."

"Girl, please, you know better."

"I'm just saying you're pregnant, and you know you can get a little crazy."

I press the gas harder, trying to get behind the car. I catch up and follow the car until it stops at Tops Grocery Market. I block the car in and get out. The chic looks all confused when I approach her. "What are you doing driving Jimmy's car?"

"Ask him!"

"Bitch, I'm gone ask you one more time before it gets stupid out here."

Someone rolls down the passenger window and says, "CC, let's just go."

"Auntie, I came to get my grocery; I'm not leaving."

The lady then says, "She just said she's stupid. We don't need this!"

Tasha lights the lady UP and tries to snatch her car door open! She talking about me; look at her little wild behind. "Tasha, leave that old lady alone!"

"She better watch her mouth, then!" They both look stuck. Blackie attempts to get back in the car.

"Oh, no, baby, that won't be happening." I slam the door back closed. "You dropping them keys."

"Let Jimmy tell me that because he gave them to me"

I call Jimmy. "Hello!"

"Hello, my ass. You have about 5 minutes to get to this store before I start busting windows." I think he got here in 2.

"Shun, what the hell is wrong with you?" Tasha is beating the bat in her hand as he walks toward me. This is about to be some foolishness.

I ask as calmly as I can, "Jimmy, who the FUCK is this?"

"Don't be talking to me like I'm a damn child!"

"Boy, FUCK ALL THAT. Either tell me who this is, or you gon' need a new set of tires and windows!"

"I wish THE FUCK YOU WOULD!"

"Ok, Tasha, hand me the bat." I raise the bat with all my might.

"WAIT! Listen, Shun. Her car is at the body shop, and the guy is taking longer than he said he would. Since I suggested she take it there, I let her borrow mine to take care of her business."

"And that's what I'm supposed to believe, huh?"

"You can believe what you want. I'm a grown-ass man, we are not together and this is my shit! If you weren't pregnant, I'd beat your ass out here clowning like this."

"Yo mama nigga!" I step around him right in her face. "Listen, broad. I'm gon' tell you since he acts like he can't talk. If I catch YOU in this CAR AGAIN, I'm gon' beat that ass. PERIOD!"

"Whatever, bitch. That's between y'all!"

"Oh, so you think it's a game?" I try and rush her, but Jimmy grabs me. "Keep getting smart, blackie. I'll bust yo shit now!"

"Shun, get your ass in that car. If something happens to my baby… I know something!"

"You don't know shit!" I give him the finger. He starts walking fast toward me. Oh hell. "Tasha, get in the car, get in the car. This nigga crazy." Once those eyes start darting back and forth, he is ready to flip, and ain't no stopping him. I don't want to hurt my baby fighting with him because he's ridiculously strong.

I look back at the chic. "You gon' catch these hands if I ever see you in this car again, pregnant and all."

I drive Tasha back home. "Tell mom I had an emergency and I will see her later."

"Ok, sis. You good?"

"I'm straight, girl. All this foolishness has given me a headache. I'm going to lay down."

"Ok, come back later if you feel better."

"Will do, baby girl." I fake smile until she gets inside.

The truth is, I know Jimmy lied to my face. I know him like a book, and he is dealing with that chic on more than a business level; he doesn't let anyone touch his car, let alone drive it. I'm going home to try and calm my nerves. I've gotten a little too worked up, and his lying self or her ugly behind are not worth my child's health. As hard as I try, I'm too wired to fall asleep. I had changed the channel on the TV a thousand times and still wasn't watching anything. Ok, lil baby, I got an old trick for you. I bet you gon' sleep after this.

I run a hot bath and pour a glass of wine; that does it every time. I'm trying to get my music set when the phone rings. "Hello!"

"Where my skins at?"

"WHAT MA!"

"I dozed off, and when I woke up, you weren't here, and neither was my stuff."

"Mom, seriously, that was hours ago!"

"Ok, don't worry. The next time you're hungry, don't call over here making no requests."

Now mama, all those kids over there, you can't send someone to the store."

"I told you to do it. And besides, these damn kids ain't got no money. They spend every dime they get on steak subs and pizza."

I laugh for the first time since that madness earlier. "Ok, Mom. I was just about to take a bath. As soon as I get out, I'll be over."

"Don't worry about it; I was just letting you know that's some bullshit.""

Mom, I said I'll bring them."

"Alright, we'll see."

As I sit in the tub, I feel the stress leaving my body. I don't know if it's mental or not, but this works every time. I put on some Mary J so she can sing to me about how low down these ninjas are, and I can definitely relate to that!

I decided against the wine since I gotta go back out now. Mom is so annoying. She does come through on the meals, though. I can't have her mad at me cause this poor child would starve, fooling with my grilled cheese, hot dogs, and hamburgers.

I feel myself drifting off from the comfort of the bath. Let me get out. All I really want to do is go lay back down. The phone rings again before I can get dressed. It's my mom again. "Ma, I told you I was getting a bath. I'm coming now."

"Don't worry about it. I got my stuff. I was trying to catch you before you left."

"Thank GOD, I'm so sleepy!"

"Yeah, Jimmy brought it. He brought me a beer, too. I love my son-in-law. He doesn't have an attitude like you."

I want to tell her I would be pretty chill, too, if I was screwing half the city with not a care in the world, but I simply say, "Whatever," and hang up the phone. He gets on my damn nerves. He is just testing the temperature to see if I had been over there raising hell. He loves my mom, no doubt—my whole family for that matter—but he ONLY went there today because he didn't want to face coming here.

I need that wine now; where's my glass? The hell with it. I grab the whole bottle.

A week has gone by, and Jimmy hasn't contacted me. I don't know if he's mad he got busted, or if he actually feels remorse for all the shit he does. I honestly think he's incapable of being with one woman! Not my problem either way; I need to focus on delivering a healthy baby. I don't care if I ever speak to him again. If he still wants to be in the baby's life, he can. If not, I got her no matter what.

His sister Joyce calls as I'm watching T.V, saying she had brought some things for the baby and asked if I could meet her at their mom's house. I want to say no because I don't want to see his face, but I didn't want to seem ungrateful. I ask her if he's at work, and she says, "I haven't seen him."

"Ok, I'm on my way."

I don't see his car when I pull up. I let out a sigh of relief. Joyce comes out and greets me in her usual upbeat spirit with bags in her hand. As I'm placing them in the seat, she tells me to open the trunk. Jimmy is bringing out a big box. I want to pass out. I give her the side eye. "Joyce, I told you I was hoping to avoid him."

"I know. But when he saw me with the box, he came downstairs and took it from me." He comes out looking nervous. He knows I will set it off anytime, anywhere. But Joyce is a Pastor, so I respect that and act cordial.

Once she walks off, Jimmy asks how I've been.

"Good!"

"Did you go to your appointment yesterday?"

"Yep!"

"I was going…"

"Look, I'm in a hurry, if you don't mind. Would you please put that in for me? I have to go." He walks to the trunk, and I get in my car. His car pulls up, and I slide off my shoes. If this broad gets out this car, it's going ALL THE WAY DOWN because I know he ain't playing with me like that. The door opens, and his brother Phillip exits. Thank goodness I don't have to show out in front of these church folks. Let me get from over here

He is still pushing and pulling on this box. "What the heck? Shun!"

"WHAT!"

"This box won't fit in here. Will it fit on my backseat?"

"No!"

"Well, tell your sister I'll pick it up later"

"She's in the house if you want to tell her yourself."

"Naw, I have to go."

"Alright, I'll let her know." He just stands there with my trunk open.

"Can you close my trunk, please?" Before his hand is completely off my car, I pull off.

I am trying to squeeze the things Joyce gave me in the guest bedroom, which is already filled to the max with my clothes and other things I've brought for the baby, when there is a knock at the door. My sister Tonya had called and said she was stopping by after work so we could catch up. Jimmy is standing there with that box when I open the door. I want to slam it in his face. NO, HE DIDN'T! Now how you gone pop up at my house without calling like you have a right? I attempt to take the box from him, and he pushes me aside.

"Move, girl. You're not about to carry this thing. Where do you want me to put it?"

"In the bedroom right there." I remain standing at the door with it open. "Shun, what have you been buying? This is not going to fit in here; NOTHING else can fit in here."

"I'll figure it out!" "Look, you need to relax; you don't need to be so angry all the time."

"Boy, I don't have the energy to listen to you act like you give a damn about me or my baby."

"YOUR BABY!"

"Yes, MY BABY! You running around doing you, you could care less about my health, or clearly, you wouldn't be entertaining other bitches, UGLY ones at that."

"What, why does it matter what she looks like?"

"You know what, Shun? I told you what that was, and I'm not about to keep explaining myself about nothing."

"I'm not asking you to."

"You can leave now!"

"Alright, cool. Call me if you need anything."

"I won't!" I slam the door behind him. He makes me sick! I look at the wine in the cabinet, then walk away. I'm not gon' allow that boy to stress me out. It takes me a few days to recoup from seeing Jimmy. I'm good as long as I don't lay eyes on him, but when I see him, it rattles me.

I'm scheduled to have my car serviced today, and I can't even have him pick me up like I had planned; I don't want to be bothered. Guess I will have to sit at the dealer for hours now. I bring my book to keep me occupied. I check in at the service desk, then go back into the waiting area where I see Jimmy walking in. Seriously!

"Hey Shun." "What are you doing here Jimmy?"

"You told me to pick you up, remember"

"Ah, yeah. Before bitches was driving your car."

"Girl, are you crazy? What does that have to do with you needing a ride? Besides, I got something to show you," he says smiling. I shake my head and follow him to the car; no need staying here if I don't have to. We ride in silence. I didn't want to sit in that dealership for that long, but I'm not going to act like we're all good, either.

I don't say a word until he takes the exit toward his house. "Where are we going?"

"You'll see in a minute." He pulls up and parks at a house on Clarence Avenue.

"Who lives here, Jimmy?"

"You, if you like it (I had been looking for a bigger place before we stopped speaking)."

"You're still going to help me move?"

"Yes, I'm a man! All that shit you got will not fit in that guest room once I start to put it together, but more importantly, I don't like that neighborhood you're in now to raise a child."

He has a point there. A year or so ago, as we were coming home late one night from Walmart grocery shopping, a cop had been shot and killed on the next street.

I smile. He broke me down a little. "Thank you, JIMMY."

"You have to see it first. The lady is up there now. You want to go in?"

"Yes!"

The apartment is AMAZING and huge. It has more stairs than I have now, but that's a small trade for all the extra space. The lady says I can move in on the first of the month. I give Jimmy a hug before we get back in the car. He may be a dog, but at least he's concerned with the safety and well-being of his child; the hug is to acknowledge that. I'm even more thankful for my family and his friends who assisted on moving day; even Charlie came by to help out. It's not a secret that I don't really care for him, but I appreciate every helping hand.

I LOVE my new place! My growing addition makes breathing a difficult task with all the stairs, but they keep my legs in shape, as they are all that's left intact on my body. My stomach, butt, and nose have gotten away from me. The hardwood floors are my favorite part. Well, second favorite; since my baby shower, I enjoy spending most of my time in Jameelah's room.

We had decided on Jameelah, the closest female name to James that's suitable. It translates to "beautiful" because despite all the turmoil, that's what this pregnancy is to me, BEAUTIFUL!

This is all happening so fast. We're still working out the details of raising a child in two separate homes; that's the reason he had found something closer to his mom's. Things are not perfect, but at least it's peace between us. No matter the number of uncertainties or how many women come and go out of this picture, this baby is coming for sure, and she needs both her parents.

Chapter 12

FROM BAD TO WORSE

In our normal dysfunctional fashion, we find our way back to casual hangout, sex partner, sleepover friends. I told Jimmy this time around we needed to be honest or nothing. If you got something else going on, just say that! He assures me he's not playing games, just trying to keep it cool so we can have a healthy delivery. We haven't had a real date since we called a truce, so tonight, we have plans to go to a comedy show.

He said he would be off around 6. I shower and start getting dressed at 5 so that I can be ready when he comes. He hates when I'm late, and I'm not trying to hear his mouth tonight. It's 5:30, and he's calling already. I'm happy I hadn't procrastinated.

"Hey, Shun, I'm going to be late."

"How late?"

"I don't know yet. Ray wants me to pick him up in Rochester."

"Why didn't you tell him we had plans, and he needs to find somebody else?"

"Ummm, he broke down. He has a flat."

"Boy, you mean to tell me, as many cars as those dude's got, he can't change a tire?"

"No, ummm, I have his jack, I borrowed it, and I have to take it to him."

"Um, hmm, I see. In Rochester, huh?"

"Yeah, I'll call you when I get back."

"Ok, babe. No problem, you be careful."

Nigga, please! I get right in my car and go around to his mom's and park out of sight. I was born at night, but not last night; you can miss me with that shit. As sure as grits are grocery, Jimmy walks out in a linen suit and dress shoes. Who the hell is changing flat tires in Keith Sweat attire? I let him get in and get a couple of car lengths ahead of me so he doesn't know I'm behind him. I trail him until he parks in front of some building. And wouldn't you know, that the burnt biscuit from the grocery store walks out and gets in the car. Now I could snatch her right now, but he may pull off before I can get her good like I want to. She was getting it first because I told her not to step foot in that car again. You claimed you didn't know about me the first time, and I let you slide, but ain't no sliding on round two; you got to come see me. I ain't worried about him. He can get at any time; if he doesn't get it tonight, I'll get him tomorrow. But I play fair; they both getting this work for sure.

I let him drive along until he gets caught at a red light and pull up next to him. They are both laughing and having a good time until they look out the passenger window! SURPRISE!! He rolls the window down and yells for me to pull over. Nah, my man, you go ahead where you going because this gon' be y'all last supper. He speeds off, running lights and cutting down streets as if I'm not used to chasing him around Buffalo. Negro, you taught me how to drive; you think I can't keep up? He finally stops at a house I'm not familiar with. I grab my bat and my razor and put them on my lap. I'm no fool, and I don't know if this is her house or what kind of trap this could be, so I sit and wait. I see Lee walk out of the back yard, and Jimmy starts talking to him and pointing at my car. I jump out! What the fuck he supposed to do?

"Wait a minute, sis. Come here. Let me talk to you."

No, fuck that. I told this nigga about playing with me. She rolls the window down and says, "You must be psychotic!"

"I am, and you're about to find out just how deep it is."

She rushes and locks the doors. "I don't have time for this!"

"You gon' make time today, bitch. You must've forgotten the window is down."

Before she could think about rolling it up, I snatched her through it, and me and this baby commenced to beating her ass. She immediately starts pulling my hair and swinging like she is swimming. Jimmy's just standing there stuck on stupid. I hope he is getting mentally prepared because his ass is next. Lee runs over and grabs me by the waist. I turn around and hook off on him, too.

Don't grab me! That allows someone to get the jump on you. He backs up, and I lay back in on her again. He screams, "Sis, you're going to hurt the baby!" I stop and back up instantly. In my fit of rage, I didn't consider the damage I could do to the baby. He takes my hand and pulls me to the side. I'm crying and screaming! He tells Jimmy, "Man, get that girl out of here."

"I was just taking her home from work. She called saying she needed a ride, and Shun came out of nowhere!"

"It doesn't matter, Jim. This girl is pregnant. You should have never let that go down."

"She grabbed her while I was talking to you; she's crazy as hell, man. I can't do nothing with her."

"Well, leave her alone then, or somebody's definitely gonna' get hurt."

"You damn right, Lee. That's what I've been telling his ass for YEARS. You can do WHATEVER you want, but you're not about to play with me! If you want other bitches, have THEM. Just stay out of my life. But if you choose to keep playing stupid ass games, you gon' win stupid prizes EVERY TIME." I don't want any female thinking she is so special that she made me snap. I give out equal-opportunity ass-whooping to ANYONE who gets disrespectful. It was never about a man; it's how you come out your mouth at ME. I try to snatch away from Lee and get in my car, but he holds my arm tight.

"No, sis. I'm not letting you go until he is gone and you calm down."

I'm crying like a baby, mad as hell that I can't get to him. When Jimmy pulls off, Lee walks me to my car and sits with me until I get myself together. "You want me to drive you home? My brother is in the house; he can follow us."

"Oh, he's in the house, not in Rochester."

"What you mean?"

"That's where that nigga said he was going, to help Ray change a tire in Rochester, in a SILK SUIT at that!"

"Get the fuck outta here, sis!"

We laugh for about ten minutes until he's in tears. "You okay for real, sis?"

"Yeah, I'm good. I'm just tired of him."

"Well, I can't tell you what to do, but what I can tell you is what you ARE doing isn't healthy at all, especially in your condition. If anything happens to my niece, both of y'all getting messed up. Now give me a hug and take your crazy ass home."

I pray all the way home that my baby is okay. Lord, I'm sorry I flipped out like that. She is innocent; please let her be okay. I pull up to my apartment, and Jimmy's car is outside. Ok, Lord, please protect her one more time because it's his turn now. I get out of the car with my bat. I'm not even about to wrestle with with this extra weight.

"Shun, I don't know what you think you about to do with that bat, but you need to chill and let me explain."

"No, because you got me fucked up!"

"Shun, listen. I know what that looked like, but she called me for a ride from work as soon as I was walking out. Her car is still messed up and I was just trying to do a favor for a friend."

"Yeah, a friend you're SLEEPING WITH!"

"That is not the case right now! I really was just giving her a ride, but I knew it was going to upset you if I told you. I was coming over here as soon as I dropped her off. I don't have to lie; that's the truth. You can take it how you want, but you need to calm down for real."

I stand there and stare at him, trying to see if his hands are shaking or if his eyes are darting back and forth; that's when he's lying. He's telling the truth this time. When Jimmy is lying or gets busted, his body language tells on him. The fact that he's here now is another indication he's being honest. When he doesn't want to deal with a situation, he disappears.

"So, you're not sleeping with her?"

"I was when shit was rocky between us and we weren't on good terms; that's when I met her. I'm not going to lie. But since we've been back chilling, I haven't, and that's my word."

"Whatever, Jimmy. Your word ain't shit. Just know what goes around comes around! And you not gon' like it if I mess around and pull my hoe boots out the closet, I promise you."

"You're grown, do you? Just let me know what it is."

He has the nerve to have bass in his voice like he mad. Boy, please. If I wasn't pregnant, I'd give him a dose of his own medicine RIGHT NOW!

"You still wanna go out?"

"What the hell you think, Jimmy?"

"Alright, come on. We'll just go to bed. I'll take you to eat tomorrow."

"No, I don't think so!"

"You don't want to go eat?"

"Oh, I always wanna eat, but you don't have to stay here. I just want to go to sleep."

"Alright, but know this. If something is wrong with my baby, you got a problem out here acting a damn fool."

"Ohhhh… I'm so scared!"

"You think it's a game if you want to with your crazy ass. I'll see you tomorrow."

"Bye, sucka!"

I'm at his mom's house at exactly 12 noon the next day to get my meal as promised; that's the least he can do, got me sore out here wrestling. I beep the horn to let him know I'm outside. His sister Paula walks by, and I wave my hand just to be polite. His little nephew P. C., who's walking with her, waves and smiles. This black heifer turns the other way. UGHHH, I can't stand her. I know they be talking about me with that light-skinned huzzy. It's a fact that if he is still talking to that burnt biscuit, he is still with her too. I'm sure that's the reason it's always tense when I'm around; ninja got one chick coming in the front and another going out the back. And here I am with my belly big, dead in love with him. I can't WAIT to have this baby; being a choice is not what's up!

I'm sitting here getting myself all worked up when there's a knock on my car window. I look over, and my very FAVORITE Gaines is grinning from ear to ear. It's his dad, Frank, whom I LOVE! He's never treated me with anything but respect, although I'm sure he knows, just like everyone else, that I'm one of many women. He's so sweet and kind every time we cross paths, and I appreciate that. I open the door and get out for a hug.

"Wow, that belly gone burst," he says with that handsome smile his son inherited. "You alright?"

"Yes, sir."

"What about my girl?" He points at my stomach.

"She's fine, just greedy."

"Her or her mama?"

We have a good laugh as Jimmy comes out of the house. I pause and stare. "I really love your son, but I don't know where this is going." I tell him the unfiltered truth and don't even know why it came out.

"I know you love him; I can tell. He'll come around one day if he has any sense. That boy wants to do what he wants to do, but you can only run from what you're supposed to be doing for so long." He winks at me. "Hang in there!"

I definitely feel his love for me and my baby girl despite my uncertainty about the future between his son and I. "Where y'all headed?" Frank asks when Jimmy walks up.

Jimmy looks at me and says, "To eat; where else?"

We all laugh this time. I'm amused that he's oblivious to our conversation moments before, but my greediness seems to be a common theme. I wobble to the passenger side telling Deddy (as he said everyone called him) I would see him later. Paula is walking back across the street as we pull off. "Jimmy, you should have let me drive so I could run her over."

"Don't make me kick your butt, Shun. What you got against my sister?"

"She doesn't like me," I say, rolling my eyes.

"She doesn't even know you!"

"Well, why is she always screw-facing me, then?"

"Probably because you are always over here acting crazy as hell. I still can't believe that shit you pulled last night!"

"I'm gon' pull it again if you try me!"

"I can't wait for you to have this baby so we can find out how tough you really are!"

I attempt to slap him, and he catches my hand. "Don't get beat down, Shun," he says with that stupid laugh he does when he's being cocky.

"Pregnant or not, boy, I will give you a run for your money."

"Can we call a truce for Chicken Slovakia?"

"Deal!" He knows that's my favorite! My face says I'm happy, but my heart is heavy. I wish it was as easy for him to settle on one woman as it is on lunch!

His pager is blowing up the whole time we're eating. "It's Charlie," he says, looking at the screen. "I need to call him."

"Right now?" I ask, pointing at the table. "We got something up! It better not be no craziness with you and that white boy, Jimmy. He's always up to 'something.'"

"Nah, he just needs me to handle something quick for him."

I'm devouring my food when he comes back asking, "What time is your doctor's appointment tomorrow?"

"2:30, why?"

"Oh, he wants to meet around 11, so I will be cool."

My stomach flips. I don't know about that. "You missed my last appointment. I am going to be pissed if you miss this one."

"I won't, girl. Now eat and hush," he says, defeating me with that smile again.

I can't wait until 2:30 to see my doctor. I think this baby may have to come out sooner; I'm in all kinds of pain. I look at my wall clock, and it's 12:15. Jimmy has been gone for over an hour. He said Charlie was meeting him at his mom's, so he wouldn't be long. I call; there was no answer. Oh well, I better wobble my way to the other room. I already take forever to get dressed, being pregnant has made it even worse. By the time I'm ready, it is right at 2:00. I check the phone. No call back from Jimmy. The doctor is only 10 minutes away, so no need to lose it yet.

I call his mom again. No answer. I pray this boy ain't going there with me today. I am too fat to be fighting. I sit on the couch and try breathing to calm my nerves. I hate to have to mess him up. As soon as I get comfortable, the phone rings; it's his mom's number. "Hello." I hear crying. "Hello," I say, panicking.

"Shun…" someone says my name. I don't recognize the voice. "Shun, it's Paula."

"Ok, what's wrong?"

"They got Jimmy!" My body goes numb and cold. "They who?" I get off the couch as quickly as my belly would allow me and grab my keys!

"The police," she says, and the line goes dead.

I run down the stairs almost falling, so I grab the rail to steady myself. My whole body is shaking. The car is barely in gear before I pull off. I race around the corner, and I'm met by a parade of people: police, bystanders, and neighbors. It's a circus. I can forget about driving. I park and jump out to run.

When I get halfway down the street, I see him lying face down on the ground, guns drawn. The jackets and uniforms belong to the FBI, ATF, and local police. I notice he's not moving. The whole scene causes me to lose my balance. Someone grabs me from behind; it's their neighbor Veronica. All I can say is, "My poor love," over and over.

"It will be alright," she says, stroking my back. I see him raise his head as they stand him up; he's in handcuffs, thank you Lord. For a minute, I thought he was shot. I try and run to him, but she stops me. All I see is pain in his beautiful eyes. I glance to the opposite side of the street and see Charlie being placed in the back of a police car. I want to spit in his face. I ALWAYS knew he was bad news. A comment Jimmy made while we were in bed last night comes to mind: "I'm going to make sure my baby girl never wants for anything." I wonder if what's taking place right now has to do with his assurance of our child's future.

I'm crying so hard my body is shaking. His mom and I might not agree on a lot of things, but we've both been telling him these streets don't love you! God is all that's certain, and then there's your family. I always warned him about the company he kept. Jimmy has two prior felonies, and this will NOT end well! My knees buckle at the thought; I think I'm going to faint. I'm shocked when Paula takes me by the hand and leads me into the house. I calm myself down so I can understand what happened. His mom says Jimmy came over a couple of hours earlier and chatted with her until he got a phone call. They walked to the door, and Charlie was outside. She went back to the kitchen and didn't think anything else of it until she heard the sirens. That was all she knew. She could hardly talk through her emotions.

I would have to wait over a week to get full details. Jimmy had called a few times to say he was okay, but it was never enough time to get the whole story. He has been cleared to have visitors, and I've been at the county jail waiting for almost two hours. After being pat searched, stripped of my jewelry, and interrogated, I feel like I have committed a crime and just want to go home. But I needed to see him, hold him, and most of all, know if he was okay. I miss him like it has been years instead of days. I'm as nervous as I could ever remember sitting here waiting for the guards to bring him out. When he finally enters the room, his presence brings tears to my eyes. I must stay strong; I know it makes him upset to see my cry. I hug him tight and lay my head on his chest.

"Have a seat," the guard yells, and I'm forced to let him go.

"How are you doing?"

"How do you think I'm doing, Jimmy?"

"I'm sorry, Shun. I fucked up!"

"You think!" I look around at our surroundings. At this moment, he looks more zoned out than the day I told him I was pregnant. My heart is aching for him. In one hour, I will be able to go home. For him, we don't know when that will be. "Well, I'm waiting!" He had promised me the truth once I was able to visit.

"I can't say what happened, Shun. I was trying to do a favor for a friend, and here I am. I really don't know how the cops found out."

"I told you the company you keep was going to get you eventually!"

"I know, I know," is all he says before his voice cracks. This brings the tears I've been trying to hold back on like a flood.

"Stop crying," he says with tears in his own eyes.

"I don't want to be a single mom, Jimmy!"

"You won't; I'm still alive," he says, trying to make light of the situation. "I need to tell you something, Shun. Stop crying." I fix my face and try to concentrate. "I've been thinking you're young, with so much more life to live. This will be my 3rd strike; I'm done. I want you to go on with your life, raise the baby, and be happy."

"Are you crazy?" I ask a little too loud, and the people around us start to stare.

"Lower your voice, Shun!"

"Listen, Jimmy. I don't play like that. I ride with you, good or bad, so whatever is happening to you, it is happening to us," I say, rubbing my stomach. I will not have a child who doesn't know her father. She will not be a statistic, at least not that kind!

The guard yells, "Time's up." I look at Jimmy for help, only this time, he can't help me; he can't even help himself. I bundle up and lace my boots tight as I exit 40 Delaware, shielding myself from the elements and preparing for the storm life's about to send our way. I set out to find him an attorney that same day. His mom knows everyone for the next five states. We are going to have to put our differences aside; we have something in common, and she's brewing in my stomach. She is way more important than either of our pride. We find an attorney we're satisfied with, and he manages to get Jimmy a bond. However, with his past history, the Feds put a hold on him. He will not be present for my delivery in a few weeks. I had family from his side as well as my own who had agreed to be there to support me, but I wanted him.

My life has seemingly come to a halt since Jimmy's been gone, but in reality, time is steadily passing by. I'm cleaning and listening to Lauren Hill when a God-awful pain shoots through my back. I credit it to an accident I had shortly after Jimmy's arrest that shook me up pretty good. It was painful, but until the baby comes, I have to tough it out. I'm getting some minor care, but I won't be able to take medication or address all the issues until she's born.

The second pain makes me call on Jesus because no one else is around. I grab the phone and call my mom when I realize I'm actually in labor. My doctor had said when I was having some Braxton Hicks' contractions a few weeks ago that I would know when it was the real thing. Boy, was she right.

Mom tells me she has my dad and sister on the way. I gather the hospital bag packed by the door and wait at the top of the stairs, too scared to risk going all the way down. Once I'm in the truck, I don't think we stop at one light! I'm prepped and taken to the labor and delivery as soon as I enter the hospital. Those were my doctor's instructions. She wanted me to get an epidural while I still had time. I refuse. I read about the risk for the baby and myself; it's a very low probability that something will go wrong, but with my luck, I'll be in the minority. My doctor tells me I'm crazy! "Suit yourself," are her last words before I'm taken to the room where I will deliver the baby. By the time I'm fully dilated, I'm looking for the epidural, a shot of Tequila, and most of all, I want Jimmy's head on a platter for doing this to me. At this point, the pain is so bad I actually think I'm going to die.

After hours of pushing, I'm exhausted! As I close my eyes and prepare for death, the doctor says she sees the head and needs me to push one last time! I take in a fresh wind; I have JUST ONE MORE left in me. If it's going to take anything more than that, she's going to have to figure it out! I give the last push all I got, my flesh rips, and I'm quite sure someone set my vagina on fire, and then it's over! Amazingly, out of all that pain comes a 7lb bundle of joy. I was wrong about her heartbeat being the most beautiful sound I will ever hear; her small cries far exceed it. The sight of her brown skin and pretty eyes makes my heart skip a beat. I had cursed Paula one too many times; she looks just like her.

I laugh at myself until everyone in the room thinks I've lost it. The nurse who was cleaning her up places her in my arms, instantly changing my laughter into tears. At this very moment, I know my life is no longer my own.

Hello, Jameelah Mone'y Gaines. Welcome to the world!

Chapter 13

READY OR NOT
HERE LIFE COMES

Everything in the world has become secondary; I am a mother now. Motherhood is not at all as scary as I thought it would be. In fact, it's quite rewarding. My sister Tonya had her daughter the very same week but still made time to coach me through my first month as this was her third child. Being an amateur, I appreciate the time she takes with me, knowing she has a newborn baby of her own. She had encouraged me to accept a new job with a Chiropractor downtown. It paid more and was closer to home. Jameelah is breastfeeding so it's logical. Visiting Jimmy will be easier as well. I'm headed there now.

I wasn't bringing her to this place until after her six-week check-up. He had waited a long time to meet her, but he understood; her safety is our main concern. More than going through this process of visiting him myself, I hate putting her through it. She is so tiny, but this doesn't matter to the guards; they still put me through hell. I think the whole point is to discourage family from visits, but that wasn't happening; nothing could keep me from someone I loved.

I'm as anxious to see him as he is to see the baby. I'm not at all disappointed when he comes out—he's like sunshine in this dark place—but I can tell he's not resting well. He kisses and hugs us both at the same time. He looks at her with so much love it makes my heart sink. "Let me see her."

I stand to hand her over the partition when the guard yells, "Have a seat!"

"I was just handing him the baby!" I yelled back.

Jimmy grabs my hand. "Don't give them the satisfaction."

I want to cry. Why do we have to go through this? Why am I handing you our precious gift with uniformed police a few feet away? I keep my thoughts to myself. I'm sure he is beating himself up enough; no need to rub it in. The look on his face when he held her chased all the sadness away.

"Yeah, this is our existence for now, but at least we still have each other."

I clear my throat to remind him I'm still here.

"Don't be jealous. I see you all the time." "Hey poom poom," He talks baby talk to her. "What kind of name is that?" "Does she sleep all night?"

"Yes, except when she wakes up to eat. I love her so much, Jimmy!"

"You are supposed to, crazy!"

"No, it's not a regular love. It's a love I never knew existed; it's unimaginable!"

"I'm just teasing you. I know exactly what you mean! I can't wait to get out of here to teach her how to fix cars!"

"Dream on, buddy. That's going to be my black beauty queen."

He smirks. "We don't need anyone else thinking the sun can't shine unless it's on them."

I laugh because that used to be so true. But he doesn't know how much that has completely changed in these last few weeks. No longer is it all about me. The reason I breathe and smile when I wake up is now lying in his arms.

"Are you excited about starting your new job?"

"Overall, yes. But I will have to leave my baby girl all day!"

"Well, at least you will have the chance to go home to her every day."

I should have chosen wiser words; I can tell that made him sad. I stroke his face. "When was the last time you slept?"

"I don't much."

"I can tell. You have to let God work it out. You just stay strong!"

"I wish that was as easy to do as it is to say!"

"It is; just have faith!"

Jameelah starts to stir; she's probably hungry. He tries to give her back to me without standing, but he bumps her head, and she starts to cry. The guard is walking over rather fast. She has a bad attitude anyways. I can tell she's about to run my blood pressure up a notch. I tell Jimmy I'm about to go; it's only a few minutes left anyways. He tries to assist me from a sitting position, but he's not much help. He is actually in the way. I decide to let him continue as this is all the assistance he will be able to give for a while. The guard makes a snide comment that I ignore. An idiot can't argue alone; no need to engage with her.

I continued preparing to leave, telling Jimmy I wouldn't be back next week because I had to figure out my work schedule. I stood and signaled the guard that I was ready to exit. Jimmy reaches for the baby and holds her face to his. I count under my breath to keep from crying. This is such a sad scene. Having my first child was supposed to be a fairytale, not a nightmare.

Although I hated leaving my baby, starting my new job was a good change of scene. Dr. Scott is a great employer, tons of fun to be around, and very handsome, I might add. My new co-workers are also very pleasant and really helpful. Usually, when there is a lot of female staff, it's plenty of drama to go with it. I'm thankful it's not the case in this office. The work itself isn't bad, either, it can be a bit tedious with all the codes and different information to learn, but I've been able to catch on quickly.

I didn't realize Thursdays are only a half day, so I will be able to visit Jimmy this week after all. We closed at noon, but visitation will not resume until after 1 pm, so I stop to get a bite to eat. When

I enter the facility, one of the front desk officers stare at me suspiciously. It makes me a little nervous, so I try not to make eye contact. I sit for almost 20 minutes until the first rounds of visitors are done. When I hear the doors to the visitation room open, I stand to start the process. Before I could take my jewelry off, Ms. Light Skin comes strolling out. Oh, hell no. I couldn't believe my eyes! After all this, this Negro is still playing games.

She walks by me, a little too closely, I might add, as she's exiting the waiting room. I KNOW she doesn't call herself staring me down! I politely tell her, "If you plan on keeping your eyes, you better redirect them." She wisely keeps walking.

The guard comes over with a stupid look on his face and says Gaines already had a visit. "No shit, Sherlock." That's why his dumb ass was staring at me the whole time I was sitting here waiting. These are some ruthless people, I tell you. I guess he was waiting for a showdown. Not happening; I have a child at home. I gather my things with tears in my eyes, but hell would freeze over before I let them fall. I won't be able to see him until next week, and best to believe it will be hell to pay.

This was the longest weekend ever. When visitation day rolled around, I was up and dressed before the sun came up. The first person in the County holding center today would be me. I was there before they unlocked the doors. I had been brewing all weekend. I left some money and the baby with my sister. I wasn't sure when I'd be back if this Negro got wrong. My whole life has been re-arranged, I hardly eat or sleep, and I'm caring for this child all alone! And here you are playing Romeo. Well, meet Nigalett; it's going down today!

Usually, I dress carefully, take extra time with my hair, and put on my sweet-smelling perfume because this is the closest we will be for a while. Today, I'm in a sweat suit and a ponytail. I didn't even bother with the perfume; he won't be able to enjoy it with a busted nose. Processing went quickly because I was early. I can tell Jimmy knows I'm here as Yvette today, not Shun. This is all business.

He walks over and just sits down in front of me. I'm not standing as usual for my hug, letting him know I haven't come in peace. I look him square in the eyes as he sits in front of me, praying he says something stupid so I can just hit him and get it over with. I am prepared to be done with Jimmy and raise my child alone, let her have him. My daughter and I will be just fine. I would tell her I was artificially inseminated.

"Hi," is all he gets out before I set it off.

"WHATEVER, NIGGA! Let me tell you this: you can have that heifer! I just came here to tell you if you want her, you can have her!"

"It's not like that, Shun."

"What the hell was she doing here, then?"

"I asked her to come. I know the last time she came with mama, you were all pissed. Since you told me you weren't coming this week, I chose to take this time to tell her how things have to be."

"Oh yeah. And I'm supposed to believe that shit, right?"

"You can believe what you want. I wouldn't play games at a time like this."

I search his eyes; he's being honest. I calm down as he continues, "I'm facing at least 10-20 years here. I would like for you both to go on with your lives, but since she and I have no ties, it's definitely best for her to start over. I understand with the baby; it's not so easy for you. So, the right thing to do, the only thing I can do, is give you peace of mind so we can try and give Jameelah as close to normal as we can."

His words just broke down the barrier I had spent the entire weekend building. I should be relieved knowing all his attention will be on me and the baby, but for some reason, I feel sorry for her now. "Jimmy, why did it take you being behind bars to choose? NO ONE wins in this madness!"

"I know, Shun, I know." He looks so defeated. I take his hand and decide to leave well enough alone. This isn't what any of us expected, but ready or not, here life comes.

After almost two years, three attorneys, preparation, and waiting, Jimmy's trial is finally set to begin. Let me tell you from the jump that a jury of your peers is a JOKE! None of those jurors looked like him or me. I didn't have a good feeling about this from the start, especially with him having two prior felonies. The first few days were the standard show me yours and I'll show you mine between the attorneys. Toward the middle of the trail, as time progressed, I realized they were trying him more on his past than his current charge. Truth be told, I don't understand, with all the crime and violence in this city, how law enforcement has time to set people up. Resources would be better expended if they would spend more time trying to solve some of the brutal crimes that are happening every day. Don't get me wrong; I believe if you do wrong, you should pay for it. We all have choices, but it seems to me it's a lot more effort put into ruining lives than it is in saving them. Just my opinion. I can't stress ENOUGH to people of color that this system isn't designed for us. It would be best to stay out of it all together! The same rules don't apply to Jimmy from the East Side as they do to Johnathan from the Suburbs.

Watching the video from the day he was arrested makes me sick to my stomach. Seeing this snake he called a friend, this dirty rat bastard who had sat at my table, had eaten our food, shook my man's hand, and called him his brother, selling him out to save his own ass sent me into a rage I never felt before! Having full knowledge of his criminal past, he knew how this would end for Jimmy, but he lied and set him up just the same. I walk outside to calm my nerves and wish like hell I could smoke a cigarette, but I'm breastfeeding, and I'm riding with Joyce who watched me like a hawk. She was doing her very best to make sure we all held it together. I returned in time to see Charlie take the stand. I thought the video had to be the worst part of it. BUT hearing him speak was as if the devil had saved the best for last.

Jimmy had held it together for the most part; this would prove to be his breaking point. The more he talked and lied about Jimmy being the mastermind behind this whole deal gone bad, the greater the look of defeat grew over Jimmy's face. With every lie that boy told, I felt all hope slipping away. Jimmy shifts uneasily in his seat. His habit of being loyal to the wrong thing has gotten him in DEEP this time. He keeps looking around as if to say, "Is anyone else hearing this BS besides me?" Jimmy had a soft spot for people, and if he considered you his friend, he would walk through fire for you. Charlie betraying his friendship in such a way pushes Jimmy over the edge. He drops his head and starts to cry, knowing his fate is sealed! In all these years of dealing with him and all the drama we had been through, I have never seen him express emotions this way! My heart is so broken for this black man right now. As if the world isn't hard enough on us for just BEING BLACK, I guess actually seeing someone you called a friend do you this way proved to be too much!

Between the video and Charlie's lies, the jury finds Jimmy guilty, and the judge sentences him to 180 months (15 years) in the Federal Penitentiary. We ALL felt that sentence; when the judge read it, I felt like my heart stopped, then I looked over at his mother, and my pain deepens. I had watched her plea, cry, and pray every day that it wouldn't turn out exactly how it just did.

Chapter 14

DOING TIME

Because of an altercation I had with that disrespectful, ignorant female guard at the holding center a few months ago, I haven't been able to see Jimmy since his sentencing. I had to wait until he was transferred to the Feds. But the look on her face when I punched her in the mouth was worth it. I had dealt with her disrespect for almost two years, and FINALLY unleashed on her when she had pushed me one day leaving the visiting room. I GUARANTEE she's learned how to keep her hands to herself now, though.

I'm a nervous wreck driving to McKean, PA, with my little girl in tow. I put on "Stand" by Donnie Mcclurkin and brace myself for the next 15 years of my life to be spent driving highways, getting pat searched, talked to crazy, and leaving my man on the other side of a gate while my child and I face this mean world alone. These tears just won't stop falling! In the midst of my pity party, I consider the fact that I could be taking flowers to a grave instead of visiting. God had at least spared his life.

I suck it up and fix my face before I arrive. We are going to have to make the most of the hand we've been dealt. Jameelah makes a sound in the backseat as if to remind me that she's in the car. I had stopped singing; she likes when I sing all loud and off-key. I force a smile and make silly faces in the mirror. I know she doesn't understand what's going on now, but one day she'll have questions, and I hope her father is prepared to answer them because I'm not equipped to explain why we're alone without breaking down.

I see the sign that reads McKean. It wasn't as bad of a drive as I had originally thought, or maybe I was just anxious to get here. After my interrogation at the desk, we were taken in and seated. I look around and examine all the other visitors and wonder how this has traumatized them. I take the money he had told me to bring to buy food and purchase things that I think he would like. I want to make it as comfortable as possible for my little family visit. I say a prayer that I hold it together when Jimmy comes out. I don't want him worrying about me being upset on the road, amongst all the other things he has to be concerned with.

My prayer that he has been well is answered. I'm relieved as he walks out the door looking as good as I've seen him in a while. Lord, he still makes my heart skip a beat, and his khakis are pressed to the nine. I give him the biggest hug, but he's not as enthusiastic; he wants to see his girl. I punch him playfully. "I should have your undivided attention after I spent all this time picking out this outfit."

"Girl, you better let me see my baby." That beautiful smile of his makes my day! After playing with Mela for a bit, he scans the food with approval. No pork... Good job. I'll bring ham sandwiches next time. He swats at my face and signals for the guard when I attempt to hit him. I'm so glad he's in a positive mood. We laugh, take a few pictures, and then discuss life as we now know it. Jameelah has fallen asleep, so we focus on each other with the little privacy we have.

"You up to this, Shun?"

"I'm down for you no matter what, Jimmy. I'm going to love you forever."

"I love you back," he says in a sad voice. I fear I'm going to lose the battle with these tears, so I excuse myself to go to the ladies' room. I give myself a pep talk, remembering I can go home and break down. He doesn't need this; it's NOTHING he can do about it right now. The cold water feels good on my face and gives me the confidence I need to finish the visit. He has Jameelah up in the air, talking baby talk to her when I exit the bathroom. I just stand by the door and stare; he's such a good guy! Even in this misfortune, I'm happy God chose that to be the man I bore a child with.

The guard yells, "15 mins left!" I hope that's enough time to get out that door before these tears come down. Jimmy asks if I got lost. "Whatever, I was watching to make sure you didn't drop my baby." I tried to make light of this terrible feeling I had about leaving him. He senses it, no matter how hard I try to conceal it.

"You're staying in a room and visiting again tomorrow, right?"

"Yes, but it will still be the same tomorrow."

"Well, let's deal with it, then. I'm just happy you made it safe, and my girls are ok." I give him a kiss and another long hug, which he returns this time. I stay in his embrace long enough to let the tears fall on his sleeve, so he wouldn't have to see me wipe my face.

I came back the next day and every weekend for a year. Sometimes with family, sometimes it was just the baby and I, and a few times without anyone. Those days he would have a fit, he didn't like me traveling alone, but at times it was just too much. He wasn't aware, but after most visits, I would have to pull over and cry for hours. My eyes would swell, and my head would pound. Sometimes I'd be so drained I would take a nap right afterwards on the highway; then head home. When Mela was with me, I felt guilty. I knew it was unsafe for one, and secondly, I was supposed to be the one comforting her cries, not drowning them out with my own. NO ONE knew how it ripped my heart apart to be without him. Doing time isn't easy for anyone, the offender or the family, but it's only two choices: give up or adjust. Then there's the question of his commitment that still nags at me. Am I doing what's best for me? Does he really love me like he says he does? Some days I wonder if he has someone else that visits on weekdays because I'm only here on the weekends, Saturdays, and sometimes Sundays if I can stay over.

The longevity of our relationship has to be discussed because, at this point, I'm going through a whole lot just to be a baby mama, and in reality, that's all I am. I mean, before he was locked up, we had dealt with our share of his infidelities. Tab was there from the start, and I basically chose to stay in that situation. But it didn't end there; through the years before his arrest, I had to deal with three or four other females that I knew of, and only God knows the ones I hadn't found out about. While he kept a low profile in the streets, I have investigative blood in my body and an intuition that won't quit. When something felt off about him to me, I put on my detective hat, and it was ALWAYS what I thought it was. Not to mention the information I got from his low-down friends, and not because they had my best interest in mind either; they wanted me for themselves. They apparently knew he had a good thing, even if he didn't realize it, but they always underestimated the depth of love I have for that man.

I always warn men that are close to me how important it is to know when you have a woman of value; it comes a time when you stop chasing. While you're out looking for new, your good thing is vulnerable to becoming new to someone too. Not me, though; my physical attraction to Jimmy is very strong. However, that's not what keeps me. I had a love for that man that dwelled somewhere deep, and although I didn't understand why or exactly when it happened, he has my soul!

For some particular reason, today our longevity is weighing heavier on me than usual. I try to keep my normal face, but he knows me so well. After a few minutes into the visit, he asks what's wrong. I playfully blow past his question, but he's adamant in wanting an answer. I figure, why not be honest? I try my best not to burden him, but I'm not sleeping much these days and being a single mother, I owe it to Jameelah to be more stable. I decide to come clean about the feelings I've been having lately as to where we stand.

He sits back for a minute, gathering his thoughts. "If you want to leave me, I understand."

"What is wrong with you, boy? No one goes through this much trouble to quit! It's just that with our history, I need to know my heart is as safe with you as yours is with me."

"YES!" he says firmly.

"How can I be sure?" I ask with tears in my eyes.

"Shun, all you can do is trust me."

"I don't want to hurt your feelings here, Jimmy, but it's hard to trust a 'boyfriend.'"

"Well, what do you want me to do? I don't know any other way to tell you that my feelings for you are real, and I respect what you're going through for me." "I just find it crazy to wait for a boyfriend who has 15 years in prison." He looks drained, and his eyes get sad.

"What do you think about getting married?"

He looks both surprised and confused. "I thought you were trying to leave me."

"Not at all, sweetheart. I'm trying to figure out a way to hold on to our love. I don't see myself waiting on a boyfriend, but for my husband, I'll wait FOREVER."

I put the plan in motion, sent for a marriage license, found rings, and carried on like we were getting married in the Waldorf Astoria. I felt resistance from both sides, his family as well as mine, and it didn't change my mind at all. Since the first day I laid eyes on this man, I knew he wouldn't be easy to forget. These prison walls aren't going to stop me from being with the love of my life. I ignored everything rational and irrational anyone had to say about our decision to get married, even though 90% of it was true. I didn't care; our truth was all that mattered to us because, in the end, we were the only two who would have to deal with any consequences there would be.

It took almost three months to get everything taken care of, and on a Wednesday, I received a letter from the facility saying what days a Chaplin would be available to perform the ceremony. You would think the letter said he was being released the way I celebrated. I was getting to marry the love of my life, and that was just as exciting to me. I arranged the ceremony for the last week of the month. I was told I would need to bring one witness, or they could allow someone from the facility to do it. I'm not having that; one khaki suit at my wedding would be enough.

Jimmy and I decided to ask Paula. Believe it or not, we had put our differences to the side once she figured out I really loved Jimmy and wasn't just a plain psycho. I only acted crazy when provoked; other than that, I'm one of the sweetest, kindest girls you will ever meet. I had picked out a formal skirt and blouse for me and a pretty little lace dress for Jameelah. I figured a gown would be a little over the top. I'm as nervous walking into the prison today as I was going into the delivery room. My whole life is about to change again, DRASTICALLY!

The ceremony was short and sweet, and I can't stop smiling. Jimmy looks both excited and nervous. He knows he has a soldier by his side, but I know giving up his player card is hard to do, even from behind these walls. We all take pictures, then Paula entertains Jameelah at a different table so we can have a few moments to ourselves. This is as close to a honeymoon as we are getting. There are no conjugal visits, nothing, just hand-holding and a kiss or two when we could sneak it; that's all the physical contact we have. I remember driving home thinking this would make everything alright, and it could only get better. I thought becoming Mrs. Gaines would give me some kind of super strength to endure. For the next 6 or 7 months, I was on cloud nine. Jimmy had found me some other wives to carpool with, so I wouldn't be so lonely on the rides down. This also saved on gas and other expenses for us all.

Our one-year anniversary comes and goes, then another... and another... and another... and another, and just like that, five years have gone by. We have put in several appeals to no avail, and my hope, along with my strength, is starting to fade. These trips are starting to take their toll. I have no life. I work, take care of my daughter, cook, clean, go visit Jimmy on the weekends. No rest.

Monday comes, and I do it all again. I realize for these past few years, I've been living on life support. I mean, I'm alive, but I don't live my OWN life. I'm operating on my determination to take care of this little girl and my husband. I'm just existing. I stopped living the day Jimmy went away. As I'm loading my things in the car that I'll need for my overnight stay this weekend, I start to cry... A cry unlike any of the others. I never really entertained the thought of giving up on us until lately. I don't know if it's healthy to continue on like this. I've decided to tell him I think it's best we go our separate ways, only the thought of leaving Jimmy feels like death to me. Good Lord, why does it hurt so bad? My life was not supposed to be this way. I had dreams of being a teacher and marrying a doctor, being adventurous, and traveling all around the world. Then maybe one day, when I was tired and ready to settle down, I would adopt a little boy and maybe a girl.

All of a sudden, I am so tickled. If you really look at it, I am traveling, and I'm married to a doctor: Dr. Feel-good! I laugh so hard I have to shut my car off and open the door. I'm literally choking and need air, but I CAN'T stop laughing. I bet my neighbors think I'm crazy as hell at this point. Oh well, I needed to get those tears out and this laughter to chase them away. Now, I must figure out how to tell the love of my life that love just ain't enough.

Chapter 15

DOES FOREVER
REALLY LAST ALWAYS

I pumped myself up the whole ride. I deserve better, and I have nothing to feel bad about. I have been better to Jimmy than he's ever been to me. All the hurt, fighting with other women, the lying… why am I feeling guilty? I tried; I'm too young for this. All the thoughts running through my head are the same things people were trying to tell me BEFORE we got married. I should have listened, now I'm going to hurt him when I should have just walked away, but my heart wouldn't let me leave him then.

I'm so consumed by my thoughts the next thing I see is MCKEAN next exit. My car must have guided itself to the facility; this familiar sign has saved me from missing this place so many times over the years. I couldn't park and get inside fast enough. I wanted to just do it, get it over with, leave and start all over; no use in prolonging the inevitable. I say a prayer that he understands. I mean, he is a player, and I'm sure he will respect the game; he probably doesn't care anyways. One down, he surely has 5 more waiting for him. I have a child to raise, I have to keep my sanity, and Jimmy is a grown man. It's not fair to Mela the way we stay held up in the house and on these highways on the weekend. Our quality of life is terrible, and it's all because of the decisions I made. She doesn't deserve this. I can no longer protect Jimmy's feelings while ignoring my own.

I sit here anticipating his reaction. I know this won't be a long visit; he'll say his peace and leave. I know him all too well. After what seemed like an eternity—20 mins was actually all it was—he came out of the back. "What's up?"

"Hey", I stand up to greet him with a hug.

"Where's my daughter?"

"I left her at home. I needed some one-on-one time with you today."

"She could have played with the toys while we talked. Why did you leave her?" He had gone through a program to be able to get a separate playroom for us when we visited, offering at least some form of privacy. We tried to make her environment as normal as possible while we were here.

"I want to talk to you alone if that's okay."

He instantly tenses up. "What's wrong?" His eyes search mine.

I lost my nerve. Who am I kidding? I could never leave him. "Nothing, I just miss you."

I see the worry start to leave his face. "I miss you too, and I'm so glad you're here." My heart aches for both of us as I feed him false hope, knowing full well my confidence in this situation is fading fast. This is not as simple as I thought. I'm trapped. I refuse to leave him with bad news, so I redirect the conversation. I ask about his week and allow myself to laugh at some of the crazy things that go on inside his world and tell him a few crazy things going on in mine. I make it through the whole visit, thinking I have successfully fooled him, until the signal to end the visit comes.

Unexpectedly, he says, "I knew this wouldn't be easy, Shun, so you do what you have to do. Don't worry about me."

"What are you talking about?" I say with a slight attitude.

"Shun, I'm not crazy. You're coming later and later every weekend. The visits are getting shorter, and you're answering your phone less."

I try to cut in, "I'm tired. I pick up extra hours here and there, you know, with taking care of the baby, paying the attorney, and trying to send you money. I'm struggling!"

"And what else?" he says as he gets up and walks away.

"Jimmy!" I call to his back with tears in my eyes. "Don't leave like that, please!"

Without turning back to face me, he says, "Handle your business!"

My heart almost leaves my chest as I imagine him fighting to hold back his own tears as I let mine freely flow. Twenty people must have asked if I was okay leaving that visiting room. I couldn't get to my car fast enough to YELL to the top of my voice, hoping that would make the pain go away. How did he know? I was so careful not to ever talk to JR in public. I ALWAYS considered Jimmy's feelings. We did talk for hours on the phone, and I told him nothing could ever happen besides a friendship because I promised Jimmy forever and I couldn't hurt him.

JR spent most of our time together telling me how I deserved better and that I shouldn't suffer for something someone else had done. He was funny and charismatic. I first encountered him in the store across the street from my apartment building and had ignored his advances and flirting for months. One day, some guys were playing basketball in the street as I was getting in my car, and the ball hit my hood. I was LIVID. I slammed my car door and walked toward the crowd of grown boys. 'WHAT THE HELL? Watch what you're doing!"

"Stuck up bitch," one of them yelled.

"Your mother," I shoot back, and the other ones laughed.

I was walking back to my car when someone said, "Don't be so mean." I turned around to give him a piece of my mind, and no words would come out. JR was standing there, smiling from ear to ear. "Why do you park so close to the hoop?"

"Because," I say in a child's voice.

"Because? What kind of answer is that?"

I smiled a little because I was acting 10. Wait a minute. I'm married! What am I doing? I gain my composure quickly and put a little pep in my voice, "Look, y'all ghetto asses should find somewhere else to be childish. I've always parked my car here, and I LIVE here."

"Girl, you need to loosen up. Kiss my… You know what, let me leave before I hurt your feelings." He smiles. "See you later, cutie!"

I don't know why, but that made my palms sweat. I get in my car and speed away to mom's for our scheduled card game. When I sit down, my sister asks, "Why you looking all crazy and spaced out?"

"Girl, get out of here and mind your business." I can't wait to get up from the table. I played the wrong card and lost the book we needed to win. Needless to say, Mom is hot with me. I don't even mind losing. I want to get up anyways and go outside to find my older brother; I need some info.

He's doing the usual clowning with his stupid friends when I pull him to the side. "What you want, Shun? I'm not walking to the store for your greedy self."

"Man, I have business to discuss this time."

"What you want, girl? I'm trying to get this dice game going."

"Ok, listen. I got a proposition for you. I need you to find out the deal on this dude that I have been seeing around the hood."

"Find out like what?"

Like where he works, does he have kids... a girlfriend. You know, stuff like that."

"Girl, get your ass out of here. Jimmy gone beat your ass if he gets wind of you out here doing dumb shit."

"Well, FIRST OF ALL (now I got an attitude because he checked me), I'm grown, and it isn't against the law to ask about someone. But for your information, he is trying to fix something at my house, and I just don't want anybody in my house around my things or my daughter."

"Yeah, OK!" He gives me the side eye, not quite convinced.

"Look, I'll pay you!"

"Oh, say no more," he says, giggling. "Who is it? How much are you paying? And can you give me a couple of days?"

"Ok, well, his name is JR, but I hear people calling him Red sometimes. And he lives—"

"Wait, stop! Tall light-skin nigga?"

"Yeah. Why?"

"Oh, you can save your money and your time. That nigga ain't the one."

"Wait, what you mean?"

"I just... Listen, sis. You're about your business, you're married, and you have a good job. That ain't the type of dude you need, not even to 'FIX' nothing, he's out of your league."

Wait, did he just check me AGAIN? "Ok, cool. Well, that's that."

"Listen, girl. Don't let me find out. You stay away from him, and I mean it!"

"Ok, Daddy. Whatever," I yell back over my shoulder.

"Ok, think I'm playing, girl!"

Boy, please.

Two months later, JR and I are hanging out and going strong. He's a gentleman, and those are hard to come by. He calls me "baby" and "honey" and kisses me goodnight, things a girl can truly get used to, especially when you're not receiving affection and it's been over 7 YEARS since you have. I feel this is getting serious, and I need to tell Jimmy that I have decided 15 years is a lot of time, and forever has turned out to be too long to wait. I mean, the last 5 years of my life, I have been a robot. I am losing myself to a man who was NEVER faithful to me. (See, when the devil gets in your head, you start to justify all your mess). I knew when I married Jimmy what his history was, and I thought our love would stand the test of time. But I'm tired of this life, and over the years, I've watched the women he's hooked me up to travel with end up brokenhearted, and I don't want that to be my story. Some of these women have done these long bids with their men only to have them come home and disrespect them, lie, and cheat. See, I'm not strong enough for that; I'm going to kill him and trade places. After all this time, money, and energy I've spent trying to make sure he's okay, it definitely wouldn't be a happy ending if he were to treat me that way. When I go see him this weekend, I'm going to let him know it's best if I go on with my life. I'm strong enough now.

It seems like the roads are longer, and time is dragging for some reason today. I left Mela with my mom again this weekend because this will not be easy. I've been crying since I left at the thought of leaving Jimmy, but it's time! Midway there, I lose my nerve... I turn the car around and head back, not even stopping to pick up Jameelah; I go straight home. I take off my clothes and lie in bed, still crying, thinking of him waiting to be called when I arrive. I feel sick from crying for the last two hours and wondering if he's worried. I could have at least done it face to face. I'm such a coward! Why didn't I go? I could have at least hugged him, kissed him, and told him I loved him more than anything in this whole world.

The phone rings, and I almost jump out of my skin. "Hello!"

"What's up?" It's JR. "Did you tell him?"

"No!"

He starts right in on me. "What you mean? You had me put my life on hold, blow up my shit, and now you don't want to leave this dude."

"FIRST OF ALL, you told me your girl was a bum bitch, she doesn't want anything in life, and you need a woman like me. I NEVER once told you to do anything. I simply said I wasn't dealing with nobody else's man, and you made a choice, so pipe the fuck down." My hurt has turned to anger, and he gon' feel it.

"Well," he says more calmly, "why didn't you tell him?"

"Because I didn't go!"

"Where you been?"

"Don't be asking me no damn question; you're not my husband!"

"Oh, it's like that!"

"Yeah, it is. Now, get the hell off my phone!" I slam the phone down so hard my hand aches. RING… RING… "Listen, Nigga. I'm about to—"

"Shun!" Oh God, it's Jimmy.

"Hey…" My heart BREAKS at the sound of his voice.

"You alright?"

"Yeah, I'm good."

"Why didn't you come? Is Jameelah okay? I been waiting for hours."

"I know… Look, I just didn't feel good today," I started there, "but I just…"

"You just what!" I can hear anger and eagerness in his voice.

BOOM BOOM BOOM… "Someone's at the door. Can you call me back?"

"Wait. Shun?"

I hang up! My mind is in a thousand places; I can't do this. I swing open the door expecting one of my aggravating siblings. I can use the distraction from my drama.

It's JR. I'm not up to this. Without me inviting him in, he pushes past me. "Look, I know this is hard on you, but you need to tell me today... If you gon' stay with him... If so, I'm gone!"

"Ok, nigga, Make tracks because this is my call to make."

He looks hurt, and I feel bad. "Okay, Shun. All I need you to understand is that I want you. We have so much in common. I want a life with you, and we both deserve better."

My eyes fill with tears. This is a new beginning standing in front of me with all the possibilities and things I've dreamed of for years. Besides, he can hold me at night and help with the bills, which allows me to pay more toward these attorney fees. I mean, I'm still helping Jimmy; it's not like I'm abandoning him. I'm just taking care of myself too. The whole time we're talking, the phone is ringing off the hook, and I'm pretending not to hear it. JR walks over suddenly, picks it up, and puts it to my ear. God, please don't let this be Jimmy on this phone. "Hello."

"Hey, Shun, what's up!"

"Hey, Jimmy."

JR says, "Tell him, or I'm done." At the same time, Jimmy is yelling into the phone to tell him what's going on before he loses it!

"Jimmy, remember the guy I was telling you about..."

"Yeah, the nigga you been 'HANGING OUT' with that's really cool."

"Yeah… Well, I… We, he…" I'm grasping here! "Listen, Jimmy. It's best if you and I are just friends because I deserve better!" I blurt it out fast so I don't lose my nerve! Silence… "HELLO! Jimmy!"

"Yeah, Shun, are you SERIOUS? I found out who that nigga is, and he's playing you. He's not who he says he is. He's not for you. Don't do this… You are smarter than this. Don't let him do this to us. I gave up a lot to be with you, and we said we would always be together…" Lord, the pain in his voice is about to KILL me.

JR is staring at me with ICE in his eyes. "I know, but I think it's best for all of us—"

Jimmy cuts me off. "FUCK IT! Let me ask you one time, and I want you to tell me what it is, and this shit is done! Is that who you want?"

"Jimmy… I don't…"

"ANSWER ME!" he yells before I can stall again.

JR turns to me. "Answer him, Shun, or I'm out!"

I chose the safest route; the man I can hold at night. "Yes, Jimmy, this is who I want to be with now." "BET!" The phone goes dead… OH GOD! I hold my chest like someone just shot me. JR attempts to come over and comfort me. I turn to him with tears in my eyes.

"Why are you so upset? I thought this was what you wanted."

"Get the hell out of here," I say in a near whisper.

"What did you say?"

"GET-THE- HELL-OUT of my house!" I yell so loud it hurts my throat. I was angry at the WHOLE world because of a decision I had just made, and right now, I want to be alone.

I called my mom and told her Jimmy's sister would be picking up Jameelah and keeping her for a couple of days. I needed to be alone, maybe even die, whichever one was easier, because, at this point, I think a bullet to my heart would be less pain than what I feel right now. The agony of waiting for the phone to ring is unbearable. I want Jimmy to call back so I can tell him that I made a mistake; this isn't what I want. The right thing couldn't feel this bad. Only he didn't call.

A week went by, and nothing. JR, who was persistent and called every day, had convinced me the pain was temporary. He came over the next day, the day after, and the day after that, banging on the door. I finally answered because I felt like the walls were closing in on me.

"Hi..."

"Hi," I leave the door ajar and walk away, ashamed of how I behaved the last time I'd seen him.

"You alright?"

"I will be."

"Where's Jameelah?"

"She's at her aunt Davida's house today."

"Oh. You want to go for a walk?"

"No, I want to die!"

"Don't say that." He pulls me close to him. "I know it hurts; it hurts me to leave her too. But sometimes moving on is the only way to get your life back."

I'm crying like a baby. "I know, but he didn't deserve that."

"Look at how he treated you for years."

"First of all, you don't know nothing about him…"

"Buffalo ain't that big, sweetheart."

"Well, if that's the case, why shouldn't I believe the things I've heard about you?"

"You know how that goes. People don't want to see people happy, and that's sad."

One thing he has on his side is the fact that I had been through A LOT of drama with Jimmy and other women. I didn't know a thing about him except the warnings my brother and Jimmy had tried to give me. He seems sincere, and I am lonely. He's been nothing but kind since we met and is eager to start a life with me. Knowing Jimmy, someone else has probably taken my place by now. Anyways, I've made my decision. I better figure out how to get on with my life.

The first time I'm intimate with JR, I feel dirty and disgusted. Not so much the sex, but my actual heart feels unclean. I want to vomit at the fact that I'm causing someone else satisfaction, while Jimmy's hurting. I drink heavily in an effort to calm my nerves, but it does nothing for my soul. The more I did it. the less I thought about it, and slowly I'm becoming someone whom I've always despised, a cheater. He is very affectionate to me and really sweet to Jameelah when I allow her to be around. I wrestled with them interacting, knowing that I had already disappointed her father seemed like enough of a betrayal. I try to curb her confusion, by limiting the time she spends around JR. Besides, something deep down is starting to sense JR is not as wonderful as he proclaimed. I mean, we still have fun, but I have an eerie feeling about things, especially when I see his lil dusty baby mother. I have about had it with her rolling her eyes and acting like a tough guy when we both know she's soft as butter. However, out of respect for both of our children, when I saw her, I always maintained my mannerism as a lady.

I had visited Jimmy a few times since our break up, and it wasn't the same, either. He treated me cold, mostly playing with Jameelah and only talking to me when absolutely necessary. I understand, though. He was angry, and he has every right to be. While we were able to maintain our relationship as parents, the hardest part of all this has been losing my best friend. We all have choices in life, though, and now I'm living with the consequences.

JR is starting to come home later and later, and it makes me furious! Not that he was playing games, but that I had trusted his lying self and broke Jimmy's heart. Tonight, when he comes in, he has some explaining to do. It's almost 10 pm, and the last time I spoke to him, he'd said he would be home by 8. Two hours is enough of a grace period. I know EXACTLY where he is. I call my brother and tell him I'm picking him up to watch Jameelah.

"Where are you going this late?"

"Mind your business, boy, and be outside when I get there." I pick him up and take him back to my house. I pull in the driveway, let them out, and tell him to put Jameelah straight to bed when they get inside, then leave again. It takes me less than 5 minutes to get to my destination. His daughter's grandmother's house, I heard they had some kind of gathering, but so what? Show your face and bring your ass home.

As sure as grits are grocery, he's propped up with his little girl in his arms and the mother looking all gloomy-eyed sitting next to him. I stop the car but leave it running because if ANTY, not ANY, ANTY body gets wrong, I'm punching them in the face and going home and sleeping like a baby.

I tap him on the shoulder. "Excuse me, family guy. Uh, what time are you planning on bringing your ass home?"

"Man, come on. —"

I cut him off! "Save the drama for your mama, nigga. It takes about eight minutes to get home doing the speed limit. See if you can be there in five." I get in my car and drive away. I hate to let broads see me out of character, but when I'm mad, it is what it is!

He walks in as I'm pouring me a glass of wine. "Did you really have to show your ass like that around them people?"

"Would you have rather me slap the shit out of you? Because that's what you deserve!"

"You still go visit that nigga every chance you get. I don't say nothing about that!"

"And you better not if you want all your teeth! I trusted you to be who you SAID you were, and you are a cold liar. I have a child with that man, it's not like he can come to us. But I tell you WHAT, either you need to bring your daughter over here, just like you do your boys, or make some visiting hours during the day; all this late night is out the gate."

He didn't want to call the child's mother and address the issue like I asked him to, so he avoided me for a few days and I know exactly what that means; he's still sleeping with her. How could I be so BLIND? I allowed my loneliness to put me in a situation I have no business being in. After a few weeks, the visiting issue blows over, and we start doing our own thing. I start to visit Jimmy more often, and not just every other weekend. That is, if he doesn't have family coming. He made it clear that I need to check and not just show up because I didn't receive first priority anymore. Meanwhile, JR continues to visit his daughter when he wants, and our conversations and time together become less and less meaningful. I feel this is coming to an end.

This weekend I'm taking a break from it all! I've planned a night out with my girl Char. Jimmy had introduced me to one of his Godsisters shortly after he and I met, and she then introduced me to her daughter. She figured her daughter and I would click since we were only one year apart, and she was right! Char cool people; she reminds me a lot of myself, real solid! A rare commodity, a diamond in the ruff, my ride or die, and whenever I need her, she's there. In these past few years, she's gone from being my friend, hair stylist, and shoulder to cry on to being my sister! If nobody else will help me party my pain away, she ALWAYS comes to the rescue!

I asked her to bring the whole crew tonight; a group of her childhood friends I had met about a year ago. She had invited me on a weekend getaway with them and we all hit it off from that moment. We have hella fun every time we get together! I moved from one confined relationship to another; FUN is what I need! I want to dance and drink a whole lot of wine, so the more people, the merrier!

We chose downtown as our destination, and I don't regret it. I dance until I can't feel my feet, then decide to call it a night. As we're saying our goodbyes, I get the strangest feeling. I tell them I have to go and race home. I practically run to Jameelah's room as soon as I get the door open; she's sound asleep. Next, I head to the guest bedroom where my brother Brandon and his girlfriend are watching a movie.

"You ok, sis?" Meech asks with a look of concern.

"I'm good, sis. Just had a bad vibe. Has JR been home?"

"I haven't heard him come in. We left the door open so I could hear Mela if she woke up. Actually, I haven't seen him since you left."

"Ok, thanks." I go up to my bedroom and call JR. No answer. I call his brother where he said he'd be; he's not there. There it is, that's the problem. He's with her, I can feel it. That woman's intuition should NEVER be underestimated; it's a real thing. He thought I would probably come home late, or in the early morning hours as usual when I hang out, but for some reason, I just wasn't feeling it. I've found my reason.

I tell my brother I'll be back, get in my car, and drive to his ex's house on the other side of town. As I suspected, his car is in her driveway, pulled all the way to the back. I shut off my lights, take off my heels and walk up the driveway. I knock on the door. No answer. I call him. No answer. I go around to the side of the house to look through a window, and I see all three of them laying in the bed, sleeping peacefully. I politely remove the license plates on the car that I had registered for him and leave a note on the windshield that reads, "I took your plates, no need to call the police, they can't even save you; your shit will be packed when you wake up. Hope you rested well!" I cry all the way home. Not about it being over between us, but that I'd hurt Jimmy despite all the warnings. I'm actually relieved this is done; in all honesty, as much as I tried to fight it, there's no denying that I'm still in love with Jimmy. I know it will be a cold day in hell before he takes me back, but at least I won't have to be so uncomfortable around him anymore once I tell him this is DONE.

I put on my Mary J and pack JR's stuff in a New York Minute. I called his brother and told him in case the wind blew the note, he needs to come to get his things. I also informed him that he'd probably need a ride because those plates were going straight to the DMV at the top of the morning. "Oh man, that's crazy," was all his brother could get out before I hung up. I place all his items on the balcony off the master bedroom on the second floor. This shit would be going down special delivery, bag by bag, whenever he did show up.

I'm so exhausted I fall asleep with my clothes on. When the phone rings, I don't even remember where I am. 9:38 am is displayed on the clock. I had only been asleep a few hours, but it felt like days.

"Hello."

"Yeah, can you let me explain?"

"Boy, get the hell on. Ain't no way you about to explain you in the bed with another broad, and you supposed to be my man." Oh, and by the way, I found your little card she brought you while I was packing your shit. The one thanking you for the new stove you got her and how she can't wait for you to see the new lingerie she bought!" Silence… "Tell that heifer to make sure she moisturizes those elbows and ankles because they are ashy EVERY time I see her!"

"Can you just come to take the deadbolt off so I can get my stuff?"

"No need. I got that order coming right up." I slide open the balcony door and throw down his belongings bag by bag, including his shoes and hats. He's so frantic you'd think I was throwing the kids. Serves his ass right! Once the last bag is on the ground, I yell down for my cousin Kev to take the deadbolt off now. If that nigga felt froggy and wanted to leap, we were ready for his ass. I grab my bat, run down the stairs, and stand in the living room praying he would get enough guts in his stomach to come into the house... off with his head. But just like I figured, he picked everything up and left without another word. He ain't about this life. I don't know why he tried that shit on a G! He better stick with them weak bitches. He's not built for a woman like ME!

Chapter 16

SELF DESTRUCTION

My life has been reduced to work and drinking, with my best effort to still be an active parent! I work as many hours of overtime as I can to cover the bills that JR and I were both paying, as well as the money I have to send Jimmy every month. Thankfully, the time JR was living here allowed me to save enough to pay off all the attorney fees; at least some good came out of the time we were together. Rain, sleet, hail, or snow, I was always going to make sure Jimmy was alright. We are in a better place now that JR and I have gone our separate ways, but I know it will never be the same. I'm very thankful that I had not lost my friend forever when I decided to leave him.

The days I'm not working, I make sure to spend with my daughter making memories. We eat out almost every day now. I know that poor baby is tired of those three dishes I was making. She also prefers dining out because we get to dress up, look pretty, and eat whatever our hearts desire. And on the nights we do stay in, I let her little cousins come over. Her playroom, which is basically a toy store within itself, keeps them busy for hours. That kid has everything in there you could imagine! I never want her to feel like she missed out on ANYTHING because her dad is not here and her mom is spiraling out of control. I will admit I overcompensate, and I know things can't replace people, but I figure if I keep buying her things, that will fill   any voids in her life. After all our dinners, play dates and once she's safely tucked away in bed, I consume alcohol; wine, liquor, beer, it doesn't matter. Anything I have on hand that will fill my own void is my drink of choice.

I've been drinking heavily lately, which led to a few meaningless escapades with men I care nothing about to try and mend my brokenness. I thought if I was in control, I could curb the pain. Once I figured out that didn't help a thing, I cut men off completely. But I can't put the bottle down; I'm on a path of self-destruction. I don't know how else to cope with my life and all the time Jimmy still has to serve. I have a sweet, healthy daughter, a great job, own my home, and a new car at the age of 29. You could say in the eye of the average person, I'm winning in life, but none of that makes me whole. Something inside of me is empty, so I drink until I can't feel anything. I wake up and repeat this routine daily, looking so put together on the outside while dying on the inside. I make it through work days strictly out of habit. The doctor often asks if I want to talk about it while I'm at work, but I just deny I have problems; I can't let anyone know I'm not the superwoman I appear to be.

I think my family's unaware of my drinking until my sisters Tasha and Kenya pop up and basically do an intervention. I suspect Brandon had snitched because he's the only one at my house all the time, and he's questioned if my drinking was healthy on more than one occasion. Otherwise, how would they know? I only go to work and then straight home; it's been over a month since I even stopped at my parents house. I mean, drinking isn't uncommon in my family, but I must admit, lately, I've been drinking enough for us all.

Tasha insists that I get out with them, but besides work, I have no desire to leave my house. A few weeks go by after their attempted intervention with me ignoring anything and everyone who told me what I was doing was unhealthy. Jameelah is spending the weekend at my mom's with her cousins, and I plan on shutting up with my sorrows. I have to get up to feed and entertain her when she's home, but when she's away, I don't move out of this spot on the couch until she returns.

I have no plans to interact with another human, yet there is a knock on the door. Tasha is standing there dressed to kill, claiming she can't get a ride to the Jay-Z after-party that I had CLEARLY told her I didn't want to attend. I offer to drop her off and pick her up; she's not having it. I know she is not leaving, so I agree to go for a little while. The quicker I get her there, the sooner I can get back home and finish drowning in my misery. I walk into my closet, and I see this white sheer get-up that Tasha and I had gotten on one of our shopping sprees. I almost didn't buy it, figuring I would never wear it, but I'm not the one to let a good sale get by. This is a perfect occasion to put it to use.

As soon as I walk in and see the strippers, I know I've made a mistake! It's a lot going on up in here, and all I want to do is drink and lay down. Tasha is instantly on the dance floor. I find the nearest available seat and watch her. The alcohol is free flowing, so I grab a cocktail as a waitress walks by. If I can't be at home in peace, I'll do something that makes me feel it's worth my while to be here.

Before I knew it, we were tearing the dance floor up together; the more I drank, the better the party became. I'm feeling the effects sooner than I thought, and I'm driving. It's time to start water to bring myself down a little before it's time to go. I'm standing at the bar when I hear a voice I haven't heard in months ask to buy me a drink. I turn around to JR, looking as sharp as ever, better than I remembered to be exact. My defense against his good looks is to tell him right off. "Boy, if you don't find the nearest bridge and jump off..."

"Wait, wait. I understand things didn't work out between us, but that doesn't mean we have to be enemies."

"Yeah, I guess you're right, but that doesn't make us friends. I'd rather go on as if we never met. It's better that way."

"Cool, I understand. Have a good night. By the way, you look nice!"

"Yo, mama," I snap back… "Now speed on!"

He says, "That's what I miss about you the most, that smart mouth."

I flip him the finger. He laughs and walks away. Never mind the water, I order a double shot of Gin and another until Tasha and I are looking at each other like, how the hell we getting home?

"We can call a cab," she suggested drunkenly.

I'm not drunk enough to leave my car anywhere. I call a few people to come and drive us home, but everyone is otherwise engaged. I feel sick, so I walk outside for some fresh air. Tasha comes out about 10 mins later with JR. "Look what I found wandering around," she says, snarling at him.

These two never got along; I'm confused as to why she has his arm. He is about to drive us home; the devil is a lie. I'm not getting in a car with him.

"Look, girl. Your sister said y'all wasted, and you can hardly stand up."

"So what! I'm still not getting in your car."

"Fine then," he walks off.

Tasha speaks with worry in her voice. "Sis, I don't think you should drive like this."

"I know that, fool. I'm drunk, not crazy. I have a daughter, and I would never jeopardize my life or yours. We just have to sleep it off in the car."

"Whatever. I'm with you, sis."

We take off, wobbling toward my car. JR comes out screaming, "WAIT!"

"Ninja, what part of I'm not getting in your car don't you understand?"

"You don't have to, smart ass. One of my boys will follow me in my car, and I'll drive you home."

Tasha sits in front to give him directions because she's getting dropped off first. I could barely keep my eyes open to tell her goodbye, but I was focused long enough to hear her threaten his life if something happened to me. We drive in silence all the way to my house. He parks and gets out to help me inside; my head is spinning so bad I can't walk without assistance. He finally gets the door open, and I make a dash to the bathroom. I'm not even past the kitchen before all that liquor makes its way back up, all over my pretty floors. GROSS! I was taught better; ladies should never get this intoxicated. I ask him to leave so I can clean up; I'm really too ashamed to look in his face. Instantly, he grabs some supplies to clean up my mess. I tell him I can clean my own house and try to snatch the mop, but I stumble. He takes my hand and gently leads me to the couch. The last thing I remember is seeing doubles of the fish tank.

I woke up a few hours later. JR's at the end of the couch, smoking a joint and staring at me.

"What are you still doing here?"

"My man had to leave. His girl was tripping because it was getting late. I told him to take my car, but I didn't want to wake you."

"Awww, that was nice of you. I can take you to get it." I attempt to stand up and stumble again.

"Sit down. It's cool. Here, smoke some of this. It will mellow you out, cause you be trippin."

This is the first time I have smiled in his presence since we went our separate ways. Every single encounter before now has been finger-flipping, shouting matches, and eye rolling. I take the joint; I do enjoy the feeling, but haven't indulged in a minute. He was right; it did bring me down a little.Out of nowhere, he starts to laugh, and it makes me laugh. "What's wrong with you?"

"I think that's Jameelah's nightgown."

It was the first thing I could find; I hadn't paid attention to what I had on. I attempt to pull it down, and he grabs my hand. "I've seen it all now!"

"Well, it's nothing you haven't seen before."

"But I do miss it," he says as he moves over and kisses my thigh. Common sense says stop him. The flesh hasn't been touched in so long and just lays back and lets it happen.

While he showers downstairs, I go up to my bathroom and cry. Why did I invite this confusion back into my heart? He is DEFINITELY not the one for me. I allow my tears to flow as I shower because he won't get the chance to even THINK I'm crying over him! I find a sweat suit to pull on, throw on a hat, and fly back downstairs to take him home or wherever he's going because he MUST get up out of here before Jimmy calls. Things are almost normal between him and I again, and I don't want anything to ruin that. JR must have the same feeling about us; this thing could never work. He is sitting on the couch waiting patiently when I come down. He asks if I'm hungry. "I'm good," I lie. In reality, my stomach is hitting my back; it's so empty. But I want to be out of his presence as quickly as possible. He directs me to his friends where his car is parked, and with a kiss on the cheek, he exits the car, off to whatever life he is living these days.

I call to check on Jameelah, and Mom fusses me out as usual, saying this isn't the first baby they've kept. I laugh and hang up, having to be satisfied with hearing her voice. I make myself some breakfast and wait for Jimmy to call; his voice makes my whole life better. I need to do laundry, but after the night I've had, I would rather curl up on the couch with a book. The OCD in me wins. I start sorting the laundry then the phone rings; it's Jimmy. I guess the laundry will have to wait.

During our calls, I like to chill; he relaxes me. I go and lay in my bed smiling like I've won money. "Good morning, baby."

"Whatever, slut. Where's my daughter?" He does that silly little laugh. Lord, my heart skipped a beat; I thought he was actually referring to what had happened earlier.

"You know she's with my mom."

"Yeah, you usually run and get her soon as your feet hit the ground."

"I know. I called, but they said to leave her, so I didn't argue. I went out last night, and I have a slight hangover."

"Where did you go?"

"To that Jay-Z after party I told you was coming up."

"Oh, the one you said you were not going to. Um, hum."

"Um, hum, WHAT?"

"Nothing, I was just calling to check on y'all. I'll call again tomorrow."

"Wait a minute. You just got on the phone."

"I know, but I gotta go."

"Jimmy, I went with my sister!"

"And you left with her too, huh?"

"As a matter of fact, I did. What's wrong?"

"I'm just saying if you were going, why'd you lie and say you weren't?"

"I didn't lie. It was a last-minute kind of thing."

"I'm sure it was. Listen, I'll talk to you tomorrow."

I know he didn't know what happened this morning, but I did, and I feel like I've cheated on him all over again. Maybe his intuition is as strong as mine. I don't get around to doing that laundry; I stay in bed all day feeling sorry for myself. I order pizza that I can't bring myself to eat and watch love stories to mourn the love that I would never have because I had hurt the only man I truly love.

I'm so glad when my baby comes home; she always makes me smile. She's my brown skin joy. Mela sees the laundry dumped out and wants to play the usual game we made up for laundry days. I put her on top of the basket, and I carry her up and down the stairs on top of each load, and she thinks it's the best thing ever. Her smile is my saving grace. I tell her we have to hurry upstairs because daddy hadn't called and we didn't want to miss him.

"I alweady talked to Daddy at Grandma's house, she says in her baby language."

"Oh, you did?"

"Yes. He said he loved me, and Mama (his mother) is going to bring me to see him."

"HE DID?" I fight back the tears as she continues.

"Yes, and will you come too, Mommy?"

"If he wants me to, baby, I sure will." I put her in the playroom and lay on her bean bag while she played. I knew if he had already talked to her, he wouldn't be calling me, and he didn't for about three weeks. I was so lost, I thought a few times about going to see him but didn't want to be embarrassed if he had someone else there, and he was surely within his rights if he did. I had never asked if he'd met someone else, I would be too hurt by the answer, so we didn't discuss it. Whenever he told me to bring Jameelah, I did, and that was that.

It's just as well. I drown myself in work and try not to think about him, which turned out to be an impossible task. I can't even use alcohol to ease my pain anymore. I think that night of the after-party, I must have gotten alcohol poisoning. In the past month, the thought of alcohol makes me nauseated and brushing my teeth is miserable. I had stopped and got a different brand of toothpaste after work yesterday. I could survive without drinking but not brushing; that ain't gon' work.

I get Jameelah dressed for school, then let her watch cartoons as I do every morning. This keeps her from being cranky when it's time to go. Then I go and get myself ready; I begin to brush my teeth and lose all the contents of my stomach. What is going on? The only time I remember puking like this is when I was... OH MY GOD! When I was pregnant with Jameelah, I would throw up every time I attempted to brush my teeth. I drop her off to school and head straight to the pharmacy for a pregnancy test. Lord God, please don't let this be. I know it's all on me, but PLEASE don't let it be what I think.

I stare at the positive result for a few minutes, then think about driving off a cliff; the thought of my baby girl is the only thing stopping me. How did I allow this to happen, why did I let JR touch me, and what am I going to tell Jimmy? JESUS! I call my job and tell them I'm sick and won't be in today. I had recently accepted a job with the Health Department's School Health Program, a position I took a Civil Service Exam for a couple of years back. I was thrilled when they called and offered me the job. There had to be hundreds of people in that room on the day of the exam and at least twelve when they actually interviewed me. When I looked around and saw I was the only black girl, I really thought it was over. But they had chosen me! As much as I hated to leave the doctors office, I really needed the benefits and life insurance the County offered for my daughter. I hate taking off being a new employee, but I have to figure this out, and quickly.

Crying was all I could manage to get done before my alarm rang, reminding me it was time to go pick up Jameelah. My eyes look a mess; she will know something is wrong. I grab my sunglasses to hide the swelling. Thank God she's still naive; she thinks I'm being cool with my shades on. Despite the house being dead quiet as I cook dinner, Mela has to keep repeating herself I'm so spaced out. After dinner, I bathe her and get ready for bed, relieved for once Jimmy has not called. I could not hide anything from him; he sensed it even over the phone. Although I hadn't figured anything out yesterday, I have to report today. I don't want to make a bad impression, and hopefully, it will get my mind off things. I know it's early enough that I can get an abortion, only I don't believe in them. I'm not a perfect Christian by far, and I know sin is sin, but it's some things I feel I couldn't live with. I know God loves us unconditionally, and He Forgives, but personally, I don't think I would be any good if I did that to a child.

The receptionist Sandra, who has quickly become my friend, is waiting and smiling as usual when I walk in. I greet her, but not in my normal happy voice; instead of stopping to chat like I always do, I head straight to my office and close the door. I don't know what to do besides cry, and I can't do that here. I take a minute to regroup in hopes that I can activate my game face, at least for these 8 hours. It's not working; I feel defeated. I lay my head on my desk and will myself to forget about it. A knock on the door reminds me that I'm getting paid to be here. It's probably my boss; I better get myself in gear. I take a deep breath and open the door. It's Sandra, but she's not smiling this time; she looks concerned. "What's wrong, gal?"

As much as I try to hold the tears, they flow freely. She rushes in and shuts the door. "Is Jameelah ok?"

"She's fine," I sob.

"What about Jimmy?" she asks.

"He's good too," I manage between tears.

"Well, Vettra, what's wrong?"

"I'm pregnant, San!"

"Oh shit!" is all she can manage. I second it with, "Exactly!"

"Anything I can do for you, sugar?"

"No, just pray for me, San. I'm going to need it."

I manage to keep myself busy for the rest of the day and give my brain a rest from the situation. Home is inviting, and I get to shut the woes of the world out! Just sitting here watching Jameelah color is so peaceful until the phone rings... It's Jimmy. I contemplate hanging up, acting like it's a bad connection, but that's not fair to him. I act as cheerful as possible in hopes he doesn't sense the heaviness in my heart. I wish he didn't know me so well.

"What's wrong, Shun?" My barrage of petty questions hadn't thrown him off as I'd hope they would've.

"Nothing. Just tired and not sleeping much lately."

"Well, go to bed earlier."

"I'm in bed by 8:30 every night."

"Well, put Mela in her own bed so you can rest better."

"It's a King bed, Jimmy. It's plenty of room for us both."

"Don't get snappy. I'm only trying to help."

"I'm not. Just assuring you none of that is the problem."

"How do you know? Just try changing your routine to see if it helps."

"Nothing will help for at least 8 months, Jimmy." I tried throwing him a hint without letting the words come out of my mouth.

"Why 8 months... Wait, Shun, don't... You pregnant?" he asks in incomplete sentences. I'm tearing up before he gets it out. I can tell from his tone he already knew the answer.

I whisper, "Yes."

"Whose is it?"

"Come on now. You know me better than that, Jimmy."

"I don't know SHIT but what you tell me, and you told me it's been over between you two for months. So, is it him?" I start to sob. "Put my daughter on the phone."

"Jimmy, wait—"

"FUCK YOU!" He yells so loud I jump, fully crying at this point.

"Please listen, Jimmy, please!"

He calmly says, "Talk, Shun. You got 2 minutes."

"Ok, I just need your help. HELP!"

"Please don't scream, Jimmy, just listen. No one knows but Tee and my friend San from work. I don't know what to do; I'm struggling. Can you please just talk to me?"

"Call that nigga. This is his headache, not mine."

"He doesn't know!"

"What the hell you mean?"

"I wanted to tell you first. I didn't want to risk telling him or anybody, and you hear it through the grapevine; I respect you more than that."

"Respect is the last thing you have for me, Shun. But wrap it up. I have to go."

"Ok. I want to know if you think I should abort this baby."

"Again, I can't give any advice. That's not my choice. Put my daughter on the phone."

"Ok," I say through sobs, "I love you."

He doesn't reply.

Almost two weeks have gone by, and he hasn't called back. I had written him a letter to ask if I could come to visit with his mom and Mela the following weekend. He said no. I was hurt, but what could I do?

I'm looking up numbers for abortion clinics when he finally calls. "Hey, Shun, how are you feeling?"

"I'm better now that I've finally decided on what to do. I was just so confused."

"Well, what are you going to do?"

"What do you think? I'm having an abortion; it's no other choice."

"It's always a choice."

"But not this time," I say with my voice cracking.

"First of all, don't start all that crying. It won't help anything. I'm sorry I haven't called. I had to have time to think this over; that messed up my head, Shun."

"I know. Mine too. Believe it or not, Jimmy, it was one night in all these months."

"The one night you went to the party, right?"

"Yes, but I promise on my life I didn't know he would be there and definitely didn't plan on leaving with him."

"Just couldn't control yourself, huh?"

"No. I just had too much to drink, and he drove me home, and one thing led to another."

"Yeah, ok. Anyways, I don't trust you to abort this baby and still be in your right mind to be a decent mother to Mela. If I was home, it would be different. But I can't have you bugging in that house with my baby all alone."

"So, you think having two kids all by myself is going to be less stressful?"

"All the kids your mama got, shit, two should be a piece of cake."

I have a good laugh and feel a little better. He's laughing himself by the time I gain my composure. "I miss you, Jimmy."

"I miss you too, tramp."

"Why are you so mean to me, Jimmy?"

"You know you full of it, Shun."

"I'm not. I was just lonely."

"I understand, and I NEVER expected you not to be with another man. I wasn't a fool, but how could you be so careless? How is that gon' make me look?"

"I know," I said in a child's voice.

"Listen, I will tell my family the baby's mine. You leave that nigga out of it ALL TOGETHER!"

"But we don't have sex, Jimmy."

"Hell, they don't know that."

"You're right, I guess."

"That's all I can figure out to save both our faces, Shun."

Even after I broke his heart by starting a relationship with another man, and being pregnant for him, he is still concerned about my reputation.

I enjoy the next couple of months in peace. I know once I start showing, the questions are going to start flying. I started visiting Jimmy regularly again; that keeps me busy and out of the way. He hardly eats when I'm here, insisting I need it more, and he doesn't fuss at me a whole lot like he used to, either. He's carrying on like this is his baby, and that makes me so sad to have to break the news to him. I let him win on the card table so he would be in a good mood to receive what I was about to tell him. He's talking plenty of junk about winning when I grab his hand and kiss it.

"Girl, don't even try it. Give me my money; you lost." (We bet with his commissary; if I won, I took that amount off what I was sending. If he wins, I add to it). He really thinks he is the greatest, but most times, I let him win because he needs the money more than I do. I tap his behind for good measure sometimes though, because he talks too much junk.

"Look at me, Jimmy."

He lays his cards down with a look of concern. "What is it, Shun?"

"Listen, I REALLY appreciate you being a man and wanting to step up, but genes don't lie. Your whole family looks alike; we may get away for a few months, but eventually, this baby is going to tell its own story, and I don't want you having to backtrack. I know it's going to be a tough pill, but it's really nobody's business but mine and yours."

He looks off in deep thought. "I guess you're right. I was just trying to help."

"I know, baby. I appreciate that and how you've allowed me back in your world because your love is where I feel the safest!"

He blushes. Sentiments are not his thing, but you can't help who you love and how you love them. We sit and stare into each other's eyes, searching for peace in this situation. We don't need any words; our eyes speak straight to each other's souls.

The guard yells, "TIME'S UP!" As I stand to leave, my shirt tucks under my stomach. As much as I'm trying to hide this growing belly, it's coming. He lays his hand on my stomach. "I will love you and this baby no matter how it turns out." I know his pride and heart are both shattered. Yet, he's choosing to stick beside me and that makes me love him more, if that's even possible.

We embrace for a good long kiss. I love him to the end of this earth. Now I have to figure out how and when I'm going to tell the actual father of the child growing inside me because he deserves to know.

I call JR the following week and ask if he could come over to discuss something important with me. He wants to know what's wrong! This is a conversation that needs to be had face-to-face.

"Alright, give me about an hour."

I haven't had a drink since I found out I was pregnant. I have to brace myself for this conversation, so I pour a glass of wine to calm my nerves. I'm on my 2nd glass when the doorbell chimes. I was a nervous wreck telling Jimmy, and he wasn't even the father. I'm really on edge right now. I know there is no future with this man. Not to mention, he has made it very clear he doesn't want more children in prior conversations we had when things were good. But still he deserves to know. Regardless of JR's reaction, Jimmy and I are at peace with it, and this baby will be loved.

He looks a little stressed but otherwise, as good as usual. "Hey!" I invite him to have a seat on the couch and pour him a glass of wine.

"How have you been?"

"Better," I reply, trying to lead into the fact that this won't be a cheerful conversation. "Look, JR, I know we're never going to be together again; that we both agree on. However, I think we need to find some civil ground, as we have a situation."

"And what's that?" he asks, looking nervous.

"JR, I'm pregnant."

He puts his head in his hand and goes silent. I allow him to absorb it for a few moments; I know it's a lot, I've known for a few months, and I still haven't quite adjusted. He finally says "You need me to pay for the abortion?"

"Absolutely not! You know I don't believe in that!"

"And you know I don't want any more kids! I'm doing all I can to keep up with the three I got."

"I understand."

"NO, YOU DON'T UNDERSTAND!"

"Hold up, nigga. Lower your voice. I didn't get pregnant by myself!"

"I thought you were on birth control!"

"I WAS. When we were together, I hadn't been with you or anyone else in almost a year, so I stopped them."

"Well, you should have told me!"

"It really wasn't like we pre-planned what happened."

"Between the alcohol and weed, my mind was clouded."

"So again, what do you want to do?" he asks.

"I'm having this baby, so the question is, what do you WANT to do?"

"I don't want any more kids, period," he says and stands.

"Cool... Go kick rocks with no socks!" I open the door and point for him to leave.

I cry myself to sleep on the couch. My head is pounding, and the ringing of the phone is not helping. It's probably my baby; I haven't talked to her since early this morning. Somewhere deep down, I hope it's JR, not for me, but for this kid. It's so sad that babies have no choice in who they are born to, but the parents can decide if they get to live or die. I'm sorry for that reason alone. As for me, I'm actually relieved he reacted the way he did. With him opting out on being a father, I get to keep my friendship with Jimmy intact; at least what we had managed to salvage after my affair with JR.

"Hello," I try sounding cheerful.

It's not my baby girl; it's her daddy. "Hi, Jimmy. What's up?"

"Why you crying?"

"I'm not..." I don't want him to think I'm crying for JR; these tears are for my baby. "I'm ok... It's just... It's just..." I can't speak.

"Listen, Shun... shhh... shhh... You're going to be sick. Just calm down."

"Ok," I say with snot running. I take a few minutes to regroup and apologize.

"You alright?" he asks in the most loving voice.

"NO."

"What's wrong?"

I rehash the conversation between JR and I, ending with, "He doesn't want the baby."

"Well, I told you what kind of nigga he was. What did you expect!"

"I know, but I'm already raising one baby by myself." My voice starts to shake again.

"Hey, don't do that. You're going to upset my baby."

"Boy, please. This is not your baby."

"It may as well be; that nigga don't want it." I start to laugh; he's so stupid. "See, I made you laugh."

"Jimmy, it's not funny."

"Nah, but it's happening, so we have to deal with it. I got you. However I can help, I always got you."

"I love you so much, Jimmy."

"I love you back, slut."

I laugh through my tears again. "Listen, I gotta go."

"Are you going to be okay?"

"Yes, I feel better now."

"Good. Seriously, you're strong; you always land on your feet."

"OK, will you call and check on me later? If I don't go out to the club tonight."

He says and chuckles,

"Bye, crazy boy!"

"Goodbye, baby."

His affectionate tone soothes my broken heart. I smile and touch my stomach. Well, kid, we have you a backup daddy; that will have to do. I call Mela and let her tiny voice remind me that I'm already a great mother. Jimmy's right; I got this! I run a hot bath and turn on my slow jams. No more wine, though. The decision is official; I'm going to be a mommy again.

It seems as if the months fly by to my 3rd trimester, and I'm bored out of my mind. I don't leave the house much. I intentionally stay out of the way as much as possible; I didn't want to embarrass Jimmy any further than I already had, so I avoid making contact with people unless it's absolutely necessary. If only I had been this careful that night, my whole life would be different, but I can't take it back now. Tasha has been asking me for a while to go dancing, and tonight, I'm taking her up on it. I missed dancing, and I need to get out of this house.

My brother and his girlfriend are downstairs as usual, so babysitting is covered. I'm going to get my boogie on. I call Tasha, and she says give her 30 minutes. She is always down to dance! I pick out an outfit that best disguises my belly and head to pick her up. We go to a local hot spot, Lee's Lounge. You can get the best drinks, pool players, and BBQ all in one stop. With the exception of a few faces I haven't seen before, it's the usual crowd in here tonight.

After I lose a $10 bet on the pool table, Tasha and I play our favorite songs on the jukebox and shoot darts. Music always makes everything better. I'm wet with sweat by the time we're preparing to leave. I had burned off some stress and had fun doing it. I'm selecting my last song on the jukebox when someone taps me on the shoulder. I turn around to this guy smiling and holding a drink.

"Hi, I'm Mr. Lee."

"Oh, the Mr. Lee!"

"That's me."

"Well, it's nice to meet you," I say, trying to slide by him.

"Hold on. I just wanted to know if you were interested in working here. I'm looking for a new barmaid."

I could use the money, and I heard they made good here. "Ok, let me think about it." I didn't want to say I'm pregnant, and I can't right now. "Let me think about it" gives me time to call back later and accept the job without explaining my long dramatic story.

"No problem. I'm always here."

I ask Tasha what she thinks, and she confirms it is indeed good money. I put his number up for later. With two kids and no man, I'm definitely going to need more money! This is my Last Hoorah before my 2nd baby girl makes her entrance into the world.

I've been uncomfortable all day; I know I'm in labor. Jameelah's Aunt Joyce picked her up early this morning. I didn't want to have to deal with getting her situated at the last minute. I pull on a dress and lay across the bed, trying to endure the contractions, but the pain doesn't subside. I can no longer wait; it's time. I call Sandra to take me to the hospital. She rushes right over; she had been on standby all day. She carried my bag to the car while her husband Woody held open the door for me to get in. As soon as I'm in the car, he starts in on me.

"Are you going to the Vet or Sister's Hospital?" He has a stupid joke every time I see him, and even being in labor doesn't stop him from giving me a hard time. I want to slap him, but the contractions are winning; I will have to get revenge in the next round. "It will be ok, sis," he says with concern in his voice. He knew if I didn't hit him with one of my quick comebacks, I was HURTING.

Chapter 17

BLESSINGS AND BETRAYALS

I had been pre-warned that this would be a big baby, but I wonder what is too big. I seem to be having the hardest time pushing this kid out. I'm in so much pain; the tears have turned into screams and threats, and it feels as if someone is cutting open my vagina. WHAT IS HAPPENING! Someone, please just shoot me. I try and lay back and close my eyes; I give up. The nurse grabs my hand and pulls me up with force; she's coming. "You can do it. Squeeze my hand and push." I said a prayer and asked God to help me.

The very next time I pushed, the second prettiest little girl I had ever seen was born. The nurse cleans her up, puts her on the scale, and gasps, "OH MY!" I fight the fatigue long enough to ask what's wrong. "Mom, you have a chubby one on your hands." I was always hungry, and now I see why she was eating everything. Her little hair was super curly, and her face was so fat it took away all the pain for the moment.

San picks her up to smell her fresh baby scent. "My God, Vettra. This is a big ass baby." All the nurses in the room join us for a good laugh. I asked the nurse if I could hold her for a few more minutes before they took her to do the pricking and poking. My father had dreaded me having another baby without a husband, yet he called EVERY single day to check on me after I had told him I was pregnant. In his honor, I name her Johnny Lahjay.

When I woke up and came to my senses, I quickly changed it to Johnia; still honoring him but allowing her a chance in the world. A girl with the name Johnny, born in 2004, would be a running joke forever. I used the L as well, being his middle name was Lee. I hadn't decided on her last name; my legal name is still Gaines, but she isn't his biological child, and I don't want her to carry a name that isn't her bloodline. I ask my mom what she thought, and she says not to ask her now, I had already named her after my father, and then flipped me the finger. I laugh so hard my stitches start to hurt. This lady is crazy, but she keeps it one hundred every day.

It's too much for me to think about. Right now, I'm just happy I delivered a healthy baby after all the emotional turmoil I went through. I had seen JR's mom when I was around seven months. She is another one that spoke her mind straight up. I had given her a hug and tried to walk away, but she wasn't having it. Pointing to my stomach, she asked, "Is that my grandbaby?"

I blushed, not wanting to lie to her. "Ask your son."

"I did after I saw you were pregnant a while back at Lee's. He said he didn't know."

"Ok, cool, Mrs. Pat. Whatever he told you, that's what it is."

"Girl," she grabs me by the arm. "Look, I don't care if y'all two never speak again, but if that's my grandchild, I would like to know."

"Fair enough. He wants a blood test, so I will have it done as soon as she's born, and I'll call you."

"Nah, call me before the test. I can save you some trouble. I know all my kids."

I laughed, gave her another hug, and kept on shopping.

When everyone leaves the room, and I have some privacy, I call her. She congratulates me and asks what hospital and room I'm in. The baby and I are sleeping soundly when the nurse shakes me to tell me I have a visitor. I asked if she knew who it was, and I think she said grandmother. My mom left a little while ago and said she wouldn't be back until tomorrow. It must be Joyce. She says she's every baby's grandmother in the family.

I tell the nurse to let her in. It's Mrs. Pat; I forgot I called her before I passed out. "Hey…"

"Hey, Mama Redd."

"Where is the baby?"

"In the bassinet. You want me to get her?"

"Now you know how many babies I have raised? Hell no. I don't need you to get her; I can pick her up."

I giggle; she reminds me of my own mom, talking mess all the time. She makes baby sounds as she picks her up. She looks dead in her face and says, "Awwww shit, this boy is crazy as hell," and lays the baby back down. I didn't know what the "awwww shit" was, and she didn't explain. She picked up the phone, and the next thing I heard her say was, "Get your ass to this hospital. I know a Redd when I see one," and hang up.

I'm quiet; I don't know what to say. She went back, picked up the baby and asked her name. "Johnia Lahjay…"

"What's her last name?"

"She doesn't have one yet."

"What kind of shit is that!"

"Well, I'm a married Gaines, so I may give her my maiden name, Fryer."

"No, you give her her daddy's name."

"I thought about giving her his last name, even if he wouldn't be around. A child should know their roots. But Mrs. Pat, he doesn't want this baby, and he would have to sign the birth certificate."

"And he WILL!"

JR walks in about an hour later, looks at the baby, and asks how I'm doing. "Good." I keep watching TV.

"Look, JR. This baby is yours, and you will sign the birth certificate!"

"Ok," is all he says to her. Well, damn, I should have called her a while ago; I could have saved myself some tears. True to his word, he came back to the hospital when it was time and signed the papers. He spends a couple of hours with Johnia, then asks when I'm being released because he needs to drop off some stuff for her once we are home. I can tell he is just as confused and unsure as I am as to how we were going to raise a baby in the strain of our situations.

Jameelah is so excited to have a new baby, as she refers to her. "Mommy, can I feed the new baby? Can I help bathe the new baby?" I keep explaining it was her sister, but she likes "new baby" better, so new baby it is! I had plenty of help the first few months, everyone gloated over this little girl, and I welcomed it. I take the time to get rest when people are around because I've started back to work. I had also taken the job at Lee's Lounge a couple of weeks ago because being on maternity leave had hit my pockets pretty hard. All money was welcome right about now.

Jimmy doesn't like me working two jobs with the kids, but the bills don't pay themselves; this is my reality. JR is keeping his word despite the uncomfortable situation. He visits the baby a few days a week and provides her with what she needs when I ask him. Slowly but surely, things are actually becoming civil between the two of us again. And by civil, I mean it's no hostility any more. Right before the baby was born, it had been ugly when we crossed paths. Between my hormones and my attitude, this baby had definitely been covered in prayer.

He was watching the girls tonight while I worked my shift at the bar. He had also brought his other daughter so she could spend time with her sister. She and Mela were busy in the playroom pushing Johnia in the stroller when I came downstairs. I stand in the door and watch them take turns pushing her. Even though they are not much older themselves, it's adorable.

"You better leave before you're late. I know how to watch them," JR says with a laugh.

"Well, three little girls might be a lot to handle for an old man."

He laughs. "Shit, I already know. I got Brandon and Jr. on the way to help". They gon' chill with me if that's okay. That is fine, I love his sons as much as I love these girls. I don't believe in falling out with the kids just because the parents can't make it.

"I really appreciate you JR."

"You know it," he says with a kiss on the cheek. I don't know how to feel about him kissing me; it kind of makes me nervous. I've had a whole baby by the man, and I don't understand why his touch is so strange to me.

I'm zoned out at the bar. Patrons have to call out their orders more than once several times; I was still a little unnerved from earlier. He only brushed my cheek with his lips, but still, I didn't like the way it made me feel. I couldn't wait until 4 am to close down and get home to my bed. JR had called and said my brother was back from the movies around 11:30, so he was taking off to get his kids home. I thanked him again and hoped he wouldn't come back for a while because I didn't want to get confused as to

BLESSINGS AND BETRAYALS | 263

what this was. We were simply co-parenting, so my child could know both sides of her family, just as Jameelah did, even though her father wasn't physically in the home. Jimmy's family made sure Mela knew exactly who they were. In fact, I had to almost fight to get her back some days. I'm not complaining, though. It is tough being the only parent in the home and working so much. I appreciate all the efforts on both of their fathers' sides. When my family wasn't available to help with Johnia, JR's mom and her aunt Rayshawn stepped in.

My love life is NON EXISTENT, but my village is on point! My little brother is MIA a lot with the weather being warm; he's doing what young men do, hanging with his friends in the streets until the birds chirp so the girls and I will have a quiet night, watching movies and eating popcorn! I don't spend as much quality time with them as I'd like, so when the other barmaid called wanting to switch nights, I was more than willing.

I forgot I had called JR two days ago to watch the girls because I was scheduled to work late. I hated bringing them out at crazy hours. It's not until he shows up that I realize I hadn't canceled once we'd switched. I feel awful when I open the door.

"You're going to be late," he says when he sees my head tie and P.J's.

I grin. "This is what I'm wearing." He looks shocked, then realizes I'm pulling his leg. "I switched days with someone, and I completely forgot to tell you I wasn't going in. I'm SO sorry!"

"It's all good. I'll just chill for a minute since I already cleared my schedule. Where's the baby?"

"She's in Jameelah's room watching Dora, of course (Jameelah is obsessed with Dora the Explorer)." He goes in, lays across the bed and starts to watch Dora with them. Good, now I can have some quiet time and not have to peek in on them every 5 minutes because I'm definitely one of those nervous moms. I separate the popcorn, to give him and Jameelah some, then go into my room.

I shut my door, pour a glass of wine, grab my book, and prepare to enjoy some me time. JR knocks on my bedroom door after about an hour. It was good while it lasted. "Come in!"

"Hey, Jameelah is sleeping, but the baby's a little fussy."

I motion for him to bring her to me. "She's probably hungry. I'll feed her."

"Just call me when you're done, and I'll put her to sleep."

Halfway through her feeding she falls asleep. I stop and burp her, tempted to just lay her next to me, but I learned from Jameelah not to let her sleep in my bed. It's tough getting them to sleep alone once you start that. Reluctantly, I call him back so he could put her down in her own room. I'm going to take advantage of this opportunity to get some rest. "Let me know if you guys need anything," I say guilt-free as I close the door behind them.

This is the first good night's sleep I've had since Johnia was born. I wake up refreshed and feeling brand new. Jameelah has gotten in my bed at some point during the night, so I ease out quietly to make breakfast without waking her. I brush my teeth and go check on Johnia, and she is not in her room. I rush down to the guest bedroom and swing open the door in a panic. JR is feeding her while talking and singing; he never looks up. I just stand there with tears in my eyes, wishing Jimmy was holding her, that she was his child, and we could ALL be in the same room. Only it wasn't. I don't know why my heartstrings are being tugged.

JR finally looks up and smiles. "Hey, sleepy head."

"Hi. Let me see this fat girl. You could have woken me up."

"Come on now, this is my 4th child." We both chuckle.

"Honestly, thank you for staying. I really needed the rest."

"I know you did. That's why I decided to hang around. Her little butt has eaten twice since you fed her. I came up the second time, and you were knocked out, so I just warmed the bottles you had pumped in the fridge."

"Thanks again. I'm going to cook if you would like breakfast."

"Sure, I'll keep her until you're done."

Jameelah is wide awake by the time I'm finished. We eat, and JR prepares to leave. Jameelah asks if she can go; he picks her up and tickles her, telling her he's on his way to work. "I'll come back tonight if it's okay with your mom."

"That's fine!"

He comes back that night like he told her he would, and plenty of other nights after that until he's not sleeping in the guest room anymore. The first night he had fallen asleep with Johnia in my bed, I got up to leave, and he grabbed my arm. "We have a baby together. Why can't you stay in bed?"

Since then, it was agreed that we work it out the best we could, because I certainly didn't want any other men besides my family around my children. With two kids and two jobs, dating definitely wasn't high on my priority list, so the arrangement doesn't interfere with my life at all! The first few times Jimmy had called, I simply didn't mention JR was there, then I started telling him it was late when I got off and he stayed the night. Now that we are practically living together again, I didn't know what to say, so I didn't say anything. I still visited him as scheduled and JR and I kind of existed with one rule. Don't EVER take my child around that ashy foot heifer because I would be a fool to think he wasn't still involved with her, nor did I care. Jimmy and I had our thing, and no one would dictate how we did what we did! I realized long ago that Jimmy had my heart and I would never get it back, but I needed human contact and help with my children. Everything was working out fine, until JR broke my one rule.

I'm using my lunch break to take Johnia for her scheduled doctor's visit, and they are particularly behind today. She needs her shots, so I don't want to reschedule. I called JR to see if he could take over and then bring her to my mom's once she was done. I also called my mom to tell her that he would be dropping her off within an hour. Two hours later, my mom called blasting me out for not bringing the baby like I said (she doesn't play about her grandkids).

"Mom, slow down. JR should have had the baby there hours ago."

"Well, she's not here!"

"Ok, let me call him." I call his phone twice, frantic. No answer. God, please don't let anything be wrong. I called the doctor's office and they said she checked out about 30 minutes after I left. I call his brother and his mom; no one has seen him. I asked my supervisor if I could leave for the day telling her I had a family emergency. I get in my car and speed to my house. Maybe she was fussy, and he just took her home, and they fell asleep.

My driveway is empty. I call his phone again. No answer. I'm in full panic mode. I lay my head on my steering wheel. Where is my baby? Suddenly, a light bulb went off. I know damn well. I speed to his girlfriend/ex-girlfriend's house, praying I'm wrong, but the first thing I see when I get there is his car. I take off my heels, grab my bat, and knock on the door. He opens the door, then quickly tries to close it when he sees me. I stick the bat in and push past him. I take my baby from her arms, put her in my car, buckle her in her seat, and call my mom with the address. "Come and get my baby."

"Whose address is this, and where are you going?"

"To jail," I reply and hang up. By the time I got back on the porch, they had locked the door. She was screaming for me to leave or she would call the police. Go ahead, but you need a reason. I knocked the glass out with the bat, unlocked the door, and proceeded to beat him right down. I don't believe in fighting a woman over a man. It was her disrespectful mouth that made me turn around and get her next. On about the third swing to those ashy legs, JR grabs my bat and she runs out the back door, gets in her car, and takes off. I get tired of wrestling with him for the bat and run outside to get my razor out of the car because he got me messed up.

My mom is pulling up with mad people in the car as I race out the door. They grab me like an animal they're trying to capture and force me into my car. I'm crying and yelling at the top of my voice; once the crazy train starts rolling, it's hard to stop it! His phone rings, and he answers on speaker out of habit or stupidity. I don't know which, but my mother hears her call me a bitch, and a new crazy train leaves the track. She tells my sisters Kenya and Ran to take Johnia and my youngest sister Fattie home. I tell mom to relax, the girl has called the police, and I see her sitting at the end of the street (it will be a remix of the Bible in rap before I leave my house running from another broad, but that's another story within itself). Mom yells for Tasha to get in the car and demands I drive. I'm about to slap this bitch because I've made it clear that no one touches or bothers my grandkids.

I just get in the car and drive. I know from experience it's no stopping her unless you want to feel her wrath, and I did not. Once we got close to the chick's car, she sped off. I stop, and mom looks at me with fire in her eyes, so I press the gas. Tasha says, "We are going to jail!" I mean, I'm all prepared to pay the price for my actions, but I don't want my mom and little sister in the cell with me.

Tasha calmly says, "Mom, we can get her later."

"Nope, I got something to tell her right now."

The red light catches us side by side, and my mom rolls down her window and yells, "You got one more—" The girl flips her off mid-sentence. Mom opens the door and tries to pull her through the window. I press the gas a little, hoping she will put her foot back in and let the girl go, but it is not happening; she has a gorilla grip on her hair. Oh God, please let this light change! I'm yelling for Tasha to grab Mom and pull her back in the car. She is NO help. She is literally stretched out on the back seat with tears running down her face laughing. I cannot take her.

The light finally changes, and Mom is forced to let her go once she presses her gas because her leg will be pulled off if she doesn't. I don't excel purposely. I pull over to reason with my mother. "Someone is going to get hurt, Ma. I am taking you home! The baby is safe, and no one was hurt. Let's just quit while we are ahead, or this gets any worse."

She is mad as hell, but it's nothing she can do. I drive her and my sister home, and pick up my kids and my brothers Brandon and Jaime. I wish that Chump would come to my house trying to explain anything; we gon' beat the brakes off him.

I feed the kids, get them settled, and turn on cartoons. I can't wait to shower this crazy day away. I'm applying my lotion and pulling on my nightgown when I hear the doorbell ring. My baby brother, who is always ready to rumble for his sisters, asks if I want him to get it. I laugh. "Nah, lil' killa. I got this one. He's probably coming to get his shit, and that's his best bet."

I open the door, ready for whatever, or so I thought! "Hello. Yvette Gaines?"

"Yes."

"I'm with the Buffalo Police. Please come out, turn around, and put your hands behind your back." It's a tow truck being hooked up to my truck.

"What is going on?"

"We have a warrant for your arrest for breaking and entering and assault with a vehicle."

"Ok, whatever. But there's no need to snatch my truck like that. I will give you the keys."

"No, it's okay. I'd rather fuck up your engine!"

I recognize the voice this time; it's the ashy broad's cousin who happens to be a Buffalo Police. I look her dead in the eyes and tell her to have fun "because I'm gon' beat your ass too as soon as I get out."

My brother is screaming for me to chill while handing me a pair of sweatpants the male officer had told him to bring me. I tell him to go back in the house and call Jimmy's mom to come to get me. I don't know how, but this woman knows everyone in the city of Buffalo. Whatever I needed, she had the answer.

As I'm being placed in the car, the female officer makes a smart remark. "All this over a man!"

"NO, all this was over disrespect. Don't run your mouth if you can't back it up!" She pushes me unnecessarily into the door. "Look, you better ask the last bitch in a uniform how I feel about people touching me."

"You want me to take the cuffs off to see if I'm like the 'last bitch?'"

"Go ahead. But believe me, one of us is going to jail, and the other one is going to the hospital! I know what I'm working with. And If you are scary like that ashy ass cousin of yours, you might just want to do your job and not be a hero." She wisely listens to her partner and places me in the back of the patrol car.

Marion Gaines had me bailed out and back home before the sun came up. When I walk in the door, Jameelah is on the couch looking sad. I pick her up and give her a tight hug.

"Where were you, Mommy?"

The look on my baby's face hurt my heart. It's official, JR and I are completely finished! Our daughter is a blessing that I can't deny, but his betrayal is one I will NEVER forget.

I did not take another call, visit for the baby, NOTHING. Co-parenting was no longer an option, either. I did take her to his mom's when she asked, she could call him to see her if she wanted to, but I made no effort at all! I put all my energy into my kids, work, and salvaging what was left of mine and Jimmy's relationship, or whatever you called it. He was livid once he found out that JR had been staying there, even if it was on occasion. I hadn't told him because I didn't want to complicate things; we were working our way back to the way we used to be. I was SURE it would never be anything else between JR and I. I just enjoyed having him around to help with the kids and bond with his daughter, and I knew Jimmy wouldn't believe that. But not telling him was STILL a lie. That drove an even bigger wedge in the gap that was left from my first indiscretion.

I haven't seen JR since that whole ordeal. I catch an instant attitude when I see him scrolling in the bar like he's the President. I know he has no idea I'm working. I switched shifts last minute. I'm not supposed to be here. We both did our best to stay out of each other's way. He didn't notice me until he sat down at the bar, and I pretended not to see him at all. If he doesn't start none, won't be none, but he better drink his spit because I ain't serving him NA-THING.

He attempts to order a drink, and I walk to the other side. He insists on calling my name, and I insist on ignoring him; I'm at work, and I'm trying to be professional. My little brother is here as my bodyguard due to several robberies that have occurred at some nearby bars at closing on the weekends. People tended to act a fool with females, so my mom had started to keep the kids on my late nights, and he would hang out with me. Tasha was chilling and keeping us company; we played darts and danced whenever it slowed down. This made my nights go faster, but tonight I wish they would have stayed home. I can feel trouble in the air.

After about the 5th attempt to order a drink, JR turns to his younger brother, who was already seated, and says, "She is just ignorant as hell."

His brother loudly responds, "Man, fuck that bitch," apparently to get a reaction out of me, unaware that my little brother is as halfcocked as I am. I immediately sit down the drink I'm making, ask the customer to excuse me, and rush toward my brother, who was all in JR's brother's face before I could get to him. Tasha locks eyes with JR like she was ready to rip his head off! A few of the other patrons walk toward the door to leave. My brother yells, "Call my sister one more bitch!" Before the next B rolled off his tongue, my brother's fist met his face. Oh Lord, guess we are about to act a fool tonight.

As soon as Brandon swings, Tasha grabs JR up by his shirt, and he smacks her hand away. I pick up a bar stool and take his legs from under him, and we go to work. He throws a bottle that barely misses our head, giving him time to get up, but we jumped him again before he made it to the door. Brandon was literally choking the brother out at this point, and it doesn't look like he planned on letting up. We release JR to try and get Brandon under control, but it's a lost cause. I look over through the open door and see Tank and Percy on the Davis's porch, and ask them to help break it up; they are laughing so hard they can offer no assistance. I hear police sirens and tell Brandon we have to go. He's hesitant, but walks outside once Tasha takes his arm. I glance around to assess the damage. There is broken glass, cracked mirrors, overturned bar stools, and spilled liquor everywhere. It's a MESS! It is clear this is my last day working at Lee's Lounge. We have literally turned it out.

I grab my purse and the keys then quickly lock up the bar before the police could enter. The first officer is at the stairs before I can make it to my car. "Ma'am, we got a call about a disturbance."

"Uhm, not here, officer!"

"So, what's with the chaos inside?"

"There was a little disagreement, but it's over. They are gone, and I'm closing down."

"Ok, so what's with these two?"

JR's brother's shirt is hanging off and he is all disheveled. My brother's collar is looking like a V-neck that keeps on going, and he still has fight in his eyes.

"Oh, they were helping me break it up." I look at them both with urgency, as to say, "Y'all either confirming this story or going to jail." They both read my face real clearly; neither say a word.

"Ok, officer, I've had a long night. Can we get going?"

"Both of them going with you?" He points at them again.

"Yep." I nod my head for JR's brother to get in the front and Brandon and Tasha to get in the back. We pull off with the officers watching closely. When I turn the corner, I ask JR's brother for directions to his house. When we arrive, he motions for my brother to step out. Here we go; I'm not sure I have another round left in me tonight. My brother jumps out before I can object, I have no choice but to follow suit.

"Man, you are like a little brother to me, and that is my sister. I hate it had to go this far, and I love y'all." He raises his arms, and my brother pulls him in for a hug; I give him one as well. I'm happy to hug it out, and I'm TIRED! He's right, though; we are like family. Liquor and pride just don't mix, that's it, that's all.

We make sure he gets in his house safely and head home. It's one-stop tonight; we are all going to my place. I want my bed. My phone rings as soon as I pull into my driveway. It's Lee, the owner.

"What happened there tonight?"

"Uhm, Mr. Lee… Let me explain."

"Well, before you do, I have cameras."

With that, I don't even bother to try to conjure up a story. A few moments of silence go by before he asks me when and where he can pick up the keys and tell me my service is no longer needed. "I'll drop them off tomorrow." I hang up the phone without even trying to change his mind. I shower and lay down, but I don't sleep, not one bit. By the time morning comes, I've decided that my time in New York has come to an end.

My mom is devastated when I tell her I'm leaving Buffalo; she is so attached to the kids. She had put her bad habits behind her, and everything she didn't offer us as a mother, she poured into our children, and I am grateful for that. I know it will be tough without my family; we literally help each other with everything, but enough is enough. It's too many regrets here, and I just want a fresh start. I put my house up for sale. My next destination will be somewhere with warm weather and good schools. Being a mom has become my main and only priority; to hell with these men. I can't be with the one I want, so I might as well be by myself; me and buffalo are finished! I had no choice in coming here, but it's all my decision to leave. The only good thing that has come from this city is my two daughters. I will take them, start fresh, and teach them there is more to life than pain and disappointment.

Chapter 18

SEASONS CHANGE

I settle on a house in South Carolina! Whenever we visited Jimmy's son Jay and his mom Shannon in Charlotte, that's where we stayed. I LOVE it there. Charlotte is nice as well, but it's too many people from Buffalo for me.

South Carolina is just as beautiful; a quieter compromise, so that will be my next destination. The house I had decided on wouldn't be ready for at least a month, so I move in with Tasha. I had hastily cleared my house and put my things in storage. I didn't want to stay in a hotel or sign another lease because I would be gone in less than 60 days. I enjoy the time with my sister. It's like the old days when she would come over and spend nights with me.

We are chilling, cooking, and singing in the kitchen when Dad calls. "Girl, turn the music down. 'It's your daddy.'" That's a running joke we have because Daddy is long-winded and hard to get off the phone. I can't make out what he is saying when I answer, he sounds like... "Dad, are you crying?"

"Yeah, Shun." I signal for everyone to get quiet. "Shun, Dott died this morning!"

"Which Dott, Daddy? You mean… your WIFE?"

"Yeah, she's gone." More sobs.

"Wait. Dad, I just spoke with her yesterday. She was on her way to a funeral."

"I know, she just died!"

"Oh my goodness, Daddy. Okay… I'm so sorry. We are on our way." I hang up, broken-hearted. I've only heard my dad cry once in my 30 years of living, and that was when his mom passed.

I call my other brothers and sisters, and we prepare to leave to go lay her to rest and comfort him. She has two kids from her previous marriage, Kim and Demetruis. I know that they are a mess. I will try and contact them in a couple of days, give them time to come to grips with it, because honey, if something happened to Sallie, I would be NO GOOD.

Dott's funeral is very sad and eye-opening, further confirming my decision to better myself; life is too short to be unhappy. We must enjoy our time here because seasons change, and sometimes unexpectedly. It has been a few weeks since we returned, and I'm getting excited as the time gets closer. I had stopped in to check on the progress of my new house while driving back from Alabama. I was assured in 3 weeks I could move in. Every call gave me anxiety, thinking it would be the one informing me that I could leave Buffalo behind for good! I was going to be on my own with two kids, that is both scary and exciting, but I'm anxious to start over.

Someone beeps a car horn, bringing me back to the moment; it's Jimmy's brother, Phillip, dropping off Jameelah. She had spent the day with him and his daughter Jae'lyn who looks more like her sister than cousin. As she gets out of the car, they hug for about 10 minutes like they will never see each other again. Just standing here looking at the two of them makes me flashback to Jimmy saying he would claim Johnia as his own. They would have laughed us out of town, and this lil white baby with curly sandy hair on my hip would not have made the cut. These Gaines got some strong genes!

We see them off, and then rush back inside so I could watch The Jeffersons. Now the phone is ringing. I hate to miss my show; I'm gone call whoever it is back. Dang, it's a number I don't recognize. Could this be good news? "Hello."

"Hey, sis."

"Hey… who is this!"

"This is Ran, girl."

It's my middle sister from Georgia. She changes her number every two weeks. Had me excited for nothing. "What you want, girl? I'm watching the Jeffersons."

"Listen, sis. I called about something serious."

"What's wrong? I sense the worry in her voice.

"It's Daddy Johnny. He's not doing so good, Shun." I sit Johnia on the couch and jump up as if that would make me hear better. "I saw him today at the gas station, and it looks like he was disoriented and hasn't eaten. He looks really sick. Y'all need to come see about him."

I hang up the phone and ask Tasha to look after the kids while I go upstairs and make a call. I call Dad; he picks up on the first ring. I tip-toe around, needing to ask if he's okay. "Hey, Daddy!"

"Hey, Shun."

I hear it immediately; he's not okay, but I don't want him to shut down, so I make small talk. "How's the weather?"

"Okay."

"Have you been back to work?"

"I can't yet."

"Ok, well, how are you doing, Daddy?"

"Not good, Shun! I feel like the walls are closing in on me every time I lay down. I can't even eat."

"I'm on my way, Dad."

"No, you got your own life. Don't worry about me, Shun. Just let me be."

"Ok, Dad. I'll call and check on you tomorrow then. Would that be ok?"

"Okay," he says, sounding defeated, and hangs up. That was my last night in Buffalo.

I pack up my two kids and what would fit in my car, and leave my storage key with Tasha in case the movers come before I get back. I hit the highway to go and see about my daddy; I think this is the fastest I've ever made that drive. I didn't stop for rest, only for gas, the restroom, and food for the girls, which they ate in the car. 15 hours later, I was knocking on my dad's door. When he answers the door, it brings tears to my eyes. In a matter of a month or so, my father is all skin and bones.

I hug him and cry for a few minutes before I'm able to gain my composure and get the kids out of the car. I think I see a slight smile cross his face, as he had never met Johnia. I hold her up for him to kiss; I'm afraid, in his frail condition, he might drop her. Jameelah had seen him a few times but was so used to my stepfather I think she's confused as to why I'm calling him, her granddad.

I help him get comfortable in the living room and get the kids settled for a nap. That was a long ride, and even though I made it a little faster than usual, a car isn't their bed or a proper place to rest. I came out and asked Dad for his doctor's phone number. He objects, saying he was fine, and I should not have come all this way; he could take care of himself. I tell him, "That may be, but you have always been there for me. It's my turn to make sure you're ok."

His eyes water as he gets up and gives me his doctor's number out of his phone book. I take the first appointment of the morning and call Ran to see if she could come over and sit with the girls.

"Sit with them where?"

"At Dad's house, fool."

"WHAT! When you get here?"

"Today! When we hung up yesterday, I was in my car a few hours later."

"Oh, ok. Of course, I can watch them. What time?"

"Be here by 9 am."

"Ok...Wait, you got the little white chick, too?"

"Girl, bye," I say, chuckling. She was referring to Johnia; the name White Chick follows her through life.

Daddy had suffered a nervous breakdown. I was sure that's what it was from the start, but I wasn't a doctor, nor did I know how to treat it. He had literally checked out on life and didn't have the will to live without his wife. I think with his parents being gone and all his children in New York, she gave him a reason to go on, and when she died, he was simply lost. It was also clear to me that my destination had changed; there was no way I was leaving my dad alone. I called South Carolina and explained the circumstances. I also canceled my moving truck because I didn't have anywhere to move the furniture too. Lastly, I called the storage company and extended my lease until I could find housing here, and I didn't know how long that would take. I lost money on a few deals, but so what? There is no amount of money that could replace my father, so I made the adjustments. He has three bedrooms, so the kids and I settle in. This is our new existence for now. We still get good weather and schools out of the current arrangement. I said every time I visited that I would never live in Alabama again; well, here I am.

It took a little persuasion, but Daddy started to eat better and gain weight slowly. Lord knows I STILL can't cook, but that's one thing I don't have to worry about in the South. People bring food to him almost every day, especially his in-laws and church family, then it's a restaurant on every strip, so it's no problem to get him to feed. Once he's a little stronger, he returns to work, and I'm glad! Daddy is a trucker at heart. After his family, his love for that road is the next best thing. I know driving will also help keep his mind from wandering all day.

With him better and back at work, it's time to think about finding a job of my own. Even though I won't be able to actually start until school resumes with him being out of the house, he's my backup for the girls when I have errands and other business to take care of. Still, I figure it can't hurt to at least put in some applications and get a feel for the job market in this area.

Finding meaningful employment is even more challenging than I had anticipated. Getting a head start on looking hadn't helped at all, and I haven't gotten any callbacks. In these small towns, it's either keep it in the family or who you know. I hit brick wall after brick wall. I have been taking out my savings since I've been here and not putting in, and it is dwindling daily; I'm starting to get frustrated.

On Saturday mornings, Dad and I enjoy coffee and hot CoCo as we catch up on our week. I'm looking forward to it this morning; it's been a LONG five days. He asks about my job search while adding a ton of sugar to his coffee.

"Dad, don't you think that's a lot?"

"Girl, don't worry about me. I asked you a question; how's the job hunt?"

"It's not going well, Dad."

"You know, they got the chicken plant... and..."

"Daddy, let me stop you right there; the devil is a lie! I'm not doing any of that. No factory work, no line work, no gas stations unh unh."

"See, that's why you can't find nothing. You can't be stuck up down here, them other jobs for the white folks."

"Daddy, WHAT! Is this Mayberry?"

"It may as well be," he says, and we both burst out in laughter. This is the first wholehearted laugh I've heard from my dad since I moved here, and it warms my soul.

A news reporter is talking about a new Homeland Security and Customs Facility being opened in Georgia. I walk over, turn up the volume, and listen. The Bulletin says they are taking applications and holding open interviews with pay starting at 13-

15hr; now they're speaking my language! Cause honey, the day I move for $6.50/hr is the day I'll be coming to the stage as candy, delicious, sexual chocolate… you get the picture.

My dad looks at me curiously while I'm scrambling for a pen and paper to write down the information. "Why are you staring, Daddy?"

"What you gon' do at a prison, Shun? You don't think that's dangerous?"

"Dad, I've walked the streets of Buffalo, NY: Genesee, Bailey, Walden, Bissell, Goodyear, Sattler, East Parade, Northampton, Spiess, Fillmore and on and on, ALONE at that; I think I can handle it. I'm more than equipped to hold my own!" I think all he'll ever see me as is his baby girl. Little did he know the things life had shown me, and I think it's best I let him keep his innocent perception of me.

I'm interviewed at the prison, and hired on the spot. I knew absolutely nothing about how a prison operated, but I did know from visiting Jimmy all those years the kind of person I wasn't going to be. Some of those nasty guards made me never want to visit him again. I vowed in my role to make people feel like humans and encourage the family to see their loved ones instead of pushing them away. Sometimes, that's all the hope those inmates had, especially the ones that were innocent in the first place or doing an unnecessary amount of time for something simple, but that too is a WHOLE OTHER story.

I caught on quickly, the training is very thorough, and by the time it's done, the supervisors ask if I was sure I never did this before. This was definitely my first time being employed at a prison, but I had been inside enough of them to know how they flowed. I focused on one motto: treat people like I would want someone treating mine. That was it.

As with any occupation, the dudes are hounds, and being a new face in town, they are extra thirsty. I had already gone out with someone briefly when I first moved here and discovered these dudes are just like the ninjas in New York with a lot of lying and scheming; that's for the birds. Anyone who came my way after that got shut down with the QUICK! I just want to do my job, stack my money, and find myself a house so I can move out of my dad's. It has been fun, but a grown woman with two kids and a daddy who still thinks she is 13 is not a good look. I be doing magic tricks, trying to hide and smoke my cigarettes. Once he found a wine bottle, and I thought my life was over. I blamed it on Ran because that was the quickest lie I could think of. She was scared to come to visit for about two weeks. I don't care how old you are; if you're not scared of your father, you weren't raised right.

I'm on a mission! They said this was a job you could advance in quickly and go all the way to the top; that is my goal. I had to check a few of these tomato-picking chicks about pressing me or thinking they were funny, which landed me in HR a couple of times, but other than that, I'm well on my way. The HR manager acts a little stuck up, but at least she doesn't look like she rolled out of bed and just came to work, which is the case for most of these females. She's not from here, I can tell. She's sharp as hell every time I see her, but she better find somebody to play with too. I didn't like her tone the last time I was there, so I'm going to be sure not to go back; I won't have a job.

I asked to be assigned to the 3rd shift and got it. This means fewer people and fewer chances of having any drama. The captains are so nice. They really trusted me on the floors more so than some seasoned people, and I think that was the issue; jealousy. One captain in particular, I think, admires more about me than my work ethic, but he's quiet and shy.

One day he's having lunch in the break room, and I ask if he minds sharing. He says, "No, you can have some," with a straight face, and keeps on eating. I was a little confused; it wasn't a letdown or a pick-up line. I usually know when men are sweet on me. I must have this wrong. Anyways, I'm not here for this. I just like to be right about things.

My hunch is wrong on this one. About an hour into the shift, Lt. Ingram comes across the radio for me to do trash detail. This brother is tripping; it's another officer on that detail. I did it at the beginning of a shift. I call for him to make a meeting so I can change it, and he tells me to follow instructions! Oh, this is about to be my last day because who is he talking to? I needed this job to stack and replace my money, but I'm back on track now. I have found a house, and I will move in next week. You can believe when this detail is done, I'm going to tell him where to go and how fast he can get there.

I roll the cans to the door and wait for my work detail to begin. The Sgt. doesn't come as usual; Captain Drew does. I was confused. Captains only run details if they don't have help and Lt. Ingram is in charge... OHHHHH, he sent him! Chris must have been too shy to approach me. How cute!!!!! I guess I can stay employed a little while longer! If he asks me, I'll definitely go out with him. He's so sweet, and that's a breath of fresh air from the last few guys I've been with.

He doesn't ask me out. I'm TOTALLY embarrassed for thinking he was interested! He talks about the job, where I'm from, my work history, you name it, but not ONCE does he inquire about anything concerning dating. Baby, the intuition has stirred me wrong. Oh well, I have other obligations. Jimmy had moved closer to us, so I didn't have to fly and drive crazy hours to see him, and Dad was demanding I learn how to cook, and that is a task within itself. He insists the girls and I eat too much take out, and that is unhealthy, so I've started to spend hours preparing meals when it used to be pick up and go. I really have no time to date. I guess I just want to know what it felt like to be hit on and told I was pretty by someone who didn't want to go to bed with me and every other woman in the next 3 counties.

Someone had put out a flier about a party at the skating rink in Eufaula. I haven't had much fun since I started working 3rd shift, and a weekend off was unheard of. I'm DEFINITELY making this party, and I'm excited about it. I'm leaving weapons training on Friday, planning an outfit out in my head, when someone calls my name. "Officer Gaines!"

I turn around, but I don't see anyone. I hear it again and look toward the armory; it's Captain Drew. "Yes, sir!"

"Oh, you're off duty. No need for that. I just wanted to ask, didn't you say you live in Eufaula?"

"Um, yea, what's wrong?"

"Well, it's a party over there tonight. Me and a couple of the captains are going to come and hang out. It's not much to do here."

"You got that right, sir!"

"Chris!"

"Ok, Chris, how can I help you?" I'm nervous thinking he's about to ask me to accompany him.

"Do you think you could give me directions? Because I'm from Tulsa, Oklahoma, and I don't know anything about these parts." That explains the accent. I'm a little disappointed again, though. Why are all the crazy, dog, playboy dudes attracted to me, but the one who genuinely appears to be a gentleman, NOTHING.

I give him directions and walk away. I don't even know why I care that he doesn't seem interested. Well, I do know; I've been praying that God gives me a NORMAL man the next time around because Jimmy stands ten toes down on being done with anything but a friendship with me. It's been more than three years since I have been in a real, healthy relationship, and that was with JR before I found out who he really was, so technically, that doesn't even count. I'm 30 with two kids, and time is ticking.

This is messing with my party mood. I dismiss the dating dilemma and head to my friend Ebony's, who watches my girls occasionally. They are busy playing when I get there, so I take a nap, content with being in the same place and seeing their faces before the party. She wakes me up to have dinner with them then practically pushes me out to go home and get dressed. I had met her a few weeks after I moved from Buffalo, and we became thick as thieves. She knows my mom and younger siblings, but somehow, we had never crossed paths. Now we are like sisters that should have been, and she's a second mom to the girls while I work. Once I moved into my own house, and Daddy was back on long distance trips, Ebony had really stepped in to help me out when my other sister's couldn't.

I begged her to come to the party with me, but she refused. She had a whole night planned with the kids; she has three of her own that are around my girls' age. She insists I go and have some fun, and I don't put up too much of a fight on my way out the door.

The bowling alley is dead when I first arrive. It's only a few male officers sitting at a table and a small group of females gathered by the DJ booth talking. I don't recognize any of them from my shift, so I find an empty table and order a drink. As I'm finishing my Long Island, someone walks up and asks to sit down. I had seen her before; she was quiet and looked mean, so I never spoke.

"Hey! You work 3rd shift, right?" I ask to see if she is here in peace or what, because it's clearly other seats she could have taken. She said, "Yes, that's why I came over. I saw you sitting alone. Everyone says you're stuck up and stuff, but I told them you are always nice to me."

I chuckle a little. I do intentionally keep my distance, so it isn't totally a lie. Females always keep up some mess, and I'm not here for it. "Yvette Gaines," I extend my hand to officially introduce myself.

"D. Price," she responds with a firm handshake.

"Well, Officer Price, now I have at least one friend at work." We both laugh and order another round. After my third drink, I'm tipsy enough to skate. It's been years, and I sure hope I don't go out here and make a fool of myself.

I'm standing at the counter waiting on my skates when I hear, "Order me a size 11," in a familiar Oklahoma accent. I do what he asks and turn to walk away. "Where are you going?"

"To sit down."

"I thought you were about to skate. I was going to join you."

"Oh no, hell, you won't laugh at me."

He giggles. "I was waiting to see if you were going out. I didn't want to interrupt you and your friend; that would have been rude."

"Well, actually, I just met her tonight. I mean, I've seen her at work, and I think she's pretty cool, but this is the first time I've talked to her."

"Oh, I couldn't tell the way you guys laughed and conversed. I didn't know you were here. I thought you had changed your mind about coming."

"Why were you looking for me?" I blush, but this big mouth decides it has no words.

He smiles and puts his skates down. "Look, I'm going to be honest. I just came to this party hoping to see you, and I did. So you want to skate or sit down and talk?"

"We can talk," I say, reverting back to a small child, as I often do when I'm nervous. My new friend is now engaged with some other officers, so he and I sit down at the table we were occupying. He asks if I want chicken wings. "I ate before I came."

He looks down and says, "It won't hurt you to gain a couple of pounds."

No, he didn't! I don't know how to take that. "Are you saying I'm too skinny?"

"I'm saying you're just right. So whatever you do, gain or lose, it would be alright with me."

OKKKKKK, so he is smooth. I got to watch him. He might be slick after all, or maybe I should just let a compliment be a compliment.

We talk for so long we are oblivious to the time until a few of the other supervisors come over to say goodbye to him. I don't see my new friend anymore; almost everyone has left, as a matter of fact. I look at my watch. "Whew, I better get out of here."

"Aren't you off tomorrow?

"And how do you know that?" I snap back.

"We are on the same card!"

"Oh!"

He looks around the table. "We have had a few, though, so maybe it is time to call it a night (the cliché would appropriately apply here, time flies when you are having fun). I live in Columbus; it took me a little over an hour to get here. Can you suggest a good hotel? I don't want to risk driving back and getting pulled over."

"Oh, you a lightweight, huh?" I ask jokingly.

"Not exactly, but I see you can handle your own."

I'm tickled again; he has a great sense of humor! Alcohol and I are really good friends. It has gotten me through some tough times, so my tolerance is high! I keep my relationship with alcohol to myself and answer his question. We may not have a lot of things in our small town, but we have plenty of hotels. I lead him to the best ones, and they are all full. I then recommend a few that he could try at his own risk. They were not the cleanest by my standards, but he is a dude, and they are a little more tolerant.

Turns out, they have no vacancies, either. After the last spot, he walks over to my car and says, "I think I'm good enough to take a chance. I've sobered up with all this driving around."

"Are you sure?" He nods, says goodnight, and turns to walk away. Something doesn't sit well with him driving even though he looks fine; I will worry all night. "Hey, listen, I have a spare bedroom, and my kids are staying over with a friend tonight. You are welcome to stay with me if you know how to behave. I carry a razor and a pistol, just so you know, but it's all yours if you want it. "

He laughs. "I can believe that you look a little crazy; I'll follow you."

I give him toiletries and point him in the direction of my spare bedroom. I wait to shower until I hear him close the bedroom door. As I exit the bathroom, I can see the light is off in his room, so I tiptoe to my room and lay there for almost an hour, thinking that he is definitely going to be a good man to somebody, but not me. He is a sweetheart, but during our conversation, he had said he didn't want kids and had no desire to ever be married. Took him right off my list, but at least I made another friend.

I offer him breakfast the next morning; he accepts. We eat and talk a little while longer, and then he's on his way. I drop off Dad's breakfast, pick up the kids, then spend the next few hours pondering what a good time I had last night. As fun as it was, I'm sure that's the last I will see of Chris Drew outside of the prison.

Chapter 19

WHERE DO I GO FROM HERE

I was wrong. On our next rotation off, Chris offers to take me to dinner. I accept the invitation and every one after that unless it coincides with the days we visit Jimmy. Unlike JR, I was upfront with Jimmy about Chris. I told him I didn't see a future because I was a mother, and he didn't want kids nor to be married, but we had gotten pretty close. He had met my daughters and was a perfect gentleman to them, as I suspected he would be. We had been intimate for the first time when Dad had taken my kids to the beach in Florida for the weekend, and a few times after when I stayed over at his place.

It was moving along nicely, and things were good except for the rumors and occasional dirty looks I got from other female staff who were itching to get next to him. He wouldn't give them the time of day, and I knew they suspected I was the reason why. We have plans to go to a movie tonight, but I'm feeling under the weather. As much as I look forward to our time together, I think I have to pass. He is such a breath of fresh air from the type of men

I'm used to being with, but I feel awful today; I think I may have a cold. I called my sister Ran to pick up the girls; she had agreed to let them come over while I went to the movies.

As soon as they leave, I call Chris to tell him I'm not coming up and that I want to rest. He lets me off the hook without hesitation, saying he would spend the day with his friend Pugh instead. All I want to do is shower and lay down. I attempt to brush my teeth before my nap and… OH NO… Here we go again. I sit in the dark for HOURS, the phone is ringing, and my mind is racing. It's a Rite-Aid at the corner of my street, but I can't bring myself to go. I already know what the test will say. However, the adult in me needs to know and not assume.

I drive up at the last minute. My cousin Julie is working and wants to laugh and crack jokes like we usually do, but I'm all messed up in the head. I pay for the test and race home to take it. NO surprise, I'm pregnant. I called Ran to see what would be a good time to pick up the girls.

"Let them stay, sis. They are having fun. I will bring them later."

I'm so exhausted, I NEED a nap! I don't answer the phone for anyone else, not even my dad. I just keep looking at the number and putting it back down until I see Jimmy's call I don't answer, but I can't put it back down, either; I just stare at it until the last ring. When it stops, the tears start; he is going to hate me!

I feel a little better after toast and OJ the next morning. The girls had decided to spend the night, but have called three times already for me to pick them up, and the phone's ringing again; I guess breakfast is over. I toss my plate, grab my keys, open the door, and almost jump out of my skin. Chris is standing on the other side of the door, looking frantic. "What's wrong?" I ask, thinking something had to happen for him to drive all this way, and we hadn't talked since yesterday.

"Nothing. I thought something was wrong with you, Yvette (he can't quite grasp the idea of calling me Shun)!"

"No, I'm fine. Just a little tired."

"Oh. Because you weren't answering your phone, I didn't know if something had happened to you, the kids, or your family. I just didn't know."

I'm touched by his concern; he had only met my dad twice and my mom once, and she broke him in with a spades game, of course. He hadn't been too anxious to go back after that. "No, I'm fine. But I'm late picking up the girls, so I better get going." I need to get away from him. I feel like he can see the baby in my stomach with X-ray vision or something. I'm tripping.

He grabs my arm. "Are you sure you're ok?"

"I'm fine. I just drank a bit too much last night."

"Wait, I thought you were sick?"

"I was, but I just needed something to put me to sleep."

He looks suspicious, but stops the questioning, and I'm relieved.

"Do you want me to ride with you?"

"No, I'm good. I have a few runs to make, and I'll be out for a while. I'll call you when I get back home."

"Ok, he gets in his car to leave. I feel really bad. I walk over and kiss him on the cheek; thank you for being so concerned." He looks a little more relaxed after that.

I avoid Chris like crazy at work and give him an excuse as to why I can't hang out every time he asks. I'm visiting Jimmy in two weeks, and I need to talk to him before I decide anything. I know abortion is not something I can withstand; I just want to know how this keeps happening. I mean, I know women who throw it back for a living, sleep with 50 men a month, and nothing. Then there are those unfortunate people who pay good money to conceive and never can. But not fertile Myrtle. I go YEARS without sex, then with one good wind… BOOM, BABY on the way!

I was on birth control the whole relationship with JR, stopped when we called it quits, and got pregnant the one time we had slept together AFTER it was over! Chris and I are careful for the most part, but there were a few times we were not and here I go. I mean, what is REALLY going on with me and these kids? I go from supposedly not being able to conceive to 2 and a damn possible; I can't deal with this.

I'm a little snappy at work; not being able to engage in my usual deep conversations with Chris is getting to me. I really miss spending time with him. As soon as I have this dreadful talk with Jimmy this weekend, hopefully, Chris will understand why I've been distant.

As much as I wanted this Saturday to come so I could talk to Jimmy now that it's here, it seems too soon. I really don't want to bring the girls, but I have to. We don't see him often, and they love to see their daddy. I had explained to Johnia, on several occasions, that JR was her dad, but gave up when she said, "I know I got two." It was a lost cause, and he didn't treat her any different from Jameelah, so I just let it be.

I tell them when we get there to be on their best behavior; Dad and I have some business to discuss. They agreed, but as soon as he walked out, they ran screaming like they didn't have any sense. I don't get too upset. I missed his beautiful smile as well. I enjoy the moment because, in a little while, it will definitely be nothing to smile about. He gives me a big hug, kisses me on the cheek, and whispers, "Me and you got a problem."

Oh Lord, can he see through my stomach! "What is it?" I ask, trying to joke and feel him out.

"You look like you've been out all night. I know you ain't been out partying and driving my kids on the highway."

I punched him in the arm. "Boy, are you crazy? I worked a double yesterday because I have to take off for a doctor's appt next week."

"Oh, in that case, I'll let it slide." He hugs me again, and I can stay in his arms forever, except these little girls hanging on both legs are hating. "Ok," he says, pushing me away, "let me talk to my kids." He puts Johnia on his lap and sits Jameelah next to him. Jameelah is not big on affection like her dad, but Johnia soaks up all the love.

I stay quiet until he asks me what's been up. I make a face that suggests it hasn't been too good. "What's up?" he asks again, looking worried.

"I'm going to send the kids to the vending machines, and then we can talk."

He sits Johnia down and tells her to find him something good. Jameelah takes the money and asks if she can get chips too. This is the first time I've smiled the whole visit. Kids are so innocent, they have no idea where we are, how horrible it is that he has to be here, but she knows there are chips. I take Jimmy's hand in mine and kiss it once they walk away. Shun, please tell me what's wrong."

"Jimmy, I'm pregnant."

He snatches his hand from mine and signals for the guard. I tear up and whisper, "PLEASE DON'T LEAVE." Still, he attempts to get the guard's attention. "Jimmy, the kids were so excited to come today. We've only been here an hour. Please don't do this to them."

He puts his hand down and leans back. I don't know if it's disgust or pain I see in his face. I'd rather it be disgust. I can take him being mad, even hating me. I can't stand for him to be in pain, yet here I am dealing another blow.

When he finally speaks, I hear pain and anger. "Shun, all I'm gon' say is don't ask me for shit. No advice, no help with a baby name, no sympathy, no understanding. I asked you if you were serious with this guy. You said you didn't know where it was going. Well, apparently, it went somewhere and fast. I should have known when you went all the way to Oklahoma to meet his family, you were lying. You haven't even known him for a year, and you lay up and get pregnant."

I wanted to tell him we had been careful for the most part, but I didn't want to set him off further. I just took whatever he was dishing out in silence. He had moved here to be closer to me and the kids, and this is how I repay him. I let him get it all off his chest without interrupting, and he continues to let me have it until the kids come back. I was thankful; that was the longest 20 minutes ever. Jameelah had warmed up his chicken wings for him, and Johnia was carefully carrying his Pepsi. "You want some chips, Mommy?" they ask simultaneously. I nod a simple no; I don't want to speak and unleash my tears.

Johnia reaches for Jameelah to pick her up because Jimmy's lap is now occupied with food. It's dead silence while they eat. I ask Jimmy if he would walk with me out to the patio area after he finishes his food. "I'm cool!"

"I just want to finish talking."

"We can do that right here."

"Ok, well, they don't know the situation, so I'll use code words."

"They will soon enough," he says rather harshly.

"Not really. I don't think I'm going through with this one. I just CAN'T have another one out of wedlock; my father will not be pleased."

"Well, that would be something to think about before you open your legs."

I give him a sharp look. "Jimmy, my kids are right next to you."

"They are MY KIDS TOO," he yells with his eyes bulging. That's when it's no more reasoning with him. I sit back and end the conversation.

When they finish eating, the kids ask to go out to the patio area and play. Without exchanging a word, Jimmy puts Jameelah on his back and picks Johnia up, and heads out the door. I stay inside and cry until visiting hours are up. I have everything packed and ready to go when they get back in. Jameelah asks if I am sad. "Just a little tired. That's all, baby."

Jimmy doesn't seem as angry once they come back inside. He puts on the kids jackets, kisses them and says "Help your mom drive back; she's a little sleepy."

They both laugh. "She sleeps A LOT, Daddy," Jameelah dry snitches.

"I bet she does," he says, picking her up for one last hug. I didn't attempt to hug him because I couldn't stand the rejection. My stomach has grumbled several times in the few minutes we've been preparing to leave. He passes me the last pack of hot wings he has left. "You need to eat."

"I'm okay," I say, looking at the floor.

He takes my chin, and kisses me on the cheek. "Take the food, Shun. That's a long drive, and you NEED IT," he emphasized.

"Thank you," I say, still looking at the floor.

"And listen; you and I are OVER! But these are still my kids, so when I call, that's what we will discuss; NOTHING else, are we clear? I will always love you, and I will NEVER forget all that you've done for me, but I can't continue to let you hurt me like this." He points to his chest. "I'm done. I still have a lot of time ahead of me. I can't handle that and think about when is gonna be the next time you'll disappoint me."

My heart shatters at the emotion in his voice! "I understand," I say through tears as the girls stand silent. It's not the first time they have seen me cry at the end of the visit. It's usually because I know he can't come with us. Today, I'm crying because he wouldn't come with me even if he could. I don't know how I'll go on without my best friend.

He gives the girls another kiss, hugs me one last time, and simply walks away.

I took off the next two days. I need to figure out where to go from here. I called Chris just to let him know the kids and I made it back safe, but put off seeing him. I tell him I need a couple of days to rest from the drive, and I'll see him at work.

Chris and I are both on 3rd shift, and I dreaded that now. I could avoid him on the phone; it was kind of hard to do at work. He's definitely good at making me feel better, though, so maybe it won't be so bad. I don't know how he's going to feel after I have this conversation with him.

My first day back, I dodged him all night. On the second day, he was waiting for me at the time clock and told me we needed to talk. I know it's about the lack of attention I've been giving him, but I just had to be sure before I burdened him with it. Jimmy had called and told me not to have an abortion because it wouldn't change a thing between him and I. I asked what we were going to do once I started showing. He had gotten so mad when the other inmates stared when I was pregnant with Johnia. They knew I was his wife, and we could not have conjugal visits; it was a rough time for him.

"You don't have to worry about that; I put in for a transfer. I'm going back up North. You go ahead and live your life." I asked about Mela. How would he see her?

"When she goes to Buffalo for the summer, my family can bring her to see me." I tried to convince him not to leave, but his mind was made up; this chapter of my life is closing unwillingly, and I'm lost!

I hang up, and for the second time in the last 5 years, I contemplate ending my life. I have to fight hard to come out of that place and force myself to keep living for my two kids and the one growing in my belly.

I had told Chris we could make a date to talk once I had a babysitter nailed down, but two weeks have gone by, and I still can't bring myself to tell him face to face, so I chicken out and call him on the phone. He answers on the first ring. I can tell he's anxious, and I feel really terrible. He didn't deserve to be avoided that way, but I didn't know how else to handle it. I start by telling him my distance isn't intentional and I have a lot going on with the kids.

"It's cool. But can I ask you a question, Yvette?"

"Sure. What's up?"

He sounds worried. "Are you seeing someone else?" I almost laugh, but the hurt in his voice is not funny.

"No, Chris. I'm not that type of person. I've told you that."

"Well, what is it, then? Because in the last few weeks, you seemed to have changed." I've learned from past experience to just come out with it, so I do.

"Chris, I'm pregnant."

Silence. Been there before, too; I just wait. "Are you sure?" he asks after a few moments.

"Yes. After having two kids, I kinda know the symptoms. But I've taken two pregnancy tests as well." Silence again.

"Well, Yvette, I really don't want nor am I in a position to have a child."

"I understand," I tell him. "I was going to abort it and not even tell you, but I think you deserve better than that. So, you can do whatever you want." He made his position on kids and marriage clear from the beginning, I'm not going to pressure him. I let him know I'm ok doing it alone! "I'm having this baby, you're welcome to be a part of their life, but I completely understand if you can't be." I hang up and lay in my bed and pray Jimmy calls. I don't care what he says; I just want to hear his voice.

After a few heated discussions, Chris decides he can't have a child in the world and walk away; he's a man through and through. By the time I start to show, we become excited about having a child. This is, after all, the biggest bond two people could share. And I love Chris for sure; I'm just not in love with him. As my stomach starts to tell the secret we need to keep quite sooner than we want, rumors start to fly more rapidly than ever. Only a few people know for sure that Chris and I are dating, but that doesn't stop the Gossip Committee from working overtime.

I'm off tonight, and thankful I didn't have to see the side eyes or walk past conversations that would stop abruptly when I came near. The ringing of the phone wakes me from a sound sleep. "Hello! Officer Gaines?"

I start to hang up because I know they are tripping, thinking I'm coming in tonight. As tempting as hanging up is, it's against the policy. You have to be willing and ready when they call. "This is she," I respond in a groggy voice.

"Hey, it's Captain J. Captain Drew has been hurt and is on his way to the hospital in Columbus via ambulance, I thought you might want to know."

I jump straight up and pull on some sweats, a tank top, and a sweater. My belly is all over the place, and I don't care. I've been hiding it at work, but right now, that wasn't on my mind. I called my sister Ran to come to sit with the kids so I could get to the hospital.

I drive that 45 min stretch in about 30 mins flat! I rush to the hospital and discover he is in X-ray, with a broken leg, they suspect. Officer James Harris, who had come with him, offered me some comforting words to calm me down as we waited. A nurse finally comes out and says he is in a room, and I take off, anxious to see him, not paying attention, and walk straight into the Chief of Security, Chris's boss. OH SHIT.

He looks at me and says, "Somehow, I knew I'd run into you here. So, the rumors are true." He looks at my belly and says, "All of them. Come on, let's check on the Captain. We can deal with that later." We walk in together, and Chris looks like he has seen a ghost. "Relax," Chief holds his hands up in a peaceful manner. "No crime has been committed. You two will just have to switch shifts. He can't be your direct supervisor; that's it!"

I sighed in relief. "I thought for sure we would be disciplined or even fired!"

"No, Ms. Gaines. That was never an option! Captain Drew is one of the best captains I've ever seen, and you're a damn good officer. No funny business is going to make me lose two of my best people," he says with a chuckle, and I smile for the first time in months. I've been squeezing this poor baby in this size six uniform, trying to hide her out of fear for our careers.

Yep, HER; it is ANOTHER GIRL. Me and God gon' have a serious conversation when the time comes.

Visiting hours are over. We say our goodbyes, and I tell him I'll be back the next day. When I walk out, Officer Harris is still there. I ask if he needs a ride. He says they are looking for someone from the facility to come get him.

"I can give you a ride if you like (we had talked a few times, and I knew he was from Eufaula)."

"Sure," he replies and even offers to drive. We became friends that night and have been ever since. Chief immediately reassigned

Chris. He would be on 2nd shift when he returned, and I remained on 3rd. That was all we ever heard from him about the matter. It was a different story with everyone else, though. It was such a BIG deal; people know they know how to mind other people's business. It was to the point I was being lied to, on, and about like NEVER before; in fact, I was almost fired. If it had not been for the HR manager Mrs. Stephanie Dunston, I would have been. She turned out to be surprisingly nice and did all she could to help me or anyone else who had a problem. My initial intel and perception of her had been inaccurate. In getting to know her, I realized she was being nailed to the cross, just as I was for being a nice-looking sister who didn't pick tomatoes and eat pig feet. Oh, hating country heifers gets on my NERVES. I had spent all this time disliking her because of the people's rumors, only to find out the very same ones were running me down every chance they got.

After discovering how low down a lot of these people are, I decide to stick to my faithful few on the security side. I now associate with about 20 people out of 450; those odds accurately reflect how much I dislike the atmosphere of this place. Then there's my friend Jamie Holland who works in administration. She's my go-to girl when I need a break from the madness on the floor. I had met her one day while turning in my unit payroll; we struck up a conversation and became inseparable. Don't get me wrong, I can communicate with anyone on an as-needed basis. I'm just careful about who I call my friend.

After days of X-rays and tests, we were told Chris had actually broken his kneecap. It broke in so many places they had to rebuild it. The road to recovery was long, but it brought us closer. He decided to move in with me because he had no family here, and I could ensure he was getting proper care if he was close to me. This did not sit well with my dad, though; he didn't believe in people living together and not being married, so you can imagine the surprise when I told him I was pregnant. Despite Dad's initial disapproval, we all got along really well.

A few months later, I gave birth to another beautiful baby girl: Jabreon Christine Drew. She joined her sisters in wrapping herself around my father's finger. He would stop by to simply see her. He didn't want to hold her, never wanted anything in particular. He would literally just come to sit on the porch in the rocking chair next to me and gaze at her while she sat in my arms. He loved my little girls as much as he loved me, and that melted my heart!

Her birth held him off for a while, and then he sat in on me about giving the kids a stable home and doing the right thing. I would in turn nag Chris about moving back to his place because I was tired of Daddy's fussing, and he didn't let up. I don't know if Daddy secretly got to him or if he genuinely loved me, but the solution was not one I was expecting at all.

I got off early to take JJ to her scheduled check-up; I had asked Chris to have her ready. I had taken a job in the administrative department because 3rd shift and a new baby didn't mix. Chris had taken off the whole day. He didn't miss one appointment, he's a good dad in every sense of the word, so he's usually ready long before the appointment time.

When I walk in, Jabreon is not sitting by the door in her car seat, ready to go like always. That's odd; Chris is very punctual. I call out his name, and he yells out he'll be right there. He brings out JJ and sits her down, then asks if I could grab her bag. Sticking out is a piece of pretty stationary, and I have no idea why it's here. "What is this?" I ask. He says read it. It was one simple line.

WOULD YOU MARRY ME?

My eyes instantly swell with tears. Chris is a wonderful father, not only to our daughter, but to my other two children as well. Not to mention he's a perfect gentleman to me. Every woman's idea of a husband is standing right here, yet the only face I see is Jimmy's flashing before me.

Chapter 20

WOUNDS IN THE WAY

Ignoring my undeniable love for Jimmy and the strong attachment we still share, I marry Chris. It's a BEAUTIFUL wedding; Chris made sure of that! Just like our relationship, he put his all into it. His family and friends had driven down from Oklahoma, making it even more special. It's important to have good supportive in-laws; marriage is hard enough without the extra pressure from the spouse's family. I had only met them twice before we got married, yet they treated me as if they had known me their whole life. Because he loved me, they did too and we all got along peacefully!

My family came from New York, and then there was our new work family that also shared the day with us. Everything was just magical! I had changed my mind about the wedding a million times in my head, especially after telling Jimmy we were getting married. I had asked to come and visit so I could tell him in person. He told me it was no need; he had already left South Carolina and was back up North. My heart was so broken. He had left without even saying goodbye or considering my feelings. We had always told each other everything. This made it all too real that I was no longer important in his life.

It was just as well, I guess. I had made my choice and was moving on with my life. After months of going back and forth with my own heart, I decided to go ahead as planned. Chris deserved a wife and not just a baby mother, and my children deserved a family. Chris is the total package, and I've never had that in a man. I believe if anyone can love me past my feelings for Jimmy, he can.

My father is pleased; his grandchildren have a complete family. He always blasted me out about being so independent and not having a husband around for the kids. I always told him, "They have YOU, Dad!"

"Yeah, but that's not the same, Shun!"

I knew that as well. I love the way Dad cares for my girls, but I know having a husband makes life more stable for them. So, I do the right thing for everyone involved except myself. Even though my heart wants Jimmy, I'm committed to giving this marriage everything I got!

Chris and I are a great power couple. We both have great careers and dominate in our field. To complete the dream, we buy a home together. The yard is beautifully fenced, the porch has a swing, and there's a Jacuzzi and gazebo in the back. I mean, it has all the fixings fit for a Southern family and is every girl's dream. If

I had asked God to let me come to Heaven and make my ideal man, I couldn't have made him any better. Chris treats me like royalty, and that didn't change because we said I DO! He cooks, cleans, pays the bills, and shows me how much he cherishes me every day, but none of it got Jimmy out of my system. I have all his pictures, the hundreds of letters we've written, as well as things he's sent me on holidays and special occasions over the years all boxed away in my closet.

Being one man's wife, and having love as fresh as morning dew on grass for another, causes conflict in my heart daily. Since Chris and I took our vows at the altar, I've been trying to convince myself that what I feel for Jimmy isn't love. Truth is, my reality is as every other cheater. No matter how deep our feelings, it's possible to be with someone else; the same way Christians love God and still sin.

We are celebrating our anniversary today, and I'm not any closer to loving Chris the way I should as a wife, as I was on this same day last year. I'm certain the problems we are experiencing is him responding to the love he doesn't feel from me. I've tried my best to force myself to fall in love with him because he deserves it, but that's a natural action; all the will in the world can't make you fall in love with someone. It seems, as of late, all we do is argue.

We are in the middle of one of our screaming matches when the phone rings. I welcome the disruption because this conversation is going around in circles. "Hello." I hear crying. "Hello," I repeat, trying to catch the voice on the other end.

Finally, a female voice says, "Shun, Deddy is gone." It's Jimmy's sister Paula.

I ask, "Has anyone told Jimmy?"

She said, "They had, and he isn't doing well."

I hold my face together as best I can because I definitely can't handle Chris's judgment right now. I tell her to let me know the arrangements as soon as she can, give her my love, and hang up. My eyes are quickly filling with tears, so I excuse myself to go pick up the kids from their play date. As soon as I left the house, I cried uncontrollably. He was not only my father-in-law; he was my friend. I can't imagine what my poor Jimmy is going through. All he talked about was his car business with his dad once he came home, and now that would never be.

I cry so much that my head hurts. I go to the park and sit until I gain my composure. How am I going to tell my little girl that she won't be seeing her grandfather this summer or ever again in Buffalo! I pick up the kids about an hour later and return home. Chris is ready to resume the argument when I get there, but I'm just not in the mood. He asks why I'm so sad, as if I'm still married to Jimmy. Little does he know he's not far from the truth. There's no need to get into that now, though; some things are best left unsaid.

When Jimmy calls the next day, the hurt in his voice breaks my heart all over again. He's very strong, and it's hard for him to show emotion, but I can tell this is cutting him like a knife, as is to be expected! I listen to him and pray for him. That's about all I can do given the circumstances. But I wish I could hold him in my arms. I can only imagine what he is feeling; the mere thought of losing my dad makes my heart bleed!

My sympathy for him, compounded with the pain I'm causing Chris, keeps me up all night! The loyalty I give Jimmy should be given to my husband, who's nothing but good to me, but no matter how much I try to completely surrender to this marriage, it's not happening. I'm booking the flights for Jameelah and I when Chris walks in and stands in a defensive stance. I complete the reservation, then ask what the hostility is about. I don't know why Mela can't go alone. I try to ignore the pain in his voice because I know exactly why it's there; he doesn't trust me and it's tearing us apart. I simply answer, "I divorced him, not them; they are still my family." That's easier than telling him I'm still in love with Jimmy, and I always will be.

I kiss him on the cheek and walk away. I can't stand to look into his eyes any longer because I know he deserves so much better.

As soon as I get my rental car, I go straight to Jimmy's mother's house to drop off Jameelah. I stay long enough to say some hello's, kiss a few babies, and then leave for my sister

Tasha's, where I will be staying while I'm here. I need a drink to ease my mind. The thought of burying my father-in-law and seeing Jimmy for the first time in 2 years is too much; I need to come down. Chris has been calling me back to back, non-stop, despite me telling him we had made it safely and I would call him when I got settled. I reach in my purse, put the phone on silent, and proceed to my sister's to drink it all away. She is in good spirits as always, and I feel better immediately seeing her and my little brother Bubba. We drink and play spades until I forget my misery, at least for the moment.

Once it's quiet, my life is still calling, and so is Chris. Let me answer before he literally blows up my phone, ringing it like crazy. "Hello," I answered, half annoyed. I know the kids are fine, and so is he. I spoke to my dad about an hour ago. I don't know why it's so important to argue at a time like this.

"You lying bitch," is all I hear on the other end.

WAIT... WHAT! "Who the hell are you talking to, Chris?"

"YOU! You told me you didn't talk to Jimmy anymore; you only kept the pictures up for your kid's sake. Well, what about the shit in this box?"

What the hell! Jimmy knew I wouldn't be home, why would he send a b... "WAIT, what box are you referring to Chris?"

"The one I found at the top of your closet."

I'm on FIRE with anger; I let him have it! "Why would you be in my personal shit?" Without giving him time to answer, I started screaming. Neither one of us gets a word in edgewise. With all the screaming and shouting, nothing is heard! I tell him not to call me again and slam the phone down. I will communicate with my dad concerning my girls for the next three days. He can go straight to hell. Nothing like being wrong and getting mad because you're busted; that would be me right now!

The next three days go by like a leaf in the wind. If I didn't have two other children, it is highly unlikely that I would even return to Alabama. Daddy was much better now, even dating again, and I don't want to put another day into a marriage I know isn't going to work. They hadn't let Jimmy attend his father's funeral, which broke him even further, but Jameelah and I had visited him before we left. All I want is to be close to him during this time. However, I have responsibilities, so I board the plane with a broken spirit and a clouded mind.

Chris is waiting at the airport when we land. Seeing him agitates me even more. I hadn't spoken to him since our argument. I assume my dad had asked him to pick us up when I called for a ride. We exchange a simple hello, he hugs Jameelah, and then we drive two and a half hours from the airport in silence. We don't discuss the box, my feelings for Jimmy, or anything else once we make it home. We just kind of existed for the next few years! Putting on smiles when we needed to, talking only when necessary, and tip-toeing around each other because we want this to work for the kids. We continue on this unhealthy path until 2011, when tragedy strikes again.

We are driving to work together as we do every morning when my phone rings. "Hey, Dad."

"Hey, Shun. Who's driving right now?"

"Chris," I respond. "What's wrong?" I had prepared Dad's breakfast and meds before I left, and he had said he was good. He never calls me on the road.

I detect sadness in his voice. "Daddy, please tell me what's wrong."

"Your mother, Shun, she didn't make it."

"Make it where?" I just talked to her last night before bed. Mom had moved back to Alabama shortly after I did. The Buffalo weather and her health were a bad mix; she missed the sunshine. She went into the hospital a few days ago to have a procedure done on her knee and was sent next door to the rehab until she would be able to walk and put pressure on it again. I had stopped by and brought her dinner two nights straight. The kids had already taken her food by the time I got off yesterday, so we just talked and laughed until we cried about how fast she ate the plate Chris sent . I told her I would be there to see her after work today, and she hadn't mentioned getting released, so I'm confused as to where she didn't make it to.

I ask him again to tell me where my mother is, a little sterner this time.

"Shun, she died a few minutes ago." I scream so loud it alarms Chris; he swerves and pulls off the road.

"What is it, Yvette?" he asks, panicking himself.

"My mother just died. Please take me home," I managed to tell him through sobs. I literally scream all the way back to Eufaula; I don't know what else to do. I thought when we buried my stepdad, who had succumbed to a stroke about a year after they moved from Buffalo, there could be no greater pain. Burying my mother proved me wrong. This is a pain I wouldn't wish on my worst enemy. Despite the rocky relationship my mother and I had growing up, she was still my mother and the best friend a girl could ask for. She had taught me things NO SCHOOL EVER COULD. We managed to mend our relationship after Jameelah was born. Once she came out of the streets and I recognized her lifestyle was more of an illness than a choice, I was able to forgive her. When I learned to see past my own pain, we became really close. She was the best grandmother to my kids that she could be; all of our kids, for that matter. I think she poured into them what she missed out on giving us, and I was okay with that. It's impossible to go back in time, but we can choose to make the most of the time we have left, and we did just that.

"Mommy!" I hear Jameelah call from the front of the house. I have been held up in my room for two days. I don't know how to function anymore. "Yes," I answer.

"My daddy is on the phone." I had told her not to tell her father about grandma dying. I asked her to let me do it. "You want to speak to him, Mommy?"

"Yes, I'm coming, sweetheart." I sit on the edge of the bed and prepare myself to tell him something else that I know will break his heart. Chris walks out of the den, closely in tow, as I make my way up front where she is. I'm sure by now they all know he's the cause of our arguments because all we do is yell.

I look at him, irritated because I don't need an escort to the phone. "Hello," I say, trying to sound normal.

"Hey, Mela said you needed to talk to me. Is everything ok?"

"No... Jimmy, my mom..." Sobs.

"Shun, please don't say that."

"Jimmy, she died," I say, almost dying myself just to hear her name and death in the same sentence. I give Jameelah back the phone because I can't even contain myself. She is crying and trying to console me; her little hands are rubbing my back.

"I know. I will, okay?" I hear her responses to her father. "Mommy, Daddy said not to cry, and he loves you."

Chris snatches the phone and says, "I can take care of my own wife," and attempts to hang up.

I snatch the phone; instantly sadness turns to anger. "Jimmy!" I called his name, hoping he didn't hang up.

"Yeah," he replies with emotion in his voice. I try to cut my tears. I should have been more mindful. My mom was his friend, as his father was mine; he loved that crazy lady. I often wondered if she knew she was my mother and not his. She always sided with him in disagreements and made sure to tell anyone who would listen that she loved Chris, but Jimmy was her only Son-in-Law. On more than one occasion, I had to remind her that I was married to someone else, whether she liked it or not. She would respond, "I don't give a damn about a piece of paper; I'm talking about your heart." It was funny how I had spent years trying to guard my heart, so no one knew Jimmy still resided there, but mom knew; mothers always know.

I called my supervisor and told him I would be extending my bereavement. I need to clear my mind, and I'm in no condition to be in a prison where you should be focused and alert at all times. I take the girls to school so I can get the house back in order. Everyone had been so wonderful assisting during mom's burial, but when the smoke clears and it's just you and the walls, it can get the best of you.

I occupy my mind deep cleaning the house from mom's repast and all the house guests. The phone rings, and I think about not answering. I'm glad I did; it's Jimmy. "Hey, Shun, how are you doing?"

"The best I can, Jimmy. How are you?"

"I'm hanging in there."

"That's great. I've been waiting for you to call so I can talk to you in peace."

"Ok, what's on your mind?"

"With the death of my mom, Chris has really been here, and through all my wrongs, he continues to be a husband. I have been very unfair in our marriage, yet he still gives me his all every day. Please try to understand that we shouldn't talk anymore. It's too hard for me to be a good wife to him when I still feel so attached to you."

"I understand."

"Are you sure? Yeah, I'm good."

He is not, I can hear it, but it's time to let go. "Take care of yourself, and I will continue to send you money every month. Just promise once your feet land on free ground, you'll let me know! Deal?"

"Deal!"

"I love you, Jimmy!"

"I love you back!" And with that, he hangs up. I cry and kiss the phone for a long time as if he can feel it and vow to give my marriage the best shot I can. I had worked myself up so much I fell asleep and missed my alarm to pick up the kids. I'm frantic when I wake up and notice the time. I rush to pick up JJ. I run to the door of the Church where the daycare is located and find Mrs. Jane getting her prepared. She is the second to the last child there. I apologize for being late, telling Mrs. Gloria, the other daycare provider, I was a little preoccupied.

"Don't worry about it, baby. Sit down."

"I'm fine," I lie through tears that keep randomly forming.

"Listen, baby. I'll bring her home. You go get yourself together."

"No, ma'am. I'm ok, really. I have to pick up my other two girls from school as well."

"I will get them too."

"I can't ask you to do that."

"You didn't ask me; I'm offering. I'll take care of the kids." And she did, that day and every day after. Me too, for that matter. Mrs. Gloria, Sister Samuel, and Sister Cunningham had gotten together with some of the other members of Tabernacle Baptist Church to bring over food and donations toward my mom's services, and I had only been attending there a little while. I thought she had done more than enough for my family. However, she continued to look after us, becoming a mom to me in the absence of my mother, and a grandmother to my children. Her whole family soon followed suit and took me in as their own. God always gives us sugar when life is pouring on the vinegar. The void of losing my mom is less painful because they made me feel welcome immediately. However, the void in my marriage isn't getting any better. Even though I have stopped communicating with Jimmy and started putting all my energy into my husband, we are still struggling.

Chris and I decide to turn to the Church to save our marriage; nothing else we've done is working. We are willing to do whatever we can to hold this thing together. Joining the Church keeps us cordial with each other, but it does nothing for the intimacy part. Church or no Church, this marriage is doomed; it's too many wounds in the way. Rededicating my life to Christ was not for nothing, though; I feel myself moving closer to God.

Chris and I eventually separate in house. No one knows, not even my father or children. We continue to go to work and attend Church as husband and wife because what's going on in our house isn't everybody's business. We interact at home, as mom and dad, but once everyone settles in for the night, I go into the other room.

Tonight, I'm extremely tired and fall asleep before I can switch. I had promised my sister Ran that we were going out, but sleep had gotten me first. I'm sure it's her calling this late to curse me out for leaving her hanging. My gospel music is still playing softly when I answer the phone. I use it to wind down at the end of each day. I'm gon' need it now for sure; this girl is crazy.

I look at the caller ID; it's my sister's number in New York. I look at the time, and it's almost midnight. This can't be good. My hand starts to shake. I thought about not answering briefly but decide against it; I'll find out later, regardless. "Hello."

"Hey, sis."

"Hey, girl. What's wrong?"

"Bubba got shot!"

I zone out. Not my baby. I raised that little boy like my own. He and Jameelah grew up like sister and older brother more than uncle and niece. I make myself ask the question, "Is he dead?"

"No, it's in the leg."

"Chris." I shake him to wake up, but he doesn't answer. I know someone who never sleeps nor slumbers. I get on my knees and thank Him for sparing yet another brother. This song hits my spirit, "Something Happens(Jesus)" by Bishop Paul Morton. I begin to sing it full of gratitude. I don't know why, but at this moment, I remember that I'm leading a song in choir tomorrow.

I text Michael, the Minister of music, and tell him I won't be able to sing in the morning. I'm exhausted from crying, and I know I won't be in any shape to sing in the next few hours. He texts back immediately, saying he understands, and as always, he forwards me a scripture and words of encouragement. He's an awesome brother in the Lord, his words give me a sense of peace, and I drift back off to sleep. By the time my alarm goes off, I'm not in the mood to go to church. I call Mrs. Gloria who is, among the many roles she plays in my life, also the Choir President. "I'm not coming to church today, Mama. I'm not feeling well."

"Baby, I don't know what's wrong, but Church is just what you need."

"Ok," I tell her, ignoring my sadness, "I'll be there." I roll out of bed, ask God for strength, and start to get myself and the kids dressed. All true worshipers know that no matter what you're going through, no matter the circumstance or how dim it seems, if you can just make it to the house of the Lord, something really does happen. God causes all the anguish you feel to be replaced with His love and unspeakable peace. And sure enough, as soon as I walk through the doors and see Sister JJ's sweet smile, I know I've made the right decision to press my way on.

I get the kids situated next to Ms. Sallie and Yolonda, who usually watches them for me when Chris is working on Sundays, and I head to the choir stand. I'm glad to be in the house of the Lord, but I still can't seem to praise Him like I want; my heart is heavy.

The choir is on to sing next. I have to be strong. My eyes swell with tears before we sing the first verse, I exit the choir stand to go get myself together. Sister Paige follows me.

"Something told me to come and see about you. I noticed something wasn't right with you in the spirit. You just weren't getting your praise on as usual."

I shared with her that my baby brother had been shot, and it was weighing on me. She gives me a much-needed hug and assures me all is well. I compose myself and return to the choir stand. As I take my seat, Michael stands up to give a testimony. Mike is known for his testimonies, and they are always long. I smile inside, thinking this is just what I need to get my mind off my situation and give me time to regroup before our next song. Instead of taking my mind off my situation, his testimony is about my text to him last night. Although he never calls my name, I know he's referring to me, and I'm grateful that God is this concerned about me. He starts with him never knowing the feeling of having a brother being shot but says he could only imagine. He says, "The spirit is leading me to do this song, and I hope that it brings Sister Yvette some comfort."

He begins to play "Something Happens(Jesus)". I almost pass out. I'm sure most of the church thinks they are tears of sorrow, but they are tears of joy. Having a personal relationship with God is unexplainable. Now, how did Michael know, except by the Holy Spirit, that this is the very song I used to get me through tough times and had gotten me through just last night? I'm not perfect; I have my faults, and even being born again doesn't exclude you from falling short. However, I feel this is certainly God's reassurance that He's always close to me and even my thoughts are in line with His. The moment I release and start to praise, I know my brother is going to be JUST FINE.

I wish that was true for my marriage. A year and a half has passed since we joined the church and nothing has changed. We are still going along, to get along. I just switched beds a little while ago with my youngest daughter. I sleep in her room and put her in the bed with her daddy. She thinks it is the coolest thing in the world when she wakes up in the morning, sort of like our little private game. She has no idea that her parents have lost any desire to be with each other; even sleeping in the same bed is too much!

My phone rings as soon as I lay down. Hmmm, it's a 716 area code, but I don't recognize the number. Lord, please don't let this be any bad news. I'm just getting back to myself from dealing with the scare with my brother.

"Hello!"

"Hey, Shun."

My whole body gets still. He has been respectful of my wishes, and we haven't spoken in over a year. However, I still sent his money and kept up with him through the family. "Jimmy, where are you calling from? Is everything ok?"

"Yes, everything is fine. I'm just calling to tell you not to send any money next month."

I sit straight up, then ask, "What do you mean?" I think I know what he's implying, but I need to hear the words. "Are you home, Jimmy?"

"Yeah, I made it… Thank you for everything you've done. I'll never forget it."

My eyes fill with tears. Thank you for making it home safely like you promised me you would."

"No doubt… You take it easy, Shun!"

"You do the same!"

He ends the call before I can say, "I love you." Maybe that's for the best. I get out of bed, get on my knees, and thank God for protecting Jimmy while allowing my pillow to catch my tears so I don't wake anyone. This has been a LONG 15 years. Lord, please let the world be kind to him; he's paid his dues and THEN SOME.

My attitude is much more positive in the next few months. I'm feeling optimistic about life. Chris, however, doesn't share my enthusiasm. Our silent separation and my brief affair with a guy in a neighboring town has taken its toll.

Work is super hectic today, and I've gotten paged three times from Central Control informing me I have a personal call. I finally make my way back to my office to see who's been calling. It's Mrs. Gloria; she left a message saying it's important. The kids' schools would have called directly, my dad is on the road, and Chris is at the restaurant we had opened after his employment had ended at the prison. I hope nothing has happened to one of my God siblings. Mrs. Gloria and her husband Tweet have three children: Star, Courtney, and a son, Maurice. They are like my sisters and brother, so she would definitely let me know if something was wrong, and this makes me nervous.

I dreadfully dial her number, not knowing what to expect. She asks me if everything is ok at the restaurant. No one is answering the phone or coming to the door, but the lights and T.V. are on.

"Let me call you back, Mama!" I called Chris 4 times. No answer. I call my sister Fattie and ask her to go by and check things out; she only lives down the street from the restaurant. She calls back within 10 minutes, saying the same thing: everything is on and Chris is not there. She says she even drove by my house, but his car was not in the driveway.

I'm panicking now. I know he was there this morning; I had stopped by on my way to work and picked up the orders for the staff at the prison as I did every morning. They would give me the money the day before. He would get up at 4 am, open up, and get them prepared before my shift started. He had given them to me and wished me a good day; he seemed fine.

I go straight to the Chief's office and tell him I have an emergency and need to leave. I'm calling Chris the whole time I'm on the highway, but I never get an answer. I pull up to the restaurant and pray before I enter. Lord, please let him be okay. I haven't been the best wife to him, but I do love him and he's my daughter's father. I'm shaking, not knowing what I will find. Everything appears normal when I go inside except the heat, T.V, and fryers are on, and no one is there. I turn them off, secure the doors, flip the open sign to close, and race home. I check the house phone first to see if there is a message since I haven't been able to reach him on his cell. Nothing!

I need to change my work attire and calm down before the kids get home; I don't want to scare them. I turn on the light, walk into my closet, remove my shoes, and that's when I see it. His whole side is empty. Not one shoe on the rack, not one piece of clothing is here, only hangers where his things used to be. I snatch open his drawers. They're empty; he has left me.

I sit on the bed in disbelief until I hear my kids' bus pulling up. I'm grateful JJ started school this fall and they are all together. I can deal with their reactions all at once. I put on my mommy face and greet them with a smile. I'm never home this early, and rarely before they are in bed for the night, so I get lots of hugs. They don't know how desperately I need them.

I'm not ready to break the news to them just yet, so I made dinner (Chris had successfully taught me how to cook finally). I'm no master chef, but at least I can feed my family. We eat, and then I put on a movie to create an atmosphere to tell them Chris is gone. I sit on the couch in the middle of them. "Girls, I have something important to discuss with you all."

I'm sure they already sense something is wrong because they have been quiet and cooperative since they've been home, and that doesn't happen voluntarily with these three little girls. "I'm sorry to say this, and I know it's going to hurt, especially you, JJ, but Chris has left, and I don't think he's coming back. As a matter of fact, I don't even know where he is," I say, fighting back tears.

"We do, Momma," they echo.

"What? Where?"

"Okahama (Oklahoma)," Jabreon says in her little baby voice.

"How do you know that?"

Jameelah says, "he told us he was going there and that he loved us this morning. He said he was moving back home because he wasn't happy here anymore, then he put his suitcases in the car."

"He brought me all these Barbie dolls this morning, too," JJ says, pulling them from her book bag.

"Ok, these are so nice," I say using my best mommy voice. "Well, girls, just know we are going to be FINE." We know mommy, they sound more assured than I feel; I didn't have a plan for this!

The three of them rally around me to give me more hugs and kisses, then ask if they can go play with the dolls now. "You sure can. Mommy is going to shower and lay down," I say with a fake smile, struggling to not to lose the battle with my tears.

I go into my bedroom and call Chris on the house phone. "Hello…" he answers this time.

"So, this is what you do!"

"Yvette, you don't love me, and I'm tired of living this way."

"SO YOU WALK OUT without any warning! No plan, no conversation, no NOTHING. Just leave me high and dry… THAT'S FUCKED UP, CHRIS!"

"You never wanted me or the life I tried so hard to give you, so you figure it OUT!" he says before hanging up. The dial tone blares for a few minutes before the shock wears off, and I'm able to put the phone down. I take off my clothes, get in the shower, and cry until the water turns cold. Then I emerge again as Superwoman. Those will be the LAST tears I cry about this!

Chapter 21

FINDING ME

I bury myself in work. Chris has only been gone a little over two months, and I'm already up for a promotion. I decline. I'm already knee-deep with juggling the restaurant, trying to be a good mom, and still remaining active in Church. With the restaurant being the most challenging, I'm in the process of selling my lease to a company that wanted it before we acquired the building. I have already cleared most of the things out, keeping only the sentimental things and selling the rest. Chris was the master behind the recipes and dishes; it was falling apart without him. Maintaining a business properly and having a full-time job has become too much.

Dad helps tremendously with the kids, but I can see he's worried about me. A promotion would mean more obligation and responsibility, and I can't handle that right now. My rhythm has been so off lately. I think Eufaula may have served its purpose; it's time to move on.

I came solely to see that my father would be ok and he's doing well; my purpose here has been served! When Jameelah graduates high school, I'm going to my original destination of South Carolina or maybe Florida. My friend Debbie moved there a few years ago and swears it's the place to be. In the meantime, I just maintain my single mom work life as I was doing before I married Chris, operating out of habit and schedule while the months fly by.

Eventually, I successfully got out from under the contract with the restaurant. That's one less stressor in my life, but I still work crazy hours at the prison. I love what I do, but it has its days. Today seems like it is going to be one of those DAYS. I haven't been on shift for 10 mins, and I'm already getting called to Administration. I have no idea what for this time, but I'm prepared for some foolishness because they are always on one with me.

I'm told to sit down and close the door when I walk in. HERE WE GO.

"Good morning!"

"Good morning," I reply, unenthused.

"Listen, Mrs. Drew. The position of Unit Manager is open again, and I want you to apply."

After I recovered from defense mode, I quickly started to explain that my life is still unraveling. Going through the divorce and just finalizing the contract on the restaurant has me spent! I want to breathe for a minute and not add more to my plate right now. He leans forward and says, "I've allowed you time to feel sorry for yourself. Divorce is a tough thing, so when you passed up the last promotion, I didn't say a word. However, I would be less than a superior to watch you throw away your career fucking around in Administration, tossing around papers." He takes off his glasses, looks me directly in the eye, and says, "GET YOUR SHIT TOGETHER; apply and do well."

I sit motionless, with tears in my eyes! After taking a few moments to gather myself, I wipe my eyes and leave his office, understanding the assignment. I passed that board with flying colors. I didn't miss ONE question.

When my promotion is announced, half the facility is thrilled! Apparently, I was the White Horse they had been waiting on since my husband and a few of the other original Captains and Lieutenants who started with us left. I take pride in what I do, and I do it flawlessly! Chris and I didn't make it as husband and wife, but we were a hell of a team on that floor. The staff knew when they saw us coming for those 8-12, sometimes 16 hours, whatever the shift was for the day; they were SAFE! He taught me everything I know, and he taught me WELL. The fact that he's no longer working with me doesn't matter. I still perform to the best of my ability. His motto was show up every day and work as if someone is watching, even if they're not. I'm working with a purpose to move on. When I do leave this area, I'll be ready for my next step, Chief of Security, and that's when I can slow down and focus more on my kids. The prison has facilities all over, and I plan to make a lasting impression so it will be easy to transfer!

As with any career, everything about this role isn't sweet. This is my 3rd promotion since I've been employed here. The work is second nature, but standing on this concrete for hours is no joke! Tonight, I'm especially feeling it; that 16 hour shift has whooped me. I take a long hot bath in Epsom Salt and crawl under my cool sheets. Sleep finds me immediately.

My phone ringing is the most unpleasant sound when I'm resting well. I decide to ignore it. It rings back-to-back three times. Knowing the rules about availability at work, I reluctantly answer in the dark. "Hello... No one says anything. I look at the caller ID; it's a New York number. I start to panic. I can feel something off in my spirit; my intuition never fails me.

"Hey, Shun," someone finally says, "Quawn was just shot and killed."

I go blank. "You mean Nephew Quawn?" I need to be sure!

"Yes," she sobs.

"Oh no," is all I can say before my own tears start to fall. We lost my nephew Jireh in 2013 in a fatal car accident, and my heart still hasn't recovered from that. Lord, I need you to give me the strength to handle this. I prepare to travel to Buffalo for the second time in a matter of weeks. I was supposed to attend my brother's wedding and had made plans to fly when I was informed that my promotion was too recent, and my request was denied. The only exception was medical necessity and death, and unfortunately, the latter has come.

My sister Ran suggested I drive with her and her children since I only have Johnia. Jabreon is in Oklahoma with Chris for the summer. After we had gotten past our anger and accepted it was things we could have both done better, he and I made amends with our failed marriage and are now the best of friends. Jameelah is already in Buffalo with Jimmy, so riding with her makes sense. Seeing my family all together is always a big deal for me, but I certainly didn't want it to be under these circumstances AGAIN!

My sister Tonya's house is the first stop when we reach Buffalo; we have to make sure she's okay before we do anything else. Losing a child is something I wouldn't wish on ANYBODY. I can only imagine what she is going through.

I'm a nervous mess; this is the first and only child loss any of the siblings have ever experienced, and I feel so sad for her. Tonya has the same spirit as my sister-in-law Bronte (Jireh's mother). They are two of the sweetest, most kind, and calmest people you will ever meet. It breaks your heart when such bad things happen to good people. I'm prepared to cry with her, drink with her, yell, scream, WHATEVER, because I know this has to be weighing on her something heavy, and whatever it takes to make her feel better, I will do it.

She's all smiles when she walks out! "Hey, sisters," she says, hugging us both and then reaching for the kids. Not at ALL the state I expected her to be in. However, I understand exactly where her calm is coming from. When God is leading you, He keeps you in Perfect Peace, and it looks like sis has discovered that place. Unexpectedly, she asks, "Have you seen Jimmy since he's been home?"

"What? No, fool. I ain't here to talk about that. I'm here to take care of you, girl."

"I know, but I'm saying he brought Jameelah by here last night. And Shun, that boy is FINE!" We all burst out laughing.

"Girl, you're a nut. That boy has been fine, ain't nothing new about that!"

"Oh nah, sis. This is some other shit, though!" We holler with laughter again. However, through all that laughter, I can still see the pain in her face, and my heart is breaking where I stand. I know none of us are exempt from life's misfortunes, but I'm just having a hard time with this one.

I start to cry and my baby sister Fattie walks up and pats me on my behind. "Somebody getting thick."

"Little girl, go on." I try to punch her in the arm before she runs off. She doubles back and hugs me from behind, and I stay in her embrace for a while; I need it. We could all use a little extra love at a time like this.

Tonya sees me falling to the emotions and yells, "Enough of this mushy stuff. Let's get some spades going."

We set the table up in the yard, next to the tent by the grill, and open a new deck of cards. Since childhood, we've been pros at making the best of bad times. I tell them to start without me. I'm going to pick up Jameelah and bring her over. Tonya says, "You might want to change. I'm telling you, her daddy is looking right!"

I laugh again. "Girl, ain't nobody thinking about that boy? We are just friends and have been for years now. Are you forgetting I'm divorced from another man?"

"EXACTLY," she and Ran say simultaneously. I flip them off and head to get Jameelah. Mela tells me she is at church with Aunt Joyce when I call her.

"Where's your father?"

"At work, I think…"

"Ok, cool. Tell Aunt Joyce I just got in town, and I'm coming to get you for a while."

I called ahead, but of course, this little girl is still not outside like I asked her to be when I pull up. I just told these ninjas I was in a hurry. Bethesda is like Fort Knox; you can forget about just walking in, so I pick up and dial Joyce's number. As soon as it rings, I see Jimmy walking from the parking lot on the corner. Good God Almighty, this boy IS fine! I should have put on my good shit… OOPS, sorry God, I didn't mean to think that at your house. Forgive me. And Lord, please let them come out before his slow-walking self makes it to this door.

"Shun," I hear him call me. I pretend I'm talking to Joyce who never answered. "Shun, is that you?"

He's too close not to answer now. "Yep, yep. It sure is. What's up?" I go into bro/sis mode. He made it REAL CLEAR years ago when I married Chris that anything else was out the gate.

I extend my hand for him to shake, and he smiles that smile that makes my knees weak! "Girl, give me a hug. We are better than that!" He leans in and takes the hand I have extended, and places it behind his back. My mind is saying don't do it, but my body doesn't listen, and as I return his hug, I feel a jolt letting me know that the man who took my heart captive in 1995 still has it under his command.

I stay glued in his arms until Mela finally opens the door and sets me free. "Ok, Jimmy, it was good seeing you!" I don't risk looking into his eyes; I just take Mela's hand and practically run toward the car.

"Bye, Dad", she says as we speed walk away.

"Shun!"

I keep walking, pretending not to hear him again. "Mom, Daddy's calling you!" She's about to get backhanded, cause I didn't ask her nothing. I turn around, almost running into him.

"You call me?"

"Yeah, where are you headed?"

"Back to Tonya's to play cards," I tell him, and start walking again.

"Ok, well, I'll stop by later when I get off."

I can't help but think that's a bad idea, but I simply say, "That would be great!"

I've been drinking nonstop since I got back; that hug had thrown me for a loop. I was here to support and lift up my sister. I can't have any confusion in the way of that. My family is a good distraction, so I focus on them and the crazy wild memories they are reliving. We are not perfect, but we love each other, and when it's a need, we got each other, if no one else got us. I had drunk enough to drown the thought of Jimmy out. I actually had forgotten he was supposed to stop by until I see Mela and Johnia fly off the porch, and my eyes follow them to his car. It's getting dark. I thought I had escaped. Thank God I had gotten myself together since earlier, because that was NOT how I wanted him to see me after all these years, but a sister is on point now.

His cologne beats him to the porch. Once he catches up, he greets everyone he hasn't seen in years, and they act like he's the President. They always carry on like that when this dude comes around. I understand, though; he is cool, about the coolest dude I've ever met besides his father and my stepdad.

He walks over to the spade table and asks who's winning.

"Us, of course," Tonya says, pointing at me, then herself.

"Ok, well, I'll take next hand!"

"Oh no, brother. We have a long day tomorrow. You're going to have to settle for, and I owe you," Tonya tells him with her unique laugh mixed with pain, and it saddens me all over again. I give Jimmy my hand to finish and excuse myself.

"Where are you going?"

"To call a cab. I drove up with my sister, and I have to get to my hotel."

"Why are you staying in a hotel?" He passes the cards to my brother Cliff who is standing next to him, and walks with me.

"Everyone is kind of full. People were already here for the wedding this weekend, and with Quawn's funeral, it's real tight at all my family's houses. I just reserved a room for Johnia and I; it's no big deal."

"Wait, who's wedding?"

"White boy getting married this weekend!"

"Get out of here!"

"Nope, for real!"

"Alright, well, go get the girls and I will take you all home."

"I'm staying on the Boulevard, just so you know."

"Nah, I'm going to ask Mama if you guys can just stay at the house." Before I can object, he is on the phone with her. "Hey, Shun and Johnia are in town, and they need somewhere to stay. Is that alright with you? Alright, here's Shun"

I side-eye him as he hands me the phone. "Hey, Mama!"

"Hey, crazy girl. How is your sister doing?"

"She's hanging in there. How are you?"

"I'm here!"

"That's good," I chuckle. That's always her answer.

"All your family here?"

"Yes, ma'am. The whole gang and then some." I avoid asking her to stay. I really don't want to be under the same roof with Jimmy. I'm hoping she continues with the small talk, and I'll pretend I forgot and just insist on going to the hotel. The very next thing she says is, "You and that lil red girl, come on and stay here. Meda is already here." She has put a D in Jameelah since she was born.

No need to fight it; I just let it ride. I chuckle again and thank her, nervous about the situation but grateful I can save a few dollars.

Mama lets us know quickly that Jimmy is to stay in one of the upstairs rooms with her, and the kids and I will take the two rooms downstairs. I catch up with the family for a bit, then go down to the room I'm sleeping in. I'm about to get under the bed, that drive from Alabama is hell. I'm so tired and the kids are fast asleep before Jimmy even brings in our luggage. "Get comfortable, Shun, because I'll be back shortly to kick your butt in a game of cards since we didn't get to play at your sister's house earlier."

Now I know he ain't thinking about no cards, and I know he can't POSSIBLY be thinking of anything else with his mom upstairs and the kids in the other room, so whatever it is, at least I'm safe. I'm sure he wants to talk and catch up, but he's too cool to say, "let's just spend some time."

About three hands in, he accidentally touches my leg and continues to do so every game after that. Between all the alcohol I've consumed and his cologne, I'm going to lose this battle. I decide to call it a night. I let him win the game and yawn, indicating it's time for him to go upstairs. When I say goodnight and stand up, he pulls me back down into his lap. Jimmy brings his face close to mine, and whispers, "Have you missed me?" I keep my head down like a child in trouble. "Shun, I asked you a question." His lips are too close to my ear.

"Yes," I say, barely audible.

"You still got that room?" I shake my head yes, realizing it's still impossible to resist him. "Get your shoes. Let's go."

I peek in on the girls who are resting soundly, grab my sandals, and follow him out the door. I'm almost as scared now as I was that first time in college. Three babies later, stretch marks and a heart full of regret, I wonder if it can possibly be the same. I stay in the shower for a long time, hoping he will fall asleep. He and my brothers had a few drinks at my sister's before we left, and he could never hold his liquor. I know my plan to outlast him has failed when I hear the shower door open.

"You good?"

"Yes, I'm almost done," I say, covering my stretch marks with my hands.

He undresses, walks into the shower, and lifts my face up to his. "What's wrong?"

I tell him the whole truth. "I'm embarrassed. You met a thin girl with a perfect body back then, no stretch marks, no stomach. I don't look the same."

He moves my hands and traces the lines on my stomach. "This just means that you're all woman now."

"Jimmy, I'm just finding myself again; I'm in a good place! I don't want to open myself up to these feelings." Without a word, he takes my face and kisses me deeply, and I say a silent prayer for God to forgive me. I had made a vow that I wouldn't sleep with another man again unless we were married and I was healed. Breaking that vow, I kiss him back and get lost in his love. Part of me hoped it would be horrible so we could finally move past each other. Not so; it is still the BOMB! This can't be real! With all these years that have passed, and everything that's happened between us, the spell has not been broken.

We barely make it home the next day before everyone wakes up; I feel like a little kid sneaking in past curfew. I'm angry and scolding myself as I get dressed for the funeral. I hadn't been in town for 24 hours and had let this boy charm me out of my panties, literally! Then again, maybe I'm being too harsh; it might be a good thing we got it over with. We were forced to bring things to an end! The judge ceased our intimate contact when he sentenced him all those years ago. He was probably curious, just as I was. Now that we've done what we did on our own terms, we can go our separate ways in peace! He'll probably carry on the next week as if I'm not even here.

I made a bad call with that assumption! He accompanied me to my nephew's funeral the following day and then my brother's wedding the day after that. We attended an Air Show in Niagara Falls with his family two days later and remained like a hand and glove every day until it was time for me to return home. It was as if 17 years hadn't passed since the last time we laid together. As we're loading the car to leave, he asks me to sit down on the porch for a minute.

"Your booty calls are over, brother," I say, laughing. But he's not smiling.

"You know you've always been more than that to me Shun," he says, taking my hand and gesturing for me to sit. I search his eyes; something is wrong.

"What is it, Jimmy?"

"I need to tell you something." My heart starts to beat fast! "Tomorrow, I'm going to Philly with a friend."

"Ok... and Jimmy, I'll be gone."

"It's a female."

Those words seemed to stop my heart momentarily. "So you've had a girlfriend this whole TIME?" I hadn't thought to ask. Not only was I staying at his mom's house during the day, I was also in bed with him EVERY NIGHT! I'm getting flashbacks. I jump up, grab my bag, and walk toward my sister's car. I had fallen for the okey doke AGAIN.

He grabs me by the arm. "Calm down. She's not my girl or anything close to it for that matter. It's nothing like that! She's just a female who held me down here and there when I got out, and this was already planned. It's not a trip for US. My man is getting married, and she offered to ride with me and pay for it, so I said why not. I didn't know you were coming. I didn't plan on any of this happening between us."

I know Jimmy like the back of my hand, and I know he's being honest. "I didn't think anything like this would EVER happen between us again, Shun! I'm starting to settle down a bit.

He's right. We haven't seen each other in years, and we barely talked; this was very unexpected. I assure him it's fine; hell, we've been over (who am I kidding). "You don't have to explain, Jimmy. As two grown people, we decided to go back down that road. Now I'm returning to Alabama, and you can carry on as you were. No harm, no foul, baby. We're good."

"You sure?" he asks, looking into my eyes.

I look him dead back in his and lie. "I'm sure, Jim," I say with a smile that I've mastered through so many years of heartache. I know there's too much water under that bridge for it to ever be the way it used to be, but it hadn't stopped a girl from hoping. And just like that, my hopes are shattered. I give him one last hug, pick up my bag, and call the kids out of the house. Mela gives him a hug and starts right back with that video game, but he and Johnia carry on ridiculously as they always do.

"Don't lose that jacket I brought you; it was expensive."

"I won't," she replies, hugging him tightly. She is his lil buddy. I can't help but admire how good he is with kids. Actually, he's a good guy all around come to think of it. He just sucks at relationships.

My sister honks the horn for me to get in the car and I'm thankful. I need assistance making my feet move. Jimmy's life is here, and I have my own to get back to, yet it's so hard letting go. He takes my bag from my hand and walks me to the car. I hug him again and tell him I love him.

"I love you back, and I'll be sure to call and check on you while you are on the road."

"No need. Let's just call it what it is, brother." I kiss him on the cheek and close the door.

"Are you ok?" My sister looks concerned as I wipe away the tears I've been holding long enough to get out of his presence.

"I'm good, girl." I smile, throw on my sunglasses, and turn up the music to drown out the sound of my breaking heart. Even though I had told him there was no need to call, he did every hour, like clockwork, until I pulled up in my driveway 18 hours later.

Chapter 22

ANOTHER ROUND

My usual escape from work is not helping remedy these feelings that have come rushing back. I haven't been able to stop thinking about Jimmy. He had called while he was in Philly, and I heard him laughing and talking with another woman. I haven't answered since. I didn't like how that made me feel, and there's no need in entertaining something that can't be. I know we have no future. As many years as I have been with him, I know he means what he says. We both needed closure, and we had gotten it. May as well let sleeping dogs lie.

Prison is definitely not a place to be inattentive; anything could happen at any time. This is about the only place my mind could escape thoughts of him, sort of. I mean, the whole reason I took my position so personally was because of his long stretch of time. It was my mission to treat the people in our custody the way I always hoped people were treating him. So at times, I would hear a story or see someone who had his mannerism and think about how badly I missed him. Other than that, those feelings had to stay outside that security gate, along with any other personal feelings, for the sake of leaving here alive and making sure everyone else under my supervision did as well. But as soon as my car door closes, thoughts of him consume me. Maybe it's the picture I keep of him on my visor. I don't know why, but I could never bring myself to take it down.

I call my friend Jaime from the mailroom to lift me up, but she is no help; she encourages me to call him. She seems more vested in this than I am. She has always said since the day I married Chris that it was a mistake. She told me she could hear my love for Jimmy when I spoke of him, and she had never met him. She also refuses to address me by the last name Drew. She insists on calling me Mrs. Gaines, and did so even in Chris's presence. I suspect that's why he never found her as wonderful as I did, but I love her to pieces. She's convinced our story isn't over, and expresses it every time we discuss him.

Today she's doubling down on her theory. "Y'all have a child, and what you're doing to yourself is unhealthy. It's ok to communicate; you're adults, Gaaaines. I love the way she drags the A in my last name. Her Richland, GA drawl makes me smile for the first time in a while.

I actually hate that she's right because it's killing me not to talk to him. All I needed was for someone to say it was ok, so I wouldn't feel like a fool. I disconnect from her, dial his number, then quickly hang up. I know we can't be just friends! I start my car and drive home. I head to the shower as soon as I walk in. I need to clear my head! I undress, then stand in the mirror, looking at myself. I touch my heart and wonder how long it will take to get Jimmy completely out of my system.

Jameelah is screaming loudly into the phone instead of turning that video game down so she can hear. I'm about to give her a good blasting because at this rate, she is going to be deaf before she turns 21. I wrap my towel around myself and walk to her door. As I'm about to open it, I hear her say, "Aunt Joyce told me."

I run and turn off the water then put my ear to her door. From the pace of the conversation, I figured out she was talking to her dad. I snatch away from the door as if he can see me; this man is a thousand miles away. I turn the water back on and step inside the shower. This boy got me stuck on stupid. Let me see if this water can help.

As I'm sliding the shower door closed, Jameelah catches it. "Girl, what the hell, you almost gave me a heart attack!"

"My dad is looking for you," she says before handing me the phone and running back to her video game. I stare at the phone, then at the water, hating I had called earlier. I have lost my nerve to talk. I'm just going to say I was checking in because I've been really busy and hang up. I take a deep breath. "Hey, what's up?" I go into my bro/sis voice again.

"Hey, Shun. I'm trying to get Jameelah a ticket to come for Christmas."

"Ok, she has her schedule, so whatever y'all decide is cool with me."

"Don't you have to drive her to Atlanta?"

"I do."

"Well, what day is best for you to do that?"

"Whatever day you guys decide. I will get her there. Listen, I have the shower running. I'm going to give Mela back the phone."

"Okay. But before you do, why haven't you answered any of my calls?"

"Because I love you. I've always loved you, and I don't know how to stop. But I know there is no chance for us," I say through tears, then I unmute the phone and simply tell him, "Work has been crazy."

"Hmph. Ok, well, let me know the day that works best for you to drive her, and I'll book the ticket."

I hang up and sit on the shower bench and cry until I feel it's safe to exit without the kids seeing my brokenness. Their mom is unbreakable to them, and I would like to keep that image! I don't ever want them to question if mom is strong enough to run this family because NOTHING will ever be as important as them and their security!

I move in slow motion getting into my PJ's then sneak to Peeta and JJ's room to check on them. Thank goodness, they have fallen asleep. I still hear Mela yelling at her TV. I don't even bother opening her door because that's some foolishness I can't deal with right now.

I climb into bed, not bothering to turn on any music or the TV; I want to lay here in silence tonight. I hear my phone beeping a voicemail and pick it up to retrieve the message. I listen in anguish to Jimmy's voice saying, "Call me back." I play it about ten times. He only said three words, and that's enough to set the tears in motion. My mind tells me his voice is a trap I can't afford to walk back into. My heart knows it's one I've never been free of.

The heart wins; I dial his number before I talk myself out of it. He answers on the first ring, and we talk until the sun comes up. I'm not even tired walking into work the next day, even though I'm working on about 2 hours of sleep. The almost hour drive it took me to get here didn't even faze me. Your day moves so much faster when your heart is happy. I call Jimmy as soon as I'm home and settled to discuss the best time to buy Mela's ticket since we didn't get around to it last night.

"I have four days off coming up this weekend when my Administrative Duty Rotation ends. Too bad Christmas isn't this week," I say as I look at my schedule.

"It can be. Why don't you come to see me?"

"I don't think so, Jimmy."

"What for?"

"What do you think?" I can't help but laugh. "I thought we both agreed to leave well enough alone, Jimmy."

"You said that. I didn't agree to anything except for the fact that you still belong to me."

I'm on a plane Friday with my work bag in hand! I told my father and the girls I was going for weekend training. This is crazy. I'm a grown-ass woman with 3 kids sneaking off to meet my ex-husband. I considered backing out more than once, but I can't say no to Jimmy now, no more than I could back then. I put my headphones in and let the music speak the words in my heart through my ears. I told him I wasn't staying with his family or mine. I don't want anyone to know I'm in Buffalo.

Punctual as always, he's waiting outside the airline gate to take me to the hotel. That beautiful smile of his was worth EVERY dime of that last minute ticket. I don't want him to know how desperately I've missed him, so I don't make a big deal. I just kiss him on the cheek as he takes my bag.

I laugh more in these three days than I have in months. We haven't left the hotel for anything but food. I'm happy to be in his arms and I don't want to spoil this wonderful time we are having, but I need to know what is happening between us, so I ask, "Jimmy, what's going on here? I'm almost 40 years old, and we are not about to start a secret love affair this far apart."

"Why do we have to call it anything, Shun? Let's just have fun."

"Negro, I have three children and a 5000 square feet yard; when I want to have fun, I go out and play with them. I need you to understand that I'm not the same girl you met back in college. I'm no longer interested in boyfriends, dating, casual sex, none of that. I came here by choice to quiet that voice telling me I made a mistake when I was here in July, that you are still the same gigolo you were back then. I broke a vow of celibacy to convince myself that our sex couldn't still be the way I remembered. I was sure this hold you have on me was physical, but this weekend, I have to face the truth. I'm still in love with you, and I know you don't feel the same. We are in two different worlds; this will never work."

"That's not fair, Shun! You know I'll always love you!"

"Yeah, I know. But loving someone and being in love are two different things. I love Chris and always will. We share a daughter, and I was once his wife, but I was never in love with him, and that's why it didn't last."

"Look, this is getting too deep." He gets out of bed and pulls me up with him. "Don't do this then leave us both upset. Can we talk about this later? Let's have a drink before your flight."

"That would be cutting it close. My flight is in 3 hours."

"Well, I'll park, come inside, and hang out until your flight leaves."

"You would go through the trouble for me, big daddy?" I try to lighten the mood.

"As long as you know my name!" He knows how to make me laugh! I grab his hand as we walk into the airport to let him know a truce has been called on the issue of "where we stand", at least for now. We laugh and drink until it's time to board.

"When will I see you again?"

"You probably won't, Jimmy. This is too hard for me! I am grateful to have my best friend back, though. No more ignoring calls, I promise!" I'm not sad when I leave this time. I believe this was what I needed; my choice, my way!

I'm so excited to see my babies. They catch me up on all the fun things granddaddy did with them. By the time the last story is finished, I have to make room to lay in my own bed. A Disney movie is still playing when the phone rings. I was too tired to find the remote and change the channel.

"Hey, baby!"

"Hey, handsome!"

"Who the hell is singing this late?"

I exit the bedroom quietly so I don't wake the kids. "It's the TV, boy." His silliness chases my fatigue away. "I miss your silly self."

"I miss you too!" I feel that familiar feeling tugging at my heart; I think the sound of his voice triggers it.

"You want to see me again?"

"No, Jimmy, I can't come back. It will be a while before I can get more days off, then leaving my children and my dad. It's too much."

"Well, how about if I come to you?"

I REALLY want him to, but I don't want him to know I'm SPRUNG again. "How will we explain you being here to our families and the kids?"

"I don't care. I'm grown. You're the one hiding."

"I'm not hiding! I'm being cautious, Jimmy. I can't afford a broken heart; mopping, sadness, none of that. I'm a single mom."

"No, you're not a single mom. I take care of my daughter and the other two as well when necessary."

"That's true, Jimmy. I guess what I mean is if I'm physically out of commission, it wouldn't be good. I'm the only parent they have HERE."

Silence. "Say something. Tell me you understand why this can't be just sex and fun. I have too much to lose, not to mention my soul."

"Alright, I get it. Let me let you go. Talk to you later." And with that, he hangs up.

I'm so damn mad for the next two weeks. "It's too much" if it couldn't be his way; so that was it! He hadn't contacted me at all, only asking Mela to tell me he said hello when they talked.

I'm relieved to be off this weekend. I plan on sleeping in and drowning my sorrows with wine. I have absolutely nothing planned, yet the girls are up early on a Saturday, dressed and ready at that. I usually have to chase them out of bed on the weekends just to complete their chores. I wonder if this is an attempt to cheer me up.

I try my best to hide my misery, but these are my children. They feel my pain just like I feel theirs, and that's why it's important to keep my priorities straight! When I'm off balance, all of us are.

Johnia comes in and gives me the biggest hug then takes my hand leading me through my closet, out on the other side of the connecting bathroom, and into Jameelah's room. The cutest outfit is laid out on Jameelah's bed, with shoes and jewelry to match. "Awe, baby, this is so nice. But Momma is saving this for a special occasion. This cost too much to wear around Eufaula."

"No, it is a special occasion, Momma," she says in her sweet little voice.

"Ok, what is the occasion?" I brainstorm quickly to see if I missed a birthday; it has been hectic lately.

"Just get dressed, Mom." She had put Jabreon's naturally curly hair up in the cutest ponytail, and Mela is all coordinated in her sparkling sandals and little sundress. Johnia is the house fashion designer, and she did all this without any help at all from me.

I give in. Forget this outfit; those smiles are well worth the dry-cleaning bill. They have activated my energy. I get dressed quickly, snatch off my scarf, shake my wrap wildly, and say, "Let's go." My silly antics entertain them, and their smiles make my whole life better. We walk toward the door hand in hand, but I have to break up this tender moment. "Where are we going?" I ask

Jameelah directly. She's the oldest, so I expect her to give it to me straight.

"To Columbus shopping!"

"Really now!". With whose money? I thought this trip was to cheer mommy up? How is spending money going to cheer me up?"

Johnia chimes in, "Granddad gave us all money already."

I have no doubt about that; he will give this little girl the shirt off his back in a snowstorm. With that settled, we get in the truck, adjust the music, and prepare to jam out on this 45-minute ride. As we approach the exit to the mall, Mela's phone rings and she turns the music down. "Yes. Yes, okay." She turns to me. "Mom, Granddad says his friend Pete is stuck at the Groome's Transportation terminal and needs a ride to Eufaula."

"Ok, what has that got to do with me? Who the heck is Pete? I'm not having some strange man riding in here with y'all. Unless he wants to wait until we're done shopping, then I can pick him up. But that will be a few hours." They look really confused or sad. Maybe upset. I can't tell. "Ok, it's not like I'm leaving Granddad. Why y'all looking crazy?"

"Well, he always does stuff for us momma, Mommy. And he would do it for you."

"Yeah, he would, wouldn't he?" These kids know how to break me down. "Ok, listen. I'll go get him, but I'm not coming back up here. So, either I can pick him up and drop him off, and we can shop tomorrow, or we can go to the mall as planned and pick him up after. What are we doing?"

"Ok, Mom. Just pick him up and we can go shopping tomorrow if you're not too tired."

"Deal!" I pass the mall exit and head to the Groome's. It's crowded when I make it there with people picking up or dropping off loved ones from the airport. It's so chaotic. How will he know we are here? I'm about to call him.

"Hello, we are outside."

"Wait a minute, Mela. How do you know this strange man's number?"

"Um, Gran—" she stops mid-sentence as her daddy comes strolling out. I smile hard at his beautiful face. These little sidekicks of his have helped him pull off his plan. I jump out, and Jimmy drops his bag to receive a hug from my outstretched arms. We stay embraced for a while until we hear a loud "Ewwwww!" from the girls. HATERS! I kiss him on the cheek and release him reluctantly.

We have a ball in Columbus then drive back to Eufaula where my father meets us under the carport. This is only the second time he's seen Jimmy. The first was when we picked up the car Dad had brought me back in college. That was almost 20 years ago, but you would never know the way they've been talking and laughing like old friends for almost an hour. I know Daddy knows how much I love Jimmy, and Jimmy certainly knows how much I love my dad. That's their connection; nothing else is needed.

My dad, Jimmy, the kids, and I enjoy each other as a family the whole week! We attended two of Mela's basketball games and Johnia's band performance, but the kids' favorite part was that we ate out every night. Dad even visited my church today with us instead of driving to St. Luke. If you didn't know any better, you'd think we're a well-put-together family. Only that's not the case, and it will all come to an end tomorrow when Jimmy leaves.

He rides with me to take the girls to school so they can say their goodbyes, and then we drive back to the airport alone; our last few hours belong to us. "Thanks for coming to see me, Jimmy."

"Girl, I came to see my kids."

"Whatever, Negro. Why didn't you sleep in one of their rooms, then?" He smiles, and I miss him already. I go silent.

"Don't start, Shun!"

I haven't even shed a tear. I'm so embarrassed by my wimpy personality. "Jimmy, I'm just worried this is not healthy."

"Shun, I honestly don't know what to do here! I'm still trying to figure it out. I just know I missed you, and I don't want you to think I don't care. I can't even process it myself."

I'm listening to a different man than the one I used to know. He's not trying to figure out how to juggle women. He's not even sure what he wants, so how can he provide my needs? As he walks toward the airport, I feel a glimmer of hope, knowing this is not one of his games; he's really trying. I just pray I'm not setting myself up for another letdown.

We've talked every day since he left, sometimes 3-4 times a day, and it has been great. It seems like it took forever for my next rotation to end; it is my time to go to him. I'm flying to Buffalo tomorrow, and our families still don't know that we're involved. Since I'm unsure as to where this is going myself, I plan on keeping it that way. The last thing I want is another round of public embarrassment.

I called our friend Tam to see if I could stay with her. I had met her through Carl when Jimmy was first sentenced to the Feds. Carl is Jimmy's friend, Mela's Godfather, and a brother to me. They have always treated me and the kids like family, and there was nothing I couldn't ask them for and vice versa.

She said I was more than welcome to stay with her usual Southern hospitable voice. It seemed like we laughed, talked, yawned, and then the weekend was over. These trips are fun, but they go by so quickly, and it's starting to add up for both of us. I kiss him at the airport, pouting that the holidays are too long to wait to be in his arms again.

"I think you can manage. I'll call you every night and sing to you." I laugh again until my face hurts. Lord, please cushion my heart. Because when this hits, it's gonna hit like a brick. That's our pattern. We love hard, but we fight even harder. Right now, I tell myself to enjoy this moment!

Christmas came quicker than I anticipated; our frequent phone conversations seems to have made the time pass faster. Jimmy arrived today to accompany me to my Job's Annual Christmas Party. He's both a hit and a mystery. Everyone knew that since Chris and I had divorced, I'd been solo. I had a brief fling with this young cutie, J, but he lived in another town. That boy was the closest to bringing me out of the spell Jimmy had on me as anyone had been in all these years, but he was much too young. I know when something seems too good to be true, it usually is! I felt it was the devil trying to get me off my track to salvation. So, I started to pray about it. And the more I prayed, the less satisfying it became. On the last weekend we spent together, we decided that the thrill had run out, and I ran back to Jesus.

These country girls are mesmerized by Jimmy's eyes, but I can't blame them. We enjoy the little while we are here because if you know me, you know I was late. We have a few drinks and just talk. Well, he talks; I just stare at him the whole time, thinking how grateful I am that he had flown down just so I didn't have to attend alone.

Two days later, he drives us all back to Buffalo to celebrate Christmas. The kids and I will stay at Bronte's house for the week. I don't want to risk being that close to Jimmy. I feel the end of the road is approaching for us. It's best to spend as little time as possible while I'm here.

I'm sitting on the couch contemplating when I should have a talk with him about ending this when his sister Nell busted in the door with her kids Chelsea and AJ, and their dad Agee clowning as usual. She's such a small girl, but loud as ever. She and his brother Reggie both live in different states. Her family is the last to arrive.

Now that everyone is here, we can start to eat. I want to get out of Jimmy's presence quickly. Once dinner is over, I ask the girls if they want to go upstairs and watch a movie. Jimmy asks me to leave them with the other kids for a minute so he could talk to me outside. I figure he just wants to take a drive and smoke a cigarette because no one else in the family does, and they always scold us, especially that lil Janae; she's the Smoke Police!

I grab my jacket and ask Paula to keep an eye on the girls. Before I can close the car door, Jimmy asks what's wrong.

"Why do you ask that?"

"Shun, I've been watching you all day; something is wrong."

"Jimmy, I'm just trying to make it through the holidays for my girls, but to be honest, after Christmas, after the New Year, when will we be able to see each other again without having a holiday as an excuse to be around?"

"Shun, you don't need an excuse! You're here because I want you to be."

"I know that. But I have this funny feeling, and I don't want to get too deep in this, and you can't even tell me what it is that we are doing here."

"Ok, listen. I know you think I keep avoiding your question, but it's too many people here and I want the kids to enjoy. It's just not the right time."

"Ok. I'm leaving in a few days, and I won't see you again until God knows when, so when do you think would be a good time for you!"

"I thought you were coming for Mike's party in February?"

"Oh, yeah, that's right!"

Technically, I planned on this being our last time seeing each other, but I wouldn't dare miss a Joyce Badger production! She throws a hell of a party, and this is for her husband. I know she gon' put on a show for Bishop; it's going to be one to remember. I'll come without the kids, enjoy the family, have a quiet evening, then tell him the way it has to be and end this before I get in any deeper than I already am.

As I drive up to Buffalo for the party, I pray it's a quiet night. I'm in a somber mood because I'm feeling some type of way about being around his family as a "friend", when I'm really not sure what we are. I'll just show my face, then go see my family and slip out of town on Sunday.

That foolish Kenny Williams spots us walking in and the quiet part goes right out the window. It's a 70's party, so he decides to dub us as Ike and Tina. That mess follows us all night. It is actually pretty fitting considering our past! Davida, Davette, and Davara can't stop laughing. I ruin my mascara laughing right with them; this family know they be with the foolishness.

I'm relieved when his other niece Nia B pulls me away for some fresh air and girl talk. We sit and catch up on all that's been going on until they announce dinner is being served. Perfect timing! I haven't seen Jimmy in over an hour. I've been socializing, and I need an excuse to get close to him without him knowing I miss him. I don't want to send mixed signals. I know we are done after this weekend, but my heart still yearns for him! So, for these next few days, I'm going to listen to my heart and have a little peace before my pain begins AGAIN.

Jimmy's sister Bronte is sitting with him when I return to the table; I sit on the opposite side of him. He takes my hand in his lap under the table, indicating he had missed me too. After dinner, Bronte and I hit the dance floor. Jimmy won't dance to save his life, but he sure enjoys watching me, and I love it when he watches; it seems as if he's the only one in the room! I dance until I'm exhausted.

"Your old butt tired now, huh?" he says, handing me a drink. I sat down to catch my breath, but that didn't happen. His two nephews, Moe and Mario, now have the mic, and they both need Jesus. They are hilarious! No one in the room has a straight face, not even Jimmy, who, in general, is usually stoic. Not tonight! We laugh at almost everything and everybody for the rest of the evening; it is some wild outfits up in here. It's some creative ones, too. My girl Pam and her husband Mel are killing it, but Jimmy and I both agree that brother Guy is the winner tonight.

We haven't had this much fun since we first met; before kids, prison, divorces. ALL THAT! The days when we were young and adventurous and would try just about anything, including doing donuts in an empty parking lot, and then dodging the police. Even in the midst of all of this laughter, the realization of this being over is overwhelming, and I can't shake it. I shouldn't have allowed myself to get this close. When I felt it a few months ago, I should have backed off. On Christmas, I should have just called it like I started too. Honestly, I'm terrified of him leaving my life again, but I know it's even more dangerous to take this risk with my heart. Jimmy will always be Jimmy, and though he is being completely honest about us, I know if we continue, it's going to end badly for me.

I thought I had put on a good enough facade during the party, but as we were walking out, Jimmy stopped me and said, "Before we go anywhere else, I need to know what's on your mind."

I was hoping to do it on my last day here, but I might as well get it over with (Now or Never). "Jimmy, this is all too much; I feel like we are living a lie. We are behaving like the cutest couple, yet your phone rings constantly when we're together. I see your

'Good morning/Good night' texts, etc... I'm clearly not the only person you're entertaining."

"So you mean to tell me I'm the only man you're dealing with?"

"That's exactly what I'm telling you!"

He immediately starts to rationalize his behavior. "Yes, I still see other people here and there. We are a thousand miles apart; that's a lot of distance between us."

"I agree! That's what I've been trying to make you see for months now, Jimmy! You're not going to move to Alabama, and I'm certainly not moving back to Buffalo, so it's no point continuing to go back and forth."

"Shun, I'm not ready to commit to a relationship."

"Oh, if anybody knows that, IT'S ME!"

"You don't get to yell or catch an attitude, Shun. It's just some things you don't forget and forgive easily."

"Like WHAT!"

"LIKE YOU HAVING TWO MORE KIDS, MARRYING ANOTHER MAN, AND FUCKING HURTING ME while I'm locked up and looking like a damn FOOL."

"Ok, THERE IT IS! That's the problem; you're still ANGRY at ME! Well, let me tell you something, mister. Try being FREE AS A DAMN bird, getting cheated on, being pregnant, and FIGHTING other women; ALL THAT! OR how about being laughed at by my family and yours for Y-E-A-R-S. I endured all that, Jimmy! Still, I married you and gave you six more years ON TOP OF IT! Excuse me for wanting a NORMAL life for my children NOW!"

"Yeah, that's all true," he says, a little calmer. "But once I married you, I vowed to be good to you the rest of my life. And you did me wrong, Shun, and I just can't forget it." He lifts my chin to look at him. His eyes are glossed with tears. "Can you understand that?"

"Yes, I understand one hundred percent. Now, can you understand that I can't spend the rest of my life paying for that either, nor am I willing to go back and forth from state to state with you? Let's just call it what it is when I leave in a couple of days."

"Bet," he says with a kiss on my forehead and a knife to my heart.

We are a perfect couple for the next two days. No bad words, no disagreements, no sadness (no sadness he could see anyways). On my last night in town, we get a hotel room away from everyone to give this twenty-year whirlwind love affair a proper goodbye. Waking up reminds me of the first time we made love. I remember thinking how that had changed my life, and here it is, changing again! I'm letting go for my own sanity because I know he doesn't have the power to let go or fully commit. I allow myself to shed a few tears before he opens his beautiful eyes, and I lose my nerve. I lay my head on his chest and pray God continues to guide and protect him as I exit his life. I pray he continues to make wise decisions and one day changes his heart to be a good man, to ONE woman, even though he didn't choose for it to be me. Someone certainly deserves to experience the wonderful person that is stuck inside of him. I can see it; I know he's there, but he's too afraid to step into who he is really meant to be. And I don't have another year, another hour, another minute to waste trying to convince him. This time, I'M CHOOSING ME! I've discovered who I am destined to be, and she deserves the best. She will never be an option AGAIN!

I get up and get dressed before I lose my nerve. I have a long drive ahead of me; I need to focus. I wake him reluctantly, as I know this is our last goodbye, but it must be done. I kiss him softly, and he grabs my hand playfully, letting me know he's awake even though his eyes are still closed. I know every single thing about this man. How will I EVER get close to another one?

That's fear talking; I shut it down! "Get up, handsome. I need to get on the road." He jumps right up, smacks my behind, and asks if I want to join him in the shower. Lord knows I do, but I simply remind him that I showered last night, and I don't like going out in the cold right out of the water. In reality, daylight has ended any chance we had of reconciling, and I will not allow my flesh to cost me my soul.

I cry the whole way home. The drive seemed to take longer than usual. I think self-consciously, I knew once I hit Alabama, Jimmy and I will never be together again. I always give myself an extra couple of days to rest after a long road trip, and I'm especially grateful for that today. I had dropped my things at the door when I got home yesterday and slept the entire day! Still, I'm physically and emotionally drained after a full day's rest. I don't know how I'm going to make it through work next week. I need to get it together.

I jump in the shower and let the water revive me. I feel a little better once I step out, but this hair AIN'T IT! I'm searching for a brush amongst this disaster of a product drawer when my cell phone rings. I've been ignoring Jimmy's calls and have directed the kids to say I'm asleep when they talk to him. It's kind of mean and selfish to keep ignoring him, but Jimmy has always had a boatload of women. I'm sure he's got plenty of other people to occupy his time. On the other hand, I also know he loves me, and this has to be affecting him to some degree, so I answer. "Hello…"

"Hey, Shun."

"Hi, Jimmy. How are you?"

"I'm good. Just wondering if you're ok."

"I'm fine. Just a little tired from the drive."

"I figured that. You haven't been answering, and the kids tell me you are sleeping every time I call."

"Well, yeah. I'm good. Thanks for checking on me. I'll talk to you later."

"Wait… I was trying to tell you that you left your gold watch here."

"Okay. Tell Paula or Joyce to mail it for me, please."

"I mailed it overnight already. That's why I was calling you."

"Ok. Haven't you talked to Jameelah since then?"

"Yeah. But you know that girl will forget to tell you, and I just want you to look out for it because it needs a signature."

"Oh, alright, will do. I'm going back to work in a couple of days, but I will have Dad look out for it if it doesn't show up by then."

"It says it should be there today."

"They always say that, but this is a small town. I highly doubt if it will be here today. But if so, I'll call and let you know."

"Go check your mailbox before we get off."

"Boy, I'm doing my hair. I'll go in a minute." I suspect he is trying to prolong the conversation; he knows if he talks long enough, I get weak. "Let me just go check so we can end this call." I wish the kids were here so I could just send them, seeing that he is not taking no for an answer. Dad had taken them to my Aunt Mary's house with him when he left earlier. I'm so grateful for my pops. The kids needed out of this house, and I've been in a funk since I got back.

My stomach is rumbling. I stop in the kitchen and put a pop tart in the toaster.

"What are you doing?"

"Getting me something to eat, boy!"

"Did you check the mail?"

"I was all the way in the back of the house. I'm getting there, chill!"

"Girl, don't get smart." His tone makes me smile. I DEFINITELY have to get off this phone. My heart is melting, just like I knew it would if I talked to him.

I move quickly to remove the locks. When I open the door, he's standing there swirling the watch with one hand, and his suitcase is in the other. "What are you doing here?" I ask, dropping the phone and jumping into his arms. He catches me and pretends I hurt his back. "You're an idiot," I say through tears.

"Damn, Shun, can I get in the house before you start crying?"

"I'm just happy to see you. But I don't know why you came. I'm doing my best to get over you!"

He steps inside, shuts the door, and pulls me into his chest. "You will never get over me," he says, then covers my lips with his. After we come up for air, he tells me Dad and the kids had picked him up from the Groome's. He had, once again, gotten my babies to help him execute his plan. They have gotten me twice, not knowing they are prolonging my misery, or maybe it's that they can see what's best for mama when she can't.

"Jimmy, we have to get dressed. I don't know when my dad and the kids will be home."

"Your father said they are going to some place called Louerviille."

"You mean Louisville."

"Yeah, whatever that country shit is."

I laugh until I cry. This is what no one else does for me; he brings laughter to my life. "You're stupid, you know that!"

"Yeah... but you love me."

"That I do, but I told you this long-distance thing doesn't work for me, Jimmy!"

"I know. I heard you in Buffalo. But I just can't let you go without a fight. So, I will stay here for two weeks. I will give this farm town a chance, and if I can make it work in any way, I'll move here. If it's too slow, you move back to Buffalo."

"Baby, I can't do Buffalo. I HATE that weather, and I will be so far from my dad. Let's try South Carolina, Florida, Atlanta... Anywhere... PLEASE!"

"Shun, I told you. I've been away from my mom too long. Either I'm staying there with her or coming here with you and the kids. I don't want to move to a strange place where neither of us have a family."

I can't argue his point, so I offer my hand to shake on it. "Ok, now let's get food. I'm starving! That pop tart had burned to hell and back."

We go to my Godsister's Courtney and Star's eatery. I introduce him and they love him. He has the same effect on everyone he meets. He's such a genuine guy and he's never met a stranger. The next two weeks are both adventurous and fun. Our days are filled with family and good food, followed by nights in the park, dancing, and dates which conclude on my front porch swinging, gazing at the stars, learning each other again, and discussing all the time we've missed.

Decision day came a little faster than either of us had hoped. At least for the past two weeks, we knew for certain that we'd be together. We had agreed to enjoy our time and discuss our fate the day before he was scheduled to leave. We didn't want to spend all our time going back and forth; it was pointless. The one thing that we were both sure of, is that THIS IS IT! We'd given it our best, and neither one of us would pursue this once he's gone if a common destination couldn't be decided upon. I can tell he is dancing around the subject every time I hint at talking about it. Finally, I just come right out and ask, "What's it going to be, Jimmy?"

He looks down for a moment. "Shun, I gave it a shot. I just can't do it. It's too slow for me. Everything is too far; shopping, entertainment, everything. I just can't."

It hurts, I won't lie, but I understand his decision. Eufaula is more of a hometown or retirement city. If you're adventurous and full of life like he is, this is a challenge; he needs hustle and bustle in his day-to-day routine. As for me, I'm content and comfortable with my simple life. Actually, I was kind of hoping that he wouldn't like it here. Deep down, I don't think he has forgiven me. He's just scared to let go. As for me, I don't trust this crazy kind of love I have for him, making me too afraid to stay. The only thing that's certain here is neither of us can withstand another heartbreak. This is not an easy choice at all!

Chapter 23
GOING HOME

It's April 2016 and I'm headed back to Buffalo. I had put my house on the market, brought my dad a smaller house that he could manage, and finalized all my affairs within the last few months. We had decided to let the kids complete the school year here, then start the next term up North. Jimmy flew down to help me get the moving truck all packed and situate my father in his new home. As soon as the movers pull off, we back out of the driveway. I have him stop to get one last look at the house that has been sufficient for this part of my life. Now it's time to go home and make new memories. I've discovered home isn't where you're born or even where you grow up; home is where your heart is, and my heart is and will always be with Jimmy. As I watch him drive and sing along to the old school we both love, then glance at my girls with their heads buried in their devices, my heart is content!

Finally, after all the tears, failed relationships, bad dates, wild sex, and encounters that only caused me more pain, I've found a real love. My whole life I've asked myself what's wrong with me, why wasn't I good enough, why didn't my relationships last, why couldn't I find JOY! When I dedicated my life to Christ, I got my answer.

He created me in His likeness; I was always good enough for HIM! I was looking for love in all the wrong places. You see, in God I found a way to love perfectly in imperfection. Falling in love with Jesus is the best thing I've ever done, and that's A LOVE THE WORLD SHOULD KNOW! God's Love has kept me down through the years, as a child, through school, from one bad relationship to the next, protected me from drug addiction, alcohol, prostitution, AIDS, suicide, depression, but most importantly He saved me from MYSELF! God placed Angels all along my path to ensure I ended up right where I should be, but still, I wasn't complete until I embraced HIS LOVE. Once I leaned into HIM, I was able to truly love myself, and attract the love I deserved!

While the love story of Shun and Jimmy is beautiful and DEFINITELY my favorite, our journey could have been a lot less difficult had we let God lead from the beginning; our appointment for love was already set! God didn't need any help! All that fighting and foolishness should have been fasting and praying. Being embedded in His word instead of the world would have gotten us here so much sooner. Tapping into God's love was how we learned to best love one another. I mean, who would know the matters of the heart better than the one who holds our heart? I pray that our future promises will be strong enough to carry us through our past hurt, but only God knows our ending. Maybe, just maybe, Jimmy and I will get it right this time. But if by chance forever is not in God's plan for us, I am blessed to even have experienced this kind of love at all.

IN SUMMARY

Ladies AND Gentlemen, the best way to find love is to first find God. His plan is for us to win from the START! True love may come, or maybe He is meant to be your only love; who knows! Either way, stay committed to Him, and He'll direct your path, providing everyone and everything you need throughout this course of life. I recklessly reached my destination, but you don't have to! My purpose of this book was to share my experience so that it may save someone from going through hell just to get to that GOOD place God already predestined for you. However, if you ever find yourself on a reckless path, or maybe you're on one right now, reach up and grab God's hand! He will save you, even from yourself... Now that's LOVE!

IN LOVING MEMORY OF:
SALLIE M. FRYER, JOHNNY LEE FRYER, JOHN D. EUTSEY, AND ELDER FRANK GAINES. JR

Special Thanks to Everyone who believed in me and contributed to making A LOVE THE WORLD SHOULD KNOW, a bestseller (speaking it into existence)! Gloria Thomas, Star Thomas, Lillie Bell Gilbert, Joyce Badger, Phillip Gaines, Nia Badger, Kermit Burkes, Jordan T. Howard, Christopher Drew, Wilma Drew, Javen K Harris, Stephanie Dunston, Angela (Cookie) Carr, Ronald Helms, Niema Erving, Demetrius Paige, and Gloria Denson Pearce. I couldn't have done it without all your love, support, and prayers throughout this process!

Lastly, to BOTH of my wild families, who I wouldn't trade for ANYTHING, thank you for always allowing me to be me… You love me unconditionally, and I love you back! However this turns out, I was and always will be just "Shun", and I'm cool with that!